Data Science

2nd Edition

by Lillian Pierson

FOREWORD BY Jake Porway

Founder and Executive Director of DataKind

for dummies®

A Wiley Brand

Data Science For Dummies®, 2nd Edition

Published by: **John Wiley & Sons, Inc.**, 111 River Street, Hoboken, NJ 07030-5774, www.wiley.com

Copyright © 2017 by John Wiley & Sons, Inc., Hoboken, New Jersey

Published simultaneously in Canada

For general information on our other products and services, please contact our Customer Care Department within the U.S. at 877-762-2974, outside the U.S. at 317-572-3993, or fax 317-572-4002. For technical support, please visit https://hub.wiley.com/community/support/dummies.

Wiley publishes in a variety of print and electronic formats and by print-on-demand. Some material included with standard print versions of this book may not be included in e-books or in print-on-demand. If this book refers to media such as a CD or DVD that is not included in the version you purchased, you may download this material at http://booksupport.wiley.com. For more information about Wiley products, visit www.wiley.com.

Library of Congress Control Number: 2017932294

ISBN 978-1-119-32763-9 (pbk); ISBN 978-1-119-32765-3 (ebk); ISBN 978-1-119-32764-6 (ebk)

Manufactured in the United States of America

10 9 8 7 6 5 4 3

Contents at a Glance

Table of Contents

Foreword

We live in exciting, even revolutionary times. As our daily interactions move from the physical world to the digital world, nearly every action we take generates data. Information pours from our mobile devices and our every online interaction. Sensors and machines collect, store, and process information about the environment around us. New, huge data sets are now open and publicly accessible.

This flood of information gives us the power to make more informed decisions, react more quickly to change, and better understand the world around us. However, it can be a struggle to know where to start when it comes to making sense of this data deluge. What data should one collect? What methods are there for reasoning from data? And, most importantly, how do we get the answers from the data to answer our most pressing questions about our businesses, our lives, and our world?

Data science is the key to making this flood of information useful. Simply put, data science is the art of wrangling data to predict our future behavior, uncover patterns to help prioritize or provide actionable information, or otherwise draw meaning from these vast, untapped data resources.

I often say that one of my favorite interpretations of the word "big" in Big Data is "expansive." The data revolution is spreading to so many fields that it is now incumbent on people working in all professions to understand how to use data, just as people had to learn how to use computers in the 80's and 90's. This book is designed to help you do that.

I have seen firsthand how radically data science knowledge can transform organizations and the world for the better. At DataKind, we harness the power of data science in the service of humanity by engaging data science and social sector experts to work on projects addressing critical humanitarian problems. We are also helping drive the conversation about how data science can be applied to solve the world's biggest challenges. From using satellite imagery to estimate poverty levels to mining decades of human rights violations to prevent further atrocities, DataKind teams have worked with many different nonprofits and humanitarian organizations just beginning their data science journeys. One lesson resounds through every project we do: The people and organizations that are most committed to using data in novel and responsible ways are the ones who will succeed in this new environment.

Just holding this book means you are taking your first steps on that journey, too. Whether you are a seasoned researcher looking to brush up on some data science techniques or are completely new to the world of data, *Data Science For Dummies* will equip you with the tools you need to show whatever you can dream up. You'll be able to demonstrate new findings from your physical activity data, to present new insights from the latest marketing campaign, and to share new learnings about preventing the spread of disease.

We truly are on the forefront of a new data age and those that learn data science will be able to take part in this thrilling new adventure, shaping our path forward in every field. For you, that adventure starts now. Welcome aboard!

Jake Porway

Founder and Executive Director of DataKind

Introduction

The power of big data and data science are revolutionizing the world. From the modern business enterprise to the lifestyle choices of today's digital citizen, data science insights are driving changes and improvements in every arena. Although data science may be a new topic to many, it's a skill that any individual who wants to stay relevant in her career field and industry needs to know.

This book is a reference manual to guide you through the vast and expansive areas encompassed by big data and data science. If you're looking to learn a little about a lot of what's happening across the entire space, this book is for you. If you're an organizational manager who seeks to understand how data science and big data implementations could improve your business, this book is for you. If you're a technical analyst, or even a developer, who wants a reference book for a quick catch-up on how machine learning and programming methods work in the data science space, this book is for you.

But, if you are looking for hands-on training in deep and very specific areas that are involved in actually implementing data science and big data initiatives, this is *not* the book for you. Look elsewhere because this book focuses on providing a brief and broad primer on *all* the areas encompassed by data science and big data. To keep the book at the For Dummies level, I do not go too deeply or specifically into any one area. Plenty of online courses are available to support people who want to spend the time and energy exploring these narrow crevices. I suggest that people follow up this book by taking courses in areas that are of specific interest to them.

Although other books dealing with data science tend to focus heavily on using Microsoft Excel to learn basic data science techniques, *Data Science For Dummies* goes deeper by introducing the R statistical programming language, Python, D3.js, SQL, Excel, and a whole plethora of open-source applications that you can use to get started in practicing data science. Some books on data science are needlessly wordy, with their authors going in circles trying to get to the point. Not so here. Unlike books authored by stuffy-toned, academic types, I've written this book in friendly, approachable language — because data science is a friendly and approachable subject!

To be honest, until now, the data science realm has been dominated by a few select data science wizards who tend to present the topic in a manner that's unnecessarily overly technical and intimidating. Basic data science isn't that confusing or difficult to understand. *Data science* is simply the practice of using a set of analytical techniques and methodologies to derive and communicate valuable and actionable insights from raw data. The purpose of data science is to optimize processes and to support improved data-informed decision making, thereby generating an increase in value — whether *value* is represented by number of lives saved, number of dollars retained, or percentage of revenues increased. In *Data Science For Dummies,* I introduce a broad array of concepts and approaches that you can use when extracting valuable insights from your data.

Many times, data scientists get so caught up analyzing the bark of the trees that they simply forget to look for their way out of the forest. This common pitfall is one that you should avoid at all costs. I've worked hard to make sure that this book presents the core purpose of each data science technique and the goals you can accomplish by utilizing them.

About This Book

In keeping with the *For Dummies* brand, this book is organized in a modular, easy-to-access format that allows you to use the book as a practical guidebook and ad hoc reference. In other words, you don't need to read it through, from cover to cover. Just take what you want and leave the rest. I've taken great care to use real-world examples that illustrate data science concepts that may otherwise be overly abstract.

Web addresses and programming code appear in monofont. If you're reading a digital version of this book on a device connected to the Internet, you can click a web address to visit that website, like this: www.dummies.com.

Foolish Assumptions

In writing this book, I've assumed that readers are at least technically minded enough to have mastered advanced tasks in Microsoft Excel — pivot tables, grouping, sorting, plotting, and the like. Having strong skills in algebra, basic statistics, or even business calculus helps as well. Foolish or not, it's my high hope that all readers have a subject-matter expertise to which they can apply the skills presented in this book. Because data scientists must be capable of intuitively understanding the implications and applications of the data insights they derive, subject-matter expertise is a major component of data science.

Icons Used in This Book

As you make your way through this book, you'll see the following icons in the margins:

TIP

The Tip icon marks tips (duh!) and shortcuts that you can use to make subject mastery easier.

REMEMBER

Remember icons mark the information that's especially important to know. To siphon off the most important information in each chapter, just skim the material represented by these icons.

TECHNICAL STUFF

The Technical Stuff icon marks information of a highly technical nature that you can normally skip.

WARNING

The Warning icon tells you to watch out! It marks important information that may save you headaches.

Beyond the Book

This book includes the following external resources:

>> **Data Science Cheat Sheet:** This book comes with a handy Cheat Sheet which lists helpful shortcuts as well as abbreviated definitions for essential processes and concepts described in the book. You can use it as a quick-and-easy reference when doing data science. To get this Cheat Sheet, simply go to www. dummies.com and search for *Data Science Cheat Sheet* in the Search box.

>> **Data Science Tutorial Datasets**: This book has a few tutorials that rely on external datasets. You can download all datasets for these tutorials from the GitHub repository for this course at https://github.com/BigDataGal/Data-Science-for-Dummies.

Where to Go from Here

Just to reemphasize the point, this book's modular design allows you to pick up and start reading anywhere you want. Although you don't need to read from cover to cover, a few good starter chapters are Chapters 1, 2, and 9.

1
Getting Started with Data Science

IN THIS PART . . .

Get introduced to the field of data science.

Define big data.

Explore solutions for big data problems.

See how real-world businesses put data science to good use.

Chapter **1**

Wrapping Your Head around Data Science

For quite some time now, *everyone* has been absolutely deluged by data. It's coming from every computer, every mobile device, every camera, and every imaginable sensor — and now it's even coming from watches and other wearable technologies. Data is generated in every social media interaction we make, every file we save, every picture we take, and every query we submit; it's even generated when we do something as simple as ask a favorite search engine for directions to the closest ice-cream shop.

Although data immersion is nothing new, you may have noticed that the phenomenon is accelerating. Lakes, puddles, and rivers of data have turned to floods and veritable tsunamis of structured, semistructured, and unstructured data that's streaming from almost every activity that takes place in both the digital and physical worlds. Welcome to the world of *big data!*

If you're anything like me, you may have wondered, "What's the point of all this data? Why use valuable resources to generate and collect it?" Although even a single decade ago, no one was in a position to make much use of most of the data that's generated, the tides today have definitely turned. Specialists known as *data engineers* are constantly finding innovative and powerful new ways to capture, collate, and condense unimaginably massive volumes of data, and other specialists, known as *data scientists,* are leading change by deriving valuable and actionable insights from that data.

In its truest form, data science represents the optimization of processes and resources. Data science produces *data insights* — actionable, data-informed conclusions or predictions that you can use to understand and improve your business, your investments, your health, and even your lifestyle and social life. Using data science insights is like being able to see in the dark. For any goal or pursuit you can imagine, you can find data science methods to help you predict the most direct route from where you are to where you want to be — and to anticipate every pothole in the road between both places.

Seeing Who Can Make Use of Data Science

The terms *data science* and *data engineering* are often misused and confused, so let me start off by clarifying that these two fields are, in fact, separate and distinct domains of expertise. *Data science* is the computational science of extracting meaningful insights from raw data and then effectively communicating those insights to generate value. *Data engineering,* on the other hand, is an engineering domain that's dedicated to building and maintaining systems that overcome data processing bottlenecks and data handling problems for applications that consume, process, and store large volumes, varieties, and velocities of data. In both data science and data engineering, you commonly work with these three data varieties:

>> **Structured:** Data is stored, processed, and manipulated in a traditional relational database management system (RDBMS).

>> **Unstructured:** Data that is commonly generated from human activities and doesn't fit into a structured database format.

>> **Semistructured:** Data doesn't fit into a structured database system, but is nonetheless structured by tags that are useful for creating a form of order and hierarchy in the data.

A lot of people believe that only large organizations that have massive funding are implementing data science methodologies to optimize and improve their business, but that's not the case. The proliferation of data has created a demand for insights, and this demand is embedded in many aspects of our modern culture — from the Uber passenger who expects his driver to pick him up exactly at the time and location predicted by the Uber application, to the online shopper who expects the Amazon platform to recommend the best product alternatives so she can compare similar goods before making a purchase. Data and the need for data-informed insights are ubiquitous. Because organizations of all sizes are beginning to recognize that they're immersed in a sink-or-swim, data-driven, competitive environment, data know-how emerges as a core and requisite function in almost every line of business.

What does this mean for the everyday person? First, it means that everyday employees are increasingly expected to support a progressively advancing set of technological requirements. Why? Well, that's because almost all industries are becoming increasingly reliant on data technologies and the insights they spur. Consequently, many people are in continuous need of re-upping their tech skills, or else they face the real possibility of being replaced by a more tech-savvy employee.

The good news is that upgrading tech skills doesn't usually require people to go back to college, or — God forbid — get a university degree in statistics, computer science, or data science. The bad news is that, even with professional training or self-teaching, it always takes extra work to stay industry-relevant and tech-savvy. In this respect, the data revolution isn't so different from any other change that has hit industry in the past. The fact is, in order to stay relevant, you need to take the time and effort to acquire only the skills that keep you current. When you're learning how to do data science, you can take some courses, educate yourself using online resources, read books like this one, and attend events where you can learn what you need to know to stay on top of the game.

Who can use data science? You can. Your organization can. Your employer can. Anyone who has a bit of understanding and training can begin using data insights to improve their lives, their careers, and the well-being of their businesses. Data science represents a change in the way you approach the world. When exacting outcomes, people often used to make their best guess, act, and then hope for their desired result. With data insights, however, people now have access to the predictive vision that they need to truly drive change and achieve the results they need.

You can use data insights to bring about changes in the following areas:

>> **Business systems:** Optimize returns on investment (those crucial ROIs) for any measurable activity.

>> **Technical marketing strategy development:** Use data insights and predictive analytics to identify marketing strategies that work, eliminate under-performing efforts, and test new marketing strategies.

>> **Keep communities safe:** Predictive policing applications help law enforcement personnel predict and prevent local criminal activities.

>> **Help make the world a better place for those less fortunate:** Data scientists in developing nations are using social data, mobile data, and data from websites to generate real-time analytics that improve the effectiveness of humanitarian response to disaster, epidemics, food scarcity issues, and more.

Analyzing the Pieces of the Data Science Puzzle

To practice data science, in the true meaning of the term, you need the analytical know-how of math and statistics, the coding skills necessary to work with data, and an area of subject matter expertise. Without this expertise, you might as well call yourself a mathematician or a statistician. Similarly, a software programmer without subject matter expertise and analytical know-how might better be considered a software engineer or developer, but not a data scientist.

Because the demand for data insights is increasing exponentially, every area is forced to adopt data science. As such, different flavors of data science have emerged. The following are just a few titles under which experts of every discipline are using data science: ad tech data scientist, director of banking digital analyst, clinical data scientist, geoengineer data scientist, geospatial analytics data scientist, political analyst, retail personalization data scientist, and clinical informatics analyst in pharmacometrics. Given that it often seems that no one without a scorecard can keep track of who's a data scientist, in the following sections I spell out the key components that are part of any data science role.

Collecting, querying, and consuming data

Data engineers have the job of capturing and collating large volumes of structured, unstructured, and semistructured *big data* — data that exceeds the processing capacity of conventional database systems because it's too big, it moves too fast, or it doesn't fit the structural requirements of traditional database architectures. Again, data engineering tasks are separate from the work that's performed in data science, which focuses more on analysis, prediction, and visualization. Despite this distinction, whenever data scientists collect, query, and consume data during the analysis process, they perform work similar to that of the data engineer (the role you read about earlier in this chapter).

Although valuable insights can be generated from a single data source, often the combination of several relevant sources delivers the contextual information required to drive better data-informed decisions. A data scientist can work from several datasets that are stored in a single database, or even in several different data warehouses. (For more about combining datasets, see Chapter 3.) At other times, source data is stored and processed on a cloud-based platform that's been built by software and data engineers.

No matter how the data is combined or where it's stored, if you're a data scientist, you almost always have to *query* data — write commands to extract relevant datasets from data storage systems, in other words. Most of the time, you use

Structured Query Language (SQL) to query data. (Chapter 16 is all about SQL, so if the acronym scares you, jump ahead to that chapter now.)

Whether you're using an application or doing custom analyses by using a programming language such as R or Python, you can choose from a number of universally accepted file formats:

» **Comma-separated values (CSV) files:** Almost every brand of desktop and web-based analysis application accepts this file type, as do commonly used scripting languages such as Python and R.

» **Scripts:** Most data scientists know how to use either the Python or R programming language to analyze and visualize data. These script files end with the extension .py or .ipynb (Python) or .r (R).

» **Application files:** Excel is useful for quick-and-easy, spot-check analyses on small- to medium-size datasets. These application files have the .xls or .xlsx extension. Geospatial analysis applications such as ArcGIS and QGIS save with their own proprietary file formats (the .mxd extension for ArcGIS and the .qgs extension for QGIS).

» **Web programming files:** If you're building custom, web-based data visualizations, you may be working in D3.js — or Data-Driven Documents, a JavaScript library for data visualization. When you work in D3.js, you use data to manipulate web-based documents using .html, .svg, and .css files.

Applying mathematical modeling to data science tasks

Data science relies heavily on a practitioner's math skills (and statistics skills, as described in the following section) precisely because these are the skills needed to understand your data and its significance. These skills are also valuable in data science because you can use them to carry out predictive forecasting, decision modeling, and hypotheses testing.

Mathematics uses deterministic methods to form a *quantitative* (or *numerical*) description of the world; *statistics* is a form of science that's derived from mathematics, but it focuses on using a *stochastic* (probabilities) approach and inferential methods to form a quantitative description of the world. More on both is discussed in Chapter 5.

Data scientists use mathematical methods to build decision models, generate approximations, and make predictions about the future. Chapter 5 presents many complex applied mathematical approaches that are useful when working in data science.

REMEMBER

In this book, I assume that you have a fairly solid skill set in basic math — it would be beneficial if you've taken college-level calculus or even linear algebra. I try hard, however, to meet readers where they are. I realize that you may be working based on a limited mathematical knowledge (advanced algebra or maybe business calculus), so I convey advanced mathematical concepts using a plain-language approach that's easy for everyone to understand.

Deriving insights from statistical methods

In data science, statistical methods are useful for better understanding your data's significance, for validating hypotheses, for simulating scenarios, and for making predictive forecasts of future events. Advanced statistical skills are somewhat rare, even among quantitative analysts, engineers, and scientists. If you want to go places in data science, though, take some time to get up to speed in a few basic statistical methods, like linear and logistic regression, naïve Bayes classification, and time series analysis. These methods are covered in Chapter 5.

Coding, coding, coding — it's just part of the game

Coding is unavoidable when you're working in data science. You need to be able to write code so that you can instruct the computer how you want it to manipulate, analyze, and visualize your data. Programming languages such as Python and R are important for writing scripts for data manipulation, analysis, and visualization, and SQL is useful for data querying. The JavaScript library D3.js is a hot new option for making cool, custom, and interactive web-based data visualizations.

Although coding is a requirement for data science, it doesn't have to be this big scary *thing* that people make it out to be. Your coding can be as fancy and complex as you want it to be, but you can also take a rather simple approach. Although these skills are paramount to success, you can pretty easily learn enough coding to practice high-level data science. I've dedicated Chapters 10, 14, 15, and 16 to helping you get up to speed in using D3.js for web-based data visualization, coding in Python and in R, and querying in SQL (respectively).

Applying data science to a subject area

Statisticians have exhibited some measure of obstinacy in accepting the significance of data science. Many statisticians have cried out, "Data science is nothing new! It's just another name for what we've been doing all along." Although I can sympathize with their perspective, I'm forced to stand with the camp of data scientists who markedly declare that data science is separate and definitely distinct from the statistical approaches that comprise it.

My position on the unique nature of data science is based to some extent on the fact that data scientists often use computer languages not used in traditional statistics and take approaches derived from the field of mathematics. But the main point of distinction between statistics and data science is the need for subject matter expertise.

Because statisticians usually have only a limited amount of expertise in fields outside of statistics, they're almost always forced to consult with a subject matter expert to verify exactly what their findings mean and to decide the best direction in which to proceed. Data scientists, on the other hand, are required to have a strong subject matter expertise in the area in which they're working. Data scientists generate deep insights and then use their domain-specific expertise to understand exactly what those insights mean with respect to the area in which they're working.

This list describes a few ways in which subject matter experts are using data science to enhance performance in their respective industries:

>> **Engineers** use machine learning to optimize energy efficiency in modern building design.

>> **Clinical data scientists** work on the personalization of treatment plans and use healthcare informatics to predict and preempt future health problems in at-risk patients.

>> **Marketing data scientists** use logistic regression to predict and preempt *customer churn* (the loss or churn of customers from a product or service to that of a competitor's). I tell you more on decreasing customer churn in Chapters 3 and 20.

>> **Data journalists** scrape websites (extract data in-bulk directly off the pages on a website, in other words) for fresh data in order to discover and report the latest breaking-news stories. (I talk more about data journalism in Chapter 18.)

>> **Data scientists in crime analysis** use spatial predictive modeling to predict, preempt, and prevent criminal activities. (See Chapter 21 for all the details on using data science to describe and predict criminal activity.)

>> **Data do-gooders** use machine learning to classify and report vital information about disaster-affected communities for real-time decision support in humanitarian response, which you can read about in Chapter 19.

Communicating data insights

As a data scientist, you must have sharp oral and written communication skills. If a data scientist can't communicate, all the knowledge and insight in the world does *nothing* for your organization. Data scientists need to be able to explain data insights in a way that staff members can understand. Not only that, data scientists need to be able to produce clear and meaningful data visualizations and written narratives. Most of the time, people need to see something for themselves in order to understand. Data scientists must be creative and pragmatic in their means and methods of communication. (I cover the topics of data visualization and data-driven storytelling in much greater detail in Chapter 9 and Chapter 18, respectively.)

Exploring the Data Science Solution Alternatives

Organizations and their leaders are still grappling with how to best use big data and data science. Most of them know that advanced analytics is positioned to bring a tremendous competitive edge to their organizations, but few of them have any idea about the options that are available or the exact benefits that data science can deliver. In this section, I introduce three major data science solution alternatives and describe the benefits that a data science implementation can deliver.

Assembling your own in-house team

Many organizations find it makes financial sense for them to establish their own dedicated in-house team of data professionals. This saves them money they would otherwise spend achieving similar results by hiring independent consultants or deploying a ready-made cloud-based analytics solution. Three options for building an in-house data science team are:

>> **Train existing employees.** If you want to equip your organization with the power of data science and analytics, data science training (the lower-cost alternative) can transform existing staff into data-skilled, highly specialized subject matter experts for your in-house team.

>> **Hire trained personnel.** Some organizations fill their requirements by either hiring experienced data scientists or by hiring fresh data science graduates. The problem with this approach is that there aren't enough of these people to go around, and if you do find people who are willing to come onboard, they have high salary requirements. Remember, in addition to the math, statistics, and coding requirements, data scientists must have a high level of subject

matter expertise in the specific field where they're working. That's why it's extraordinarily difficult to find these individuals. Until universities make data literacy an integral part of every educational program, finding highly specialized and skilled data scientists to satisfy organizational requirements will be nearly impossible.

>> **Train existing employees and hire some experts.** Another good option is to train existing employees to do high-level data science tasks and then bring on a few experienced data scientists to fulfill your more advanced data science problem-solving and strategy requirements.

Outsourcing requirements to private data science consultants

Many organizations prefer to outsource their data science and analytics requirements to an outside expert, using one of two general strategies:

>> **Comprehensive:** This strategy serves the entire organization. To build an advanced data science implementation for your organization, you can hire a private consultant to help you with a comprehensive strategy development. This type of service will likely cost you, but you can receive tremendously valuable insights in return. A strategist will know about the options available to meet your requirements, as well as the benefits and drawbacks of each on. With strategy in hand and an on-call expert available to help you, you can much more easily navigate the task of building an internal team.

>> **Individual:** You can apply piecemeal solutions to specific problems that arise, or that have arisen, within your organization. If you're not prepared for the rather involved process of comprehensive strategy design and implementation, you can contract out smaller portions of work to a private data science consultant. This spot-treatment approach could still deliver the benefits of data science without requiring you to reorganize the structure and financials of your entire organization.

Leveraging cloud-based platform solutions

A cloud-based solution can deliver the power of data analytics to professionals who have only a modest level of data literacy. Some have seen the explosion of big data and data science coming from a long way off. Although it's still new to most, professionals and organizations in the know have been working fast and furiously to prepare. New, private cloud applications such as Trusted Analytics Platform, or TAP (`http://trustedanalytics.org`) are dedicated to making it easier and faster for organizations to deploy their big data initiatives. Other cloud services, like Tableau, offer code-free, automated data services — from basic clean-up and statistical modeling to analysis and data visualization. Though you still need to understand the statistical, mathematical, and substantive relevance of the data insights, applications such as Tableau can deliver powerful results without requiring users to know how to write code or scripts.

REMEMBER

If you decide to use cloud-based platform solutions to help your organization reach its data science objectives, you still need in-house staff who are trained and skilled to design, run, and interpret the quantitative results from these platforms. The platform will not do away with the need for in-house training and data science expertise — it will merely augment your organization so that it can more readily achieve its objectives.

Letting Data Science Make You More Marketable

Throughout this book, I hope to show you the power of data science and how you can use that power to more quickly reach your personal and professional goals. No matter the sector in which you work, acquiring data science skills can transform you into a more marketable professional. The following list describes just a few key industry sectors that can benefit from data science and analytics:

>> **Corporations, small- and medium-size enterprises (SMEs), and e-commerce businesses:** Production-costs optimization, sales maximization, marketing ROI increases, staff-productivity optimization, customer-churn reduction, customer lifetime-value increases, inventory requirements and sales predictions, pricing model optimization, fraud detection, collaborative filtering, recommendation engines, and logistics improvements

>> **Governments:** Business-process and staff-productivity optimization, management decision-support enhancements, finance and budget forecasting, expenditure tracking and optimization, and fraud detection

>> **Academia:** Resource-allocation improvements, student performance-management improvements, dropout reductions, business process optimization, finance and budget forecasting, and recruitment ROI increases

Chapter **2**

Exploring Data Engineering Pipelines and Infrastructure

There's a lot of hype around big data these days, but most people don't really know or understand what it is or how they can use it to improve their lives and livelihoods. This chapter defines the term big data, explains where big data comes from and how it's used, and outlines the roles that data engineers and data scientists play in the big data ecosystem. In this chapter, I introduce the fundamental big data concepts that you need in order to start generating your own ideas and plans on how to leverage big data and data science to improve your lifestyle and business workflow (*Hint:* You'd be able to improve your lifestyle by mastering some of the technologies discussed in this chapter — which would certainly lead to more opportunities for landing a well-paid position that also offers excellent lifestyle benefits.)

Defining Big Data by the Three Vs

Big data is data that exceeds the processing capacity of conventional database systems because it's too big, it moves too fast, or it doesn't fit the structural requirements of traditional database architectures. Whether data volumes rank in the terabyte or petabyte scales, data-engineered solutions must be designed to meet requirements for the data's intended destination and use.

TECHNICAL STUFF

When you're talking about regular data, you're likely to hear the words *kilobyte* and *gigabyte* used as measurements — 10^3 and 10^9 bytes, respectively. In contrast, when you're talking about big data, words like *terabyte* and *petabyte* are thrown around instead — 10^{12} and 10^{15} bytes, respectively. A *byte* is an 8-bit unit of data.

Three characteristics (known as "the three Vs") define big data: volume, velocity, and variety. Because the three Vs of big data are continually expanding, newer, more innovative data technologies must continuously be developed to manage big data problems.

REMEMBER

In a situation where you're required to adopt a big data solution to overcome a problem that's caused by your data's velocity, volume, or variety, you have moved past the realm of regular data — you have a big data problem on your hands.

Grappling with data volume

The lower limit of big data volume starts as low as 1 terabyte, and it has no upper limit. If your organization owns at least 1 terabyte of data, it's probably a good candidate for a big data deployment.

WARNING

In its raw form, most big data is *low value* — in other words, the value-to-data-quantity ratio is low in raw big data. Big data is composed of huge numbers of very small transactions that come in a variety of formats. These incremental components of big data produce true value only after they're aggregated and analyzed. Data engineers have the job of rolling it up, and data scientists have the job of analyzing it.

Handling data velocity

A lot of big data is created through automated processes and instrumentation nowadays, and because data storage costs are relatively inexpensive, system velocity is, many times, the limiting factor. Big data is low-value. Consequently, you need systems that are able to ingest a lot of it, on short order, to generate timely and valuable insights.

In engineering terms, *data velocity* is data volume per unit time. Big data enters an average system at velocities ranging between 30 kilobytes (K) per second to as much as 30 *gigabytes* (GB) per second. Many data-engineered systems are required to have latency less than 100 milliseconds, measured from the time the data is created to the time the system responds. Throughput requirements can easily be as high as 1,000 messages per second in big data systems! High-velocity, real-time moving data presents an obstacle to timely decision making. The capabilities of data-handling and data-processing technologies often limit data velocities.

REMEMBER

Data ingestion tools come in a variety of flavors. Some of the more popular ones are described in this list:

>> **Apache Sqoop:** You can use this data transference tool to quickly transfer data back and forth between a relational data system and the *Hadoop distributed file system (HDFS)* — it uses clusters of commodity servers to store big data. HDFS makes big data handling and storage financially feasible by distributing storage tasks across clusters of inexpensive commodity servers. It is the main storage system that's used in big data implementations.

>> **Apache Kafka:** This distributed messaging system acts as a message broker whereby messages can quickly be pushed onto, and pulled from, HDFS. You can use Kafka to consolidate and facilitate the data calls and pushes that consumers make to and from the HDFS.

>> **Apache Flume:** This distributed system primarily handles log and event data. You can use it to transfer massive quantities of unstructured data to and from the HDFS.

Dealing with data variety

Big data gets even more complicated when you add unstructured and semistructured data to structured data sources. This *high-variety* data comes from a multitude of sources. The most salient point about it is that it's composed of a combination of datasets with differing underlying structures (either structured, unstructured, or semistructured). Heterogeneous, high-variety data is often composed of any combination of graph data, JSON files, XML files, social media data, structured tabular data, weblog data, and data that's generated from click-streams.

Structured data can be stored, processed, and manipulated in a traditional relational database management system (RDBMS). This data can be generated by humans or machines, and is derived from all sorts of sources, from click-streams and web-based forms to point-of-sale transactions and sensors. *Unstructured* data comes completely unstructured — it's commonly generated from human activities and doesn't fit into a structured database format. Such data could be derived from blog posts, emails, and Word documents. *Semistructured* data doesn't fit into a structured database system, but is nonetheless structured by tags that are useful for creating a form of order and hierarchy in the data. Semistructured data is commonly found in databases and file systems. It can be stored as log files, XML files, or JSON data files.

TIP

Become familiar with the term *data lake* — this term is used by practitioners in the big data industry to refer to a nonhierarchical data storage system that's used to hold huge volumes of multi-structured data within a flat storage architecture. HDFS can be used as a data lake storage repository, but you can also use the Amazon Web Services S3 platform to meet the same requirements on the cloud (the Amazon Web Services S3 platform is a cloud architecture that's available for storing big data).

Identifying Big Data Sources

Big data is being continually generated by humans, machines, and sensors everywhere. Typical sources include data from social media, financial transactions, health records, click-streams, log files, and the *Internet of things* — a web of digital connections that joins together the ever-expanding array of electronic devices we use in our everyday lives. Figure 2-1 shows a variety of popular big data sources.

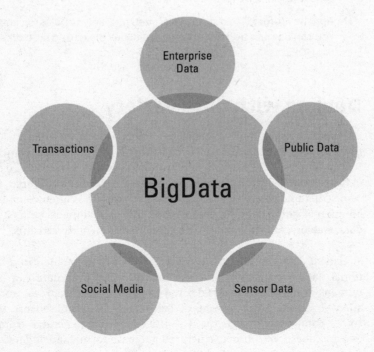

FIGURE 2-1: Popular sources of big data.

Grasping the Difference between Data Science and Data Engineering

Data science and data engineering are two different branches within the *big data paradigm* — an approach wherein huge velocities, varieties, and volumes of structured, unstructured, and semistructured data are being captured, processed, stored, and analyzed using a set of techniques and technologies that is completely novel compared to those that were used in decades past.

Both are useful for deriving knowledge and actionable insights from raw data. Both are essential elements for any comprehensive decision-support system, and both are extremely helpful when formulating robust strategies for future business management and growth. Although the terms *data science* and *data engineering* are often used interchangeably, they're distinct domains of expertise. In the following sections, I introduce concepts that are fundamental to data science and data engineering, and then I show you the differences in how these two roles function in an organization's data processing system.

Defining data science

If *science* is a systematic method by which people study and explain domain-specific phenomenon that occur in the natural world, you can think of *data science* as the scientific domain that's dedicated to knowledge discovery via data analysis.

TECHNICAL STUFF

With respect to data science, the term *domain-specific* refers to the industry sector or subject matter domain that data science methods are being used to explore.

Data scientists use mathematical techniques and algorithmic approaches to derive solutions to complex business and scientific problems. Data science practitioners use its predictive methods to derive insights that are otherwise unattainable. In business and in science, data science methods can provide more robust decision making capabilities:

>> **In business,** the purpose of data science is to empower businesses and organizations with the data information that they need in order to optimize organizational processes for maximum efficiency and revenue generation.

>> **In science,** data science methods are used to derive results and develop protocols for achieving the specific scientific goal at hand.

Data science is a vast and multidisciplinary field. To call yourself a true data scientist, you need to have expertise in math and statistics, computer programming, and your own domain-specific subject matter.

Using data science skills, you can do things like this:

» Use machine learning to optimize energy usages and lower corporate carbon footprints.

» Optimize tactical strategies to achieve goals in business and science.

» Predict for unknown contaminant levels from sparse environmental datasets.

» Design automated theft- and fraud-prevention systems to detect anomalies and trigger alarms based on algorithmic results.

» Craft site-recommendation engines for use in land acquisitions and real estate development.

» Implement and interpret predictive analytics and forecasting techniques for net increases in business value.

Data scientists must have extensive and diverse quantitative expertise to be able to solve these types of problems.

TECHNICAL STUFF

Machine learning is the practice of applying algorithms to learn from, and make automated predictions about, data.

Defining data engineering

If *engineering* is the practice of using science and technology to design and build systems that solve problems, you can think of *data engineering* as the engineering domain that's dedicated to building and maintaining data systems for overcoming data-processing bottlenecks and data-handling problems that arise due to the high volume, velocity, and variety of big data.

Data engineers use skills in computer science and software engineering to design systems for, and solve problems with, handling and manipulating big datasets. Data engineers often have experience working with and designing real-time processing frameworks and massively parallel processing (MPP) platforms (discussed later in this chapter), as well as RDBMSs. They generally code in Java, C++, Scala, and Python. They know how to deploy Hadoop MapReduce or Spark to handle, process, and refine big data into more manageably sized datasets. Simply put, with respect to data science, the purpose of data engineering is to engineer big data solutions by building coherent, modular, and scalable data processing platforms from which data scientists can subsequently derive insights.

Most engineered systems are *built* systems — they are constructed or manufactured in the physical world. Data engineering is different, though. It involves designing, building, and implementing software solutions to problems in the data world — a world that can seem abstract when compared to the physical reality of the Golden Gate Bridge or the Aswan Dam.

Using data engineering skills, you can, for example:

>> Build large-scale Software-as-a-Service (SaaS) applications.

>> Build and customize Hadoop and MapReduce applications.

>> Design and build relational databases and highly scaled distributed architectures for processing big data.

>> Build an integrated platform that simultaneously solves problems in data ingestion, data storage, machine learning, and system management — all from one interface.

Data engineers need solid skills in computer science, database design, and software engineering to be able to perform this type of work.

Software-as-a-Service (SaaS) is a term that describes cloud-hosted software services that are made available to users via the Internet.

Comparing data scientists and data engineers

The roles of data scientist and data engineer are frequently completely confused and intertwined by hiring managers. If you look around at most position descriptions for companies that are hiring, they often mismatch the titles and roles or simply expect applicants to do both data science and data engineering.

If you're hiring someone to help make sense of your data, be sure to define the requirements clearly before writing the position description. Because data scientists must also have subject-matter expertise in the particular areas in which they work, this requirement generally precludes data scientists from also having expertise in data engineering (although some data scientists do have experience using engineering data platforms). And, if you hire a data engineer who has data science skills, that person generally won't have much subject-matter expertise outside of the data domain. Be prepared to call in a subject-matter expert to help out.

Because many organizations combine and confuse roles in their data projects, data scientists are sometime stuck spending a lot of time learning to do the job of a data engineer, and vice versa. To get the highest-quality work product in the least amount of time, hire a data engineer to process your data and a data scientist to make sense of it for you.

Lastly, keep in mind that data engineer and data scientist are just two small roles within a larger organizational structure. Managers, middle-level employees, and organizational leaders also play a huge part in the success of any data-driven initiative. The primary benefit of incorporating data science and data engineering into your projects is to leverage your external and internal data to strengthen your organization's decision-support capabilities.

Making Sense of Data in Hadoop

Because big data's three Vs (volume, velocity, and variety) don't allow for the handling of big data using traditional relational database management systems, data engineers had to become innovative. To get around the limitations of relational systems, data engineers turn to the Hadoop data processing platform to boil down big data into smaller datasets that are more manageable for data scientists to analyze.

REMEMBER

When you hear people use the term *Hadoop* nowadays, they're generally referring to a Hadoop ecosystem that includes the HDFS (for data storage), MapReduce (for bulk data processing), Spark (for real-time data processing), and YARN (for resource management).

In the following sections, I introduce you to MapReduce, Spark, and the Hadoop distributed file system. I also introduce the programming languages you can use to develop applications in these frameworks.

Digging into MapReduce

MapReduce is a parallel distributed processing framework that can be used to process tremendous volumes of data *in-batch* — where data is collected and then processed as one unit with processing completion times on the order of hours or days. MapReduce works by converting raw data down to sets of tuples and then combining and reducing those tuples into smaller sets of tuples (with respect to MapReduce, *tuples* refer to key-value pairs by which data is grouped, sorted, and processed). In layman's terms, MapReduce uses parallel distributed computing to transform big data into manageable-size data.

Parallel distributed processing refers to a powerful framework where data is processed very quickly via the distribution and parallel processing of tasks across clusters of commodity servers.

MapReduce jobs implement a sequence of map- and reduce-tasks across a distributed set of servers. In the *map task*, you delegate data to key-value pairs, transform it, and filter it. Then you assign the data to nodes for processing. In the *reduce task*, you aggregate that data down to smaller-size datasets. Data from the reduce step is transformed into a standard *key-value format* — where the *key* acts as the record identifier and the *value* is the value being identified by the key. The clusters' computing nodes process the map tasks and reduce tasks that are defined by the user.

This work is done in two steps:

1. **Map the data.**

    The incoming data must first be delegated into key-value pairs and divided into fragments, which are then assigned to map tasks. Each *computing cluster* (a group of nodes that are connected to each other and perform a shared computing task) is assigned a number of map tasks, which are subsequently distributed among its nodes. Upon processing of the key-value pairs, intermediate key-value pairs are generated. The intermediate key-value pairs are sorted by their key values, and this list is divided into a new set of fragments. Whatever count you have for these new fragments, it will be the same as the count of the reduce tasks.

2. **Reduce the data.**

    Every reduce task has a fragment assigned to it. The reduce task simply processes the fragment and produces an output, which is also a key-value pair. Reduce tasks are also distributed among the different nodes of the cluster. After the task is completed, the final output is written onto a file system.

In short, you can use MapReduce as a batch-processing tool, to boil down and begin to make sense of a huge volume, velocity, and variety of data by using map and reduce tasks to tag the data by (key, value) pairs, and then reduce those pairs into smaller sets of data through *aggregation operations* — operations that combine multiple values from a dataset into a single value. A diagram of the MapReduce architecture is shown in Figure 2-2.

If your data doesn't lend itself to being tagged and processed via keys, values, and aggregation, map-and-reduce *generally* isn't a good fit for your needs.

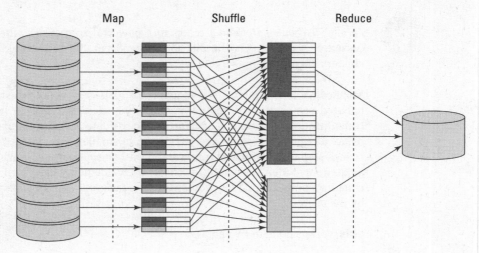

Map   Shuffle   Reduce

FIGURE 2-2:
The MapReduce
architecture.

Stepping into real-time processing

Do you recall that MapReduce is a batch processor and can't process real-time, streaming data? Well, sometimes you might need to query big data streams in real-time — and you just can't do this sort of thing using MapReduce. In these cases, use a real-time processing framework instead.

A *real-time processing framework* is — as its name implies — a framework that processes data in real-time (or near – real-time) as that data streams and flows into the system. Real-time frameworks process data in microbatches — they return results in a matter of seconds rather than hours or days, like MapReduce. Real-time processing frameworks either

>> **Lower the overhead of MapReduce tasks to increase the overall time efficiency of the system:** Solutions in this category include Apache Storm and Apache Spark for near–real-time stream processing.

>> **Deploy innovative querying methods to facilitate the real-time querying of big data:** Some solutions in this category are Google's Dremel, Apache Drill, Shark for Apache Hive, and Cloudera's Impala.

Although MapReduce was historically the main processing framework in a Hadoop system, Spark has recently made some major advances in assuming MapReduce's position. *Spark* is an in-memory computing application that you can use to query, explore, analyze, and even run machine learning algorithms on incoming, streaming data in near–real-time. Its power lies in its processing speed — the ability to process and make predictions from streaming big data sources in three seconds flat is no laughing matter. Major vendors such as Cloudera have been pushing for the advancement of Spark so that it can be used as a complete MapReduce replacement, but it isn't there yet.

Real-time, stream-processing frameworks are quite useful in a multitude of industries — from stock and financial market analyses to e-commerce optimizations, and from real-time fraud detection to optimized order logistics. Regardless of the industry in which you work, if your business is impacted by real-time data streams that are generated by humans, machines, or sensors, a real-time processing framework would be helpful to you in optimizing and generating value for your organization.

Storing data on the Hadoop distributed file system (HDFS)

The Hadoop distributed file system (HDFS) uses clusters of commodity hardware for storing data. Hardware in each cluster is connected, and this hardware is composed of *commodity servers* — low-cost, low-performing generic servers that offer powerful computing capabilities when run in parallel across a shared cluster. These commodity servers are also called *nodes*. Commoditized computing dramatically decreases the costs involved in storing big data.

The HDFS is characterized by these three key features:

>> **HDFS blocks:** In data storage, a *block* is a storage unit that contains some maximum number of records. HDFS blocks are able to store 64MB of data, by default.

>> **Redundancy:** Datasets that are stored in HDFS are broken up and stored on blocks. These blocks are then replicated (three times, by default) and stored on several different servers in the cluster, as backup, or *redundancy*.

>> **Fault-tolerance:** A system is described as *fault tolerant* if it is built to continue successful operations despite the failure of one or more of its subcomponents. Because the HDFS has built-in redundancy across multiple servers in a cluster, if one server fails, the system simply retrieves the data from another server.

WARNING

Don't pay storage costs on data you don't need. Storing big data is relatively inexpensive, but it is definitely not free. In fact, storage costs range up to $20,000 per commodity server in a Hadoop cluster. For this reason, only relevant data should be ingested and stored.

Putting it all together on the Hadoop platform

The Hadoop platform is the premier platform for large-scale data processing, storage, and management. This open-source platform is generally composed of the HDFS, MapReduce, Spark, and YARN, all working together.

Within a Hadoop platform, the workloads of applications that run on the HDFS (like MapReduce and Spark) are divided among the nodes of the cluster, and the output is stored on the HDFS. A Hadoop cluster can be composed of thousands of nodes. To keep the costs of input/output (I/O) processes low, MapReduce jobs are performed as close to the data as possible — the reduce tasks processors are positioned as closely as possible to the outgoing map task data that needs to be processed. This design facilitates the sharing of computational requirements in big data processing.

Hadoop also supports hierarchical organization. Some of its nodes are classified as master nodes, and others are categorized as slaves. The master service, known as *JobTracker*, is designed to control several slave services. A single slave service (also called *TaskTracker*) is distributed to each node. The JobTracker controls the Task-Trackers and assigns Hadoop MapReduce tasks to them. YARN, the resource manager, acts as an integrated system that performs resource management and scheduling functions.

Identifying Alternative Big Data Solutions

Looking past Hadoop, alternative big data solutions are on the horizon. These solutions make it possible to work with big data in real-time or to use alternative database technologies to handle and process it. In the following sections, I introduce you to massively parallel processing (MPP) platforms and the NoSQL databases that allow you to work with big data outside of the Hadoop environment.

REMEMBER

ACID compliance stands for *a*tomicity, *c*onsistency, *i*solation, and *d*urability compliance, a standard by which accurate and reliable database transactions are guaranteed. In big data solutions, most database systems are not ACID compliant, but this does not necessarily pose a major problem, because most big data systems use a decision support system (DSS) that batch-processes data before that data is read out. A DSS is an information system that is used for organizational decision support. A nontransactional DSS demonstrates no real ACID compliance requirements.

Introducing massively parallel processing (MPP) platforms

Massively parallel processing (MPP) platforms can be used instead of MapReduce as an alternative approach for distributed data processing. If your goal is to deploy parallel processing on a traditional data warehouse, an MPP may be the perfect solution.

To understand how MPP compares to a standard MapReduce parallel-processing framework, consider that MPP runs parallel computing tasks on costly, custom hardware, whereas MapReduce runs them on inexpensive commodity servers. Consequently, MPP processing capabilities are cost restrictive. MPP is quicker and easier to use, however, than standard MapReduce jobs. That's because MPP can be queried using Structured Query Language (SQL), but native MapReduce jobs are controlled by the more complicated Java programming language.

Introducing NoSQL databases

A traditional RDBMS isn't equipped to handle big data demands. That's because it is designed to handle only relational datasets constructed of data that's stored in clean rows and columns and thus is capable of being queried via SQL. RDBMSs are not capable of handling unstructured and semistructured data. Moreover, RDBMSs simply don't have the processing and handling capabilities that are needed for meeting big data volume and velocity requirements.

This is where NoSQL comes in. *NoSQL* databases are non-relational, distributed database systems that were designed to rise to the big data challenge. NoSQL databases step out past the traditional relational database architecture and offer a much more scalable, efficient solution. NoSQL systems facilitate non-SQL data querying of non-relational or schema-free, semistructured and unstructured data. In this way, NoSQL databases are able to handle the structured, semistructured, and unstructured data sources that are common in big data systems.

NoSQL offers four categories of non-relational databases: graph databases, document databases, key-values stores, and column family stores. Because NoSQL offers native functionality for each of these separate types of data structures, it offers very efficient storage and retrieval functionality for most types of non-relational data. This adaptability and efficiency makes NoSQL an increasingly popular choice for handling big data and for overcoming processing challenges that come along with it.

The NoSQL applications Apache Cassandra and MongoDB are used for data storage and real-time processing. Apache Cassandra is a popular type of key-value store NoSQL database, and MongoDB is a document-oriented type of NoSQL database. It uses dynamic schemas and stores JSON-esque documents. MongoDB is the most popular type of document store on the NoSQL market.

TECHNICAL STUFF

Some people argue that the term *NoSQL* stands for Not Only SQL, and others argue that it represents Non-SQL databases. The argument is rather complex, and there is no cut-and-dried answer. To keep things simple, just think of NoSQL as a class of non-relational systems that do not fall within the spectrum of RDBMSs that are queried using SQL.

Data Engineering in Action: A Case Study

A Fortune 100 telecommunications company had large datasets that resided in separate *data silos* — data repositories that are disconnected and isolated from other data storage systems used across the organization. With the goal of deriving data insights that lead to revenue increases, the company decided to connect all of its data silos and then integrate that shared source with other contextual, external, non-enterprise data sources as well.

Identifying the business challenge

The Fortune 100 company was stocked to the gills with all the traditional enterprise systems: ERP, ECM, CRM — you name it. Slowly, over many years, these systems grew and segregated into separate information silos. (Check out Figure 2-3 to see what I mean.) Because of the isolated structure of the data systems, otherwise useful data was lost and buried deep within a mess of separate, siloed storage systems. Even if the company knew what data it had, it would be like pulling teeth to access, integrate, and utilize it. The company rightfully believed that this restriction was limiting its business growth.

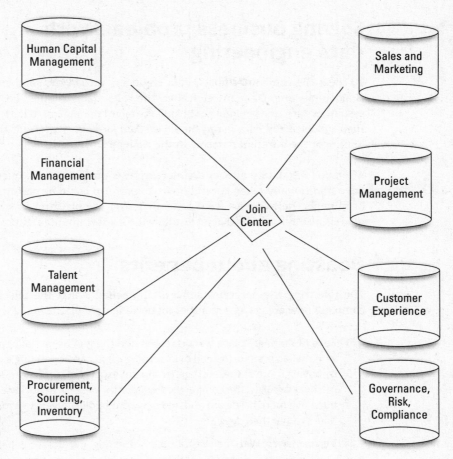

FIGURE 2-3:
Data silos, joined
by a common
join point.

To optimize its sales and marketing return on investments, the company wanted to integrate external, open datasets and relevant social data sources that would provide deeper insights into its current and potential customers. But to build this 360-degree view of the target market and customer base, the company needed to develop a sophisticated platform across which the data could be integrated, mined, and analyzed.

The company had the following three goals in mind for the project:

» Manage and extract value from disparate, isolated datasets.

» Take advantage of information from external, non-enterprise, or social data sources to provide new, exciting, and useful services that create value.

» Identify specific trends and issues in competitor activity, product offerings, industrial customer segments, and sales team member profiles.

Solving business problems with data engineering

To meet the company's goals, data engineers moved the company's datasets to Hadoop clusters. One cluster hosted the sales data, another hosted the human resources data, and yet another hosted the talent management data. Data engineers then modeled the data using the *linked data format* — a format that facilitates a joining of the different datasets in the Hadoop clusters.

After this big data platform architecture was put into place, queries that would have traditionally taken several hours to perform could be performed in a matter of minutes. New queries were generated after the platform was built, and these queries also returned efficient results within a few minutes' time.

Boasting about benefits

The following list describes some of the benefits that the telecommunications company now enjoys as a result of its new big data platform:

>> **Ease of scaling:** Scaling is much easier and cheaper using Hadoop than it was with the old system. Instead of increasing capital and operating expenditures by buying more of the latest generation of expensive computers, servers, and memory capacity, the company opted to grow wider instead. It was able to purchase more hardware and add new commodity servers in a matter of hours rather than days.

>> **Performance:** With their distributed processing and storage capabilities, the Hadoop clusters deliver insights faster and produce more data insight for less cost.

>> **High availability and reliability:** The company has found that the Hadoop platform is providing data protection and high availability while the clusters grow in size. Additionally, the Hadoop clusters have increased system reliability because of their *automatic failover* configuration — a configuration that facilitates an automatic switch to redundant, backup data-handling systems in instances where the primary system might fail.

Chapter **3**

Applying Data-Driven Insights to Business and Industry

To the nerds and geeks out there, data science is interesting in its own right, but to most people, it's interesting only because of the benefits it can generate. Most business managers and organizational leaders couldn't care less about coding and complex statistical algorithms. They are, on the other hand, extremely interested in finding new ways to increase business profits by increasing sales rates and decreasing inefficiencies. In this chapter, I introduce the concept of business-centric data science, discuss how it differs from traditional business intelligence, and talk about how you can use data-derived business insights to increase your business's bottom line.

The modern business world is absolutely deluged with data. That's because every line of business, every electronic system, every desktop computer, every laptop, every company-owned cellphone, and every employee is continually creating new business-related data as a natural and organic output of their work. This data is structured or unstructured some of it is big and some of it is small, fast or slow; maybe it's tabular data, or video data, or spatial data, or data that no one has come up with a name for yet. But though there are many varieties and variations between the types of datasets produced, the challenge is only one — to extract data insights that add value to the organization when acted upon. In this chapter, I walk you through the challenges involved in deriving value from actionable insights that are generated from raw business data.

Benefiting from Business-Centric Data Science

Business is complex. Data science is complex. At times, it's easy to get so caught up looking at the trees that you forget to look for a way out of the forest. That's why, in all areas of business, it's extremely important to stay focused on the end goal. Ultimately, no matter what line of business you're in, true north is always the same: business profit growth. Whether you achieve that by creating greater efficiencies or by increasing sales rates and customer loyalty, the end goal is to create a more stable, solid profit–growth rate for your business. The following list describes some of the ways that you can use business–centric data science and business intelligence to help increase profits:

>> **Decrease financial risks.** A business-centric data scientist can decrease financial risk in e-commerce business by using time series anomaly-detection methods for real-time fraud detection — to decrease Card-Not-Present fraud and to decrease the incidence of account takeovers, to take two examples.

>> **Increase the efficiencies of systems and processes.** This is a business systems optimization function that's performed by both the business-centric data scientist and the business analyst. Both use analytics to optimize business processes, structures, and systems, but their methods and data sources differ. The end goal here should be to decrease needless resource expenditures and to increase return on investment for justified expenditures.

>> **Increase sales rates.** To increase sales rates for your offerings, you can employ a business-centric data scientist to help you find the best ways to upsell and cross-sell, increase customer loyalty, increase conversions in each layer of the funnel, and exact-target your advertising and discounts. It's likely that your business is already employing many of these tactics, but a business-centric data scientist can look at all data related to the business and, from that, derive insights that supercharge these efforts.

Converting Raw Data into Actionable Insights with Data Analytics

Turning your raw data into actionable insights is the first step in the progression from the data you've collected to something that actually benefits you. Business-centric data scientists use *data analytics* to generate insights from raw data.

Types of analytics

Listed here, in order of increasing complexity, are the four types of data analytics you'll most likely encounter:

>> **Descriptive analytics:** This type of analytics answers the question, "What happened?" Descriptive analytics are based on historical and current data. A business analyst or a business-centric data scientist bases modern-day business intelligence on descriptive analytics.

>> **Diagnostic analytics:** You use this type of analytics to find answers to the question, "Why did this particular something happen?" or "What went wrong?" Diagnostic analytics are useful for deducing and inferring the success or failure of subcomponents of any data-driven initiative.

>> **Predictive analytics:** Although this type of analytics is based on historical and current data, predictive analytics go one step further than descriptive analytics. *Predictive analytics* involve complex model-building and analysis in order to predict a future event or trend. In a business context, these analyses would be performed by the business-centric data scientist.

>> **Prescriptive analytics:** This type of analytics aims to optimize processes, structures, and systems through informed action that's based on predictive analytics — essentially telling you what you should do based on an informed estimation of what will happen. Both business analysts and business-centric data scientists can generate prescriptive analytics, but their methods and data sources differ.

REMEMBER

Ideally, a business should engage in all four types of data analytics, but prescriptive analytics is the most direct and effective means by which to generate value from data insights.

Common challenges in analytics

Analytics commonly pose at least two challenges in the business enterprise. First, organizations often have difficulty finding new hires with specific skill sets that include analytics. Second, even skilled analysts often have difficulty communicating complex insights in a way that's understandable to management decision makers.

To overcome these challenges, the organization must create and nurture a culture that values and accepts analytics products. The business must work to educate all levels of the organization so that management has a basic concept of analytics and the success that can be achieved by implementing them. Conversely, business-centric data scientists must have a solid working knowledge about business in general and, in particular, a solid understanding of the business at hand. A strong business knowledge is one of the three main requirements of any business-centric data scientist; the other two are a strong coding acumen and strong quantitative analysis skills via math and statistical modeling.

Data wrangling

Data wrangling is another important portion of the work that's required in order to convert data to insights. To build analytics from raw data, you'll almost always need to use *data wrangling* — the processes and procedures that you use to clean and convert data from one format and structure to another so that the data is accurate and in the format that analytics tools and scripts require for consumption. The following list highlights a few of the practices and issues I consider most relevant to data wrangling:

>> **Data extraction:** The business-centric data scientist must first identify which datasets are relevant to the problem at hand and then extract sufficient quantities of the data that's required to solve the problem. (This extraction process is commonly referred to as *data mining*.)

>> **Data preparation:** Data preparation involves cleaning the raw data extracted through data mining and then converting it into a format that allows for a more convenient consumption of the data. Six steps are involved, as you see in the next paragraph.

>> **Data governance:** Data governance standards are used as a quality control measure to ensure that manual and automated data sources conform to the data standards of the model at hand. Data governance standards must be applied so that the data is at the right granularity when it's stored and made ready for use.

REMEMBER

Granularity is a measure of a dataset's level of detail. Data granularity is determined by the relative size of the subgroupings into which the data is divided.

>> **Data architecture:** IT architecture is the key. If your data is isolated in separate, fixed repositories — those infamous *data silos* everybody complains about — then it's available to only a few people within a particular line of business. Siloed data structures result in scenarios where a majority of an organization's data is simply unavailable for use by the organization at large. (Needless to say, siloed data structures are incredibly wasteful and inefficient.)

TIP

When preparing to analyze data, follow this 6-step process for data preparation:

1. **Import.** Read relevant datasets into your application.

2. **Clean.** Remove strays, duplicates, and out-of-range records, and also standardizing casing.

3. **Transform.** In this step, you treat missing values, deal with outliers, and scale your variables.

4. **Process.** Processing your data involves data parsing, recoding of variables, concatenation, and other methods of reformatting your dataset to prepare it for analysis.

5. **Log in.** In this step, you simply create a record that describes your dataset. This record should include descriptive statistics, information on variable formats, data source, collection methods, and more. Once you generate this log, make sure to store it in a place you'll remember, in case you need to share these details with other users of the processed dataset.

6. **Back up.** The last data preparation step is to store a backup of this processed dataset so that you have a clean, fresh version — no matter what.

Taking Action on Business Insights

After wrangling your data down to actionable insights, the second step in the progression from raw data to value-added is to take decisive actions based on those insights. In business, the only justifiable purpose for spending time deriving insights from raw data is that the actions should lead to an increase in business profits. Failure to take action on data-driven insights results in a complete and total loss of the resources that were spent deriving them, at no benefit whatsoever to the organization. An organization absolutely must be ready and equipped to change, evolve, and progress when new business insights become available.

What I like to call the *insight-to-action arc* — the process of taking decisive actions based on data insights — should be formalized in a written action plan and then rigorously exercised to affect continuous and iterative improvements to your organization — *iterative* because these improvements involve a successive round of deployments and testing to optimize all areas of business based on actionable insights that are generated from organizational data. This action plan is not something that should be tacked loosely on the side of your organization and then never looked at again.

To best prepare your organization to take action on insights derived from business data, make sure you have the following people and systems in place and ready to go:

>> **Right data, right time, right place:** This part isn't complicated: You just have to have the right data, collected and made available at the right places and the right times, when it's needed the most.

>> **Business-centric data scientists and business analysts:** Have business-centric data scientists and business analysts in place and ready to tackle problems when they arise.

>> **Educated and enthusiastic management:** Educate and encourage your organization's leaders so that you have a management team that understands, values, and makes effective use of business insights gleaned from analytics.

>> **Informed and enthusiastic organizational culture:** If the culture of your organization reflects a naïveté or lack of understanding about the value of data, begin fostering a corporate culture that values data insights and analytics. Consider using training, workshops, and events.

>> **Written procedures with clearly designated chains of responsibility:** Have documented processes in place and interwoven into your organization so that when the time comes, the organization is prepared to respond. New insights are generated all the time, but growth is achieved only through iterative adjustments and actions based on constantly evolving data insights. The organization needs to have clearly defined procedures ready to accommodate these changes as necessary.

>> **Advancement in technology:** Your enterprise absolutely must keep up-to-date with rapidly changing technological developments. The analytics space is changing fast — very fast! There are many ways to keep up. If you keep in-house experts, you can assign them the ongoing responsibility of monitoring industry advancements and then suggesting changes that are needed to keep your organization current. An alternative way to keep current is to purchase cloud-based Software-as-a-Service (SaaS) subscriptions and then rely on SaaS platform upgrades to keep you up to speed on the most innovative and cutting-edge technologies.

WARNING

When relying on SaaS platforms to keep you current, you're taking a leap of faith that the vendor is working hard to keep on top of industry advancements and not just letting things slide. Ensure that the vendor has a long-standing history of maintaining up-to-date and reliable services over time. Although you could try to follow the industry yourself and then check back with the vendor on updates as new technologies emerge, that is putting the onus on you. Unless you're a data technology expert with a lot of free time to research and inquire about advancements in industry standards, it's better to choose a reliable vendor that has an excellent reputation for delivering up-to-date, cutting-edge technologies to customers.

Distinguishing between Business Intelligence and Data Science

Business-centric data scientists and business analysts who do business intelligence are like cousins: They both use data to work toward the same business goal, but their approach, technology, and function differ by measurable degrees. In the following sections, I define, compare, and distinguish between business intelligence and business-centric data science.

Business intelligence, defined

The purpose of business intelligence is to convert raw data into business insights that business leaders and managers can use to make data-informed decisions. Business analysts use business intelligence tools to create decision-support products for business management decision making. If you want to build decision-support dashboards, visualizations, or reports from complete medium-size sets of structured business data, you can use business intelligence tools and methods to help you.

Business intelligence (BI) is composed of

>> **Mostly internal datasets:** By *internal,* I mean business data and information that's supplied by your organization's own managers and stakeholders.

>> **Tools, technologies, and skillsets:** Examples here include online analytical processing, ETL (*e*xtracting, *t*ransforming, and *l*oading data from one database into another), data warehousing, and information technology for business applications.

The kinds of data used in business intelligence

Insights that are generated in business intelligence (BI) are derived from standard-size sets of structured business data. BI solutions are mostly built off of *transactional data* — data that's generated during the course of a transaction event, like data generated during a sale or during a money transfer between bank accounts, for example. Transactional data is a natural byproduct of business activities that occur across an organization, and all sorts of inferences can be derived from it. The following list describes the possible questions you can answer by using BI to derive insights from these types of data:

>> **Customer service:** "What areas of business are causing the largest customer wait times?"

>> **Sales and marketing:** "Which marketing tactics are most effective and why?"

>> **Operations:** "How efficiently is the help desk operating? Are there any immediate actions that must be taken to remedy a problem there?"

>> **Employee performance:** "Which employees are the most productive? Which are the least?"

Technologies and skillsets that are useful in business intelligence

To streamline BI functions, make sure that your data is organized for optimal ease of access and presentation. You can use multidimensional databases to help you. Unlike relational, or *flat* databases, *multidimensional* databases organize data into cubes that are stored as multidimensional arrays. If you want your BI staff to be able to work with source data as quickly and easily as possible, you can use multidimensional databases to store data in a cube rather than store the data across several relational databases that may or may not be compatible with one another.

This cubic data structure enables *Online Analytical Processing (OLAP)* — a technology through which you can quickly and easily access and use your data for all sorts of different operations and analyses. To illustrate the concept of OLAP, imagine that you have a cube of sales data that has three dimensions: time, region, and business unit. You can *slice* the data to view only one rectangle — to view one sales region, for instance. You can *dice* the data to view a smaller cube made up of some subset of time, region(s), and business unit(s). You can *drill down* or *drill up* to view either highly detailed or highly summarized data, respectively. And you can *roll up,* or total, the numbers along one dimension — to total business unit numbers, for example, or to view sales across time and region only.

OLAP is just one type of *data warehousing system* — a centralized data repository that you can use to store and access your data. A more traditional data warehouse system commonly employed in business intelligence solutions is a *data mart* — a data storage system that you can use to store one particular focus area of data, belonging to only one line of business in the enterprise. *Extract, transform, and load (ETL)* is the process that you'd use to extract data, transform it, and load it into your database or data warehouse. Business analysts generally have strong backgrounds and training in business and information technology. As a discipline, BI relies on traditional IT technologies and skills.

Defining Business-Centric Data Science

Within the business enterprise, data science serves the same purpose that business intelligence does — to convert raw data into business insights that business leaders and managers can use to make data-informed decisions. If you have large sets of structured and unstructured data sources that may or may not be complete and you want to convert those sources into valuable insights for decision support across the enterprise, call on a data scientist. Business-centric data science is multidisciplinary and incorporates the following elements:

REMEMBER

>> **Quantitative analysis:** Can be in the form of mathematical modeling, multivariate statistical analysis, forecasting, and/or simulations.

The term *multivariate* refers to more than one variable. A multivariate statistical analysis is a simultaneous statistical analysis of more than one variable at a time.

>> **Programming skills:** You need the necessary programming skills to analyze raw data *and* to make this data accessible to business users.

>> **Business knowledge:** You need knowledge of the business and its environment so that you can better understand the relevancy of your findings.

Data science is a pioneering discipline. Data scientists often employ the scientific method for data exploration, hypotheses formation, and hypothesis testing (through simulation and statistical modeling). Business-centric data scientists generate valuable data insights, often by exploring patterns and anomalies in business data. Data science in a business context is commonly composed of

>> **Internal and external datasets:** Data science is flexible. You can create business data mash-ups from internal and external sources of structured and unstructured data fairly easily. (A *data mash-up* is combination of two or more data sources that are then analyzed together in order to provide users with a more complete view of the situation at hand.)

>> **Tools, technologies, and skillsets:** Examples here could involve using cloud-based platforms, statistical and mathematical programming, machine learning, data analysis using Python and R, and advanced data visualization.

Like business analysts, business-centric data scientists produce decision-support products for business managers and organizational leaders to use. These products include analytics dashboards and data visualizations, but generally not tabular data reports and tables.

Kinds of data that are useful in business-centric data science

You can use data science to derive business insights from standard-size sets of structured business data (just like BI) or from structured, semi-structured, and unstructured sets of big data. Data science solutions are not confined to transactional data that sits in a relational database; you can use data science to create valuable insights from all available data sources. These data sources include

>> **Transactional business data:** A tried-and-true data source, transactional business data is the type of structured data used in traditional BI and it includes management data, customer service data, sales and marketing data, operational data, and employee performance data.

>> **Social data related to the brand or business:** A more recent phenomenon, the data covered by this rubric includes the unstructured data generated through emails, instant messaging, and social networks such as Twitter, Facebook, LinkedIn, Pinterest, and Instagram.

>> **Machine data from business operations:** Machines automatically generate this unstructured data, like SCADA data, machine data, or sensor data.

TECHNICAL STUFF

The acronym SCADA refers to Supervisory Control and Data Acquisition. SCADA systems are used to control remotely operating mechanical systems and equipment. They generate data that is used to monitor the operations of machines and equipment.

>> **Audio, video, image, and PDF file data:** These well-established formats are all sources of unstructured data.

TIP

You may have heard of *dark data* — operational data that most organizations collect and store but then never use. Storing this data and then not using it is pure detriment to a business. On the other hand, with a few sharp data scientists and data engineers on staff, the same organization could use this data resource for optimization security, marketing, business processes, and more. If your organization has dark data, someone should go ahead and turn the light on.

Technologies and skillsets that are useful in business-centric data science

Since the products of data science are often generated from big data, cloud-based data platform solutions are common in the field. Data that's used in data science is often derived from data-engineered big data solutions, like Hadoop, MapReduce, Spark, and massively parallel processing (MPP) platforms. (For more on these technologies, check out Chapter 2.) Data scientists are innovative forward-thinkers who must often think outside the box in order to exact solutions to the problems they solve. Many data scientists tend toward open-source solutions, when available. From a cost perspective, this approach benefits the organizations that employ these scientists.

Business-centric data scientists often use machine learning techniques to find patterns in (and derive predictive insights from) huge datasets that are related to a line of business or the business at large. They're skilled in math, statistics, and programming, and they often use these skills to generate predictive models. They generally know how to program in Python or R. Most of them know how to use SQL to query relevant data from structured databases. They are usually skilled at communicating data insights to end users — in business-centric data science, end users are business managers and organizational leaders. Data scientists must be skillful at using verbal, oral, and visual means to communicate valuable data insights.

REMEMBER

Although business-centric data scientists serve a decision-support role in the enterprise, they're different from the business analyst in that they usually have strong academic and professional backgrounds in math, science, or engineering — or all of the above. This said, business-centric data scientists also have a strong substantive knowledge of business management.

Making business value from machine learning methods

A discussion of data science in business would be incomplete without a description of the popular machine learning methods being used to generate business value, as described in this list:

>> **Linear regression:** You can use linear regression to make predictions for sales forecasts, pricing optimization, marketing optimization, and financial risk assessment.

>> **Logistic regression:** Use logistic regression to predict customer churn, to predict response-versus-ad spending, to predict the lifetime value of a

customer, and to monitor how business decisions affect predicted churn rates.

» **Naïve Bayes:** If you want to build a spam detector, analyze customer sentiment, or automatically categorize products, customers, or competitors, you can do that using a Naïve Bayes classifier.

» **K-means clustering:** K-means clustering is useful for cost modeling and customer segmentation (for marketing optimization purposes).

» **Hierarchical clustering:** If you want to model business processes, or to segment customers based on survey responses, hierarchical clustering will probably come in handy.

» **k-nearest neighbor classification:** k-nearest neighbor is a type of instance-based learning. You can use it for text document classification, financial distress prediction modeling, and competitor analysis and classification.

» **Principal component analysis:** Principal component analysis is a dimensionality reduction method that you can use for detecting fraud, for speech recognition, and for spam detection.

TIP

If you want to know more about how these machine learning algorithms work, keep reading! They're explained in detail in Part 2 of this book.

Differentiating between Business Intelligence and Business-Centric Data Science

The similarities between BI and business-centric data science are glaringly obvious; it's the differences that most people have a hard time discerning. The purpose of both BI and business-centric data science is to convert raw data into actionable insights that managers and leaders can use for support when making business decisions.

BI and business-centric data science differ with respect to approach. Although BI can use forward-looking methods like forecasting, these methods are generated by making simple inferences from historical or current data. In this way, BI extrapolates from the past and present to infer predictions about the future. It looks to present or past data for relevant information to help monitor business operations and to aid managers in short- to medium-term decision making.

In contrast, business–centric data science practitioners seek to make new discoveries by using advanced mathematical or statistical methods to analyze and generate predictions from vast amounts of business data. These predictive insights are generally relevant to the long–term future of the business. The business–centric data scientist attempts to discover new paradigms and new ways of looking at the data to provide a new perspective on the organization, its operations, and its relations with customers, suppliers, and competitors. Therefore, the business–centric data scientist must know the business and its environment. She must have business knowledge to determine how a discovery is relevant to a line of business or to the organization at large.

Other prime differences between BI and business–centric data science are

>> **Data sources:** BI uses only structured data from relational databases, whereas business-centric data science may use structured data and unstructured data, like that generated by machines or in social media conversations.

>> **Outputs:** BI products include reports, data tables, and decision-support dashboards, whereas business-centric data science products involve either dashboard analytics or another type of advanced data visualization, but rarely tabular data reports. Data scientists generally communicate their findings through words or data visualizations, but not tables and reports. That's because the source datasets from which data scientists work are generally more complex than a typical business manager would be able to understand.

>> **Technology:** BI runs off of relational databases, data warehouses, OLAP, and ETL technologies, whereas business-centric data science often runs off of data from data-engineered systems that use Hadoop, MapReduce, or massively parallel processing.

>> **Expertise:** BI relies heavily on IT and business technology expertise, whereas business-centric data science relies on expertise in statistics, math, programming, and business.

Knowing Whom to Call to Get the Job Done Right

Since most business managers don't know how to do advanced data work themselves, it's definitely beneficial to at least know which types of problems are best suited for a business analyst and which problems should be handled by a data scientist instead.

If you want to use enterprise data insights to streamline your business so that its processes function more efficiently and effectively, bring in a business analyst. Organizations employ business analysts so that they have someone to cover the responsibilities associated with requirements management, business process analysis, and improvements-planning for business processes, IT systems, organizational structures, and business strategies. Business analysts look at enterprise data and identify what processes need improvement. They then create written specifications that detail exactly what changes should be made for improved results. They produce interactive dashboards and tabular data reports to supplement their recommendations and to help business managers better understand what is happening in the business. Ultimately, business analysts use business data to further the organization's strategic goals and to support them in providing guidance on any procedural improvements that need to be made.

In contrast, if you want to obtain answers to very specific questions on your data, and you can obtain those answers only via advanced analysis and modeling of business data, bring in a business-centric data scientist. Many times, a data scientist may support the work of a business analyst. In such cases, the data scientist might be asked to analyze very specific data-related problems and then report the results back to the business analyst to support him in making recommendations. Business analysts can use the findings of business-centric data scientists to help them determine how to best fulfill a requirement or build a business solution.

Exploring Data Science in Business: A Data-Driven Business Success Story

Southeast Telecommunications Company was losing many of its customers to *customer churn* — the customers were simply moving to other telecom service providers. Because it's significantly more expensive to acquire new customers than it is to retain existing customers, Southeast's management wanted to find a way to decrease the churn rates. So, Southeast Telecommunications engaged Analytic Solutions, Inc. (ASI), a business-analysis company. ASI interviewed Southeast's employees, regional managers, supervisors, frontline employees, and help desk employees. After consulting with personnel, they collected business data that was relevant to customer retention.

ASI began examining several years' worth of Southeast's customer data to develop a better understanding of customer behavior and why some people left after years of loyalty while others continued to stay on. The customer datasets contained records for the number of times a customer had contacted Southeast's help desk, the number of customer complaints, and the number of minutes and megabytes of data each customer used per month. ASI also had demographic and personal data (credit score, age, and region, for example) that was contextually relevant to the evaluation.

By looking at this customer data, ASI discovered the following insights. Within the 1-year time interval before switching service providers

>> Eighty-four percent of customers who left Southeast had placed two or more calls into its help desk in the nine months before switching providers.

>> Sixty percent of customers who switched showed drastic usage drops in the six months before switching.

>> Forty-four percent of customers who switched had made at least one complaint to Southeast in the six months before switching. (The data showed significant overlap between these customers and those who had called into the help desk.)

Based on these results, ASI fitted a logistic regression model to the historical data in order to identify the customers who were most likely to churn. With the aid of this model, Southeast could identify and direct retention efforts at the customers that it was most likely to lose. These efforts helped Southeast improve its services by identifying sources of dissatisfaction; increase returns on investment by restricting retention efforts to only those customers at risk of churn (rather than all customers); and, most importantly, decrease overall customer churn, thus preserving the profitability of the business at large.

What's more, Southeast didn't make these retention efforts a one-time event: The company incorporated churn analysis into its regular operating procedures. By the end of that year, and in the years since, it has seen a dramatic reduction in overall customer churn rates.

2

Using Data Science to Extract Meaning from Your Data

IN THIS PART . . .

Master the basics behind machine learning approaches.

Explore the importance of math and statistics for data science.

Work with clustering and instance-based learning algorithms.

Examine how Internet-of-things analytics are revolutionizing the world.

Chapter **4**

Machine Learning: Learning from Data with Your Machine

If you've been watching any news lately, there's no doubt that you've heard of something called *machine learning*. It's often referenced when reporters are covering stories on some new and amazing invention from artificial intelligence. In this chapter, you dip your toes into the area called machine learning, and in Chapter 8, you get a view on how machine learning works within this new world of artificial intelligence inventions.

Defining Machine Learning and Its Processes

Machine learning is the practice of applying algorithmic models to data, in an iterative manner, so that your computer discovers hidden patterns or trends that you can use to make predictions. It's also called *algorithmic learning.* Machine learning has a vast and ever-expanding assortment of use cases, including

- » Real-time Internet advertising
- » Internet marketing personalization
- » Internet search
- » Spam filtering
- » Recommendation engines
- » Natural language processing and sentiment analysis
- » Automatic facial recognition
- » Customer churn prediction
- » Credit score modeling
- » Survival analysis for mechanical equipment

Walking through the steps of the machine learning process

Three main steps are involved in machine learning: setting up, learning, and application. Setting up involves acquiring data, preprocessing it, feature selection (the process of selecting the most appropriate variables for the task at hand), and breaking the data into training and test datasets. You use the *training data* to train the model, and the *test data* to test the accuracy of the model's predictions. The learning step involves model experimentation, training, building, and testing. The application step involves model deployment and prediction.

REMEMBER

A good rule of thumb when breaking data into test and training sets is to apply random sampling to take two-thirds of the original dataset to use as data to train the model. Use the remaining one-third of the data as test data, for evaluating the model's predictions.

Getting familiar with machine learning terms

Before getting too deep into a discussion on machine learning methods, you need to know about the sometimes confusing vocabulary associated with the field. Because machine learning is an offshoot of both traditional statistics and computer science, it has adopted terms from both fields and added a few of its own. Here is what you need to know:

>> **Instance:** The same as a *row* (in a data table), an *observation* (in statistics), and a *data point*. Machine learning practitioners are also known to call an instance a *case*.

>> **Feature:** The same as a *column* or *field* (in a data table) and a *variable* (in statistics). In regression methods, a feature is also called an *independent variable* (IV).

>> **Target variable:** The same as a *predictant* or *dependent variable* (DV) in statistics.

REMEMBER

In machine learning, *feature selection* is a somewhat straightforward process for selecting appropriate variables; for *feature engineering*, you need substantial domain expertise and strong data science skills to manually design input variables from the underlying dataset. You use feature engineering in cases where your model needs a better representation of the problem being solved than is available in the raw dataset.

Considering Learning Styles

There are three main styles within machine learning: supervised, unsupervised, and semisupervised. Supervised and unsupervised methods are behind most modern machine learning applications, and semisupervised learning is an up-and-coming star.

Learning with supervised algorithms

Supervised learning algorithms require that input data has labeled features. These algorithms learn from known features of that data to produce an output model that successfully predicts labels for new incoming, unlabeled data points. You use supervised learning when you have a labeled dataset composed of historical values that are good predictors of future events. Use cases include survival analysis and fraud detection, among others. Logistic regression is a type of supervised learning algorithm, and you can read more on that topic in the next section.

Learning with unsupervised algorithms

Unsupervised learning algorithms accept unlabeled data and attempt to group observations into categories based on underlying similarities in input features, as shown in Figure 4-1. Principal component analysis, k-means clustering, and singular value decomposition are all examples of unsupervised machine learning algorithms. Popular use cases include recommendation engines, facial recognition systems, and customer segmentation.

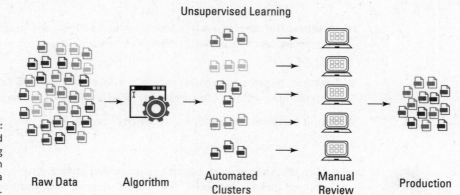

FIGURE 4-1:
Unsupervised machine learning breaks down unlabeled data into subgroups.

Unsupervised Learning

Raw Data   Algorithm   Automated Clusters   Manual Review   Production

Learning with reinforcement

Reinforcement learning (or *semisupervised* learning) is a behavior-based learning model. It is based on a mechanic similar to how humans and animals learn. The model is given "rewards" based on how it behaves, and it subsequently learns to maximize the sum of its rewards by adapting the decisions it makes to earn as many rewards as possible. Reinforcement learning is an up-and-coming concept in data science.

Seeing What You Can Do

Whether you're just getting familiar with the algorithms that are involved in machine learning or you're looking to find out more about what's happening in cutting-edge machine learning advancements, this section has something for you. First I give you an overview of machine learning algorithms, broken down by function, and then I describe more about the advanced areas of machine learning that are embodied by deep learning and Apache Spark.

Selecting algorithms based on function

When you need to choose a class of machine learning algorithms, it's helpful to consider each model class based on its functionality. For the most part, algorithmic functionality falls into the categories shown in Figure 4-2.

>> **Regression algorithm:** You can use this type of algorithm to model relationships between features in a dataset. You can read more on linear and logistic regression methods and ordinary least squares in Chapter 5.

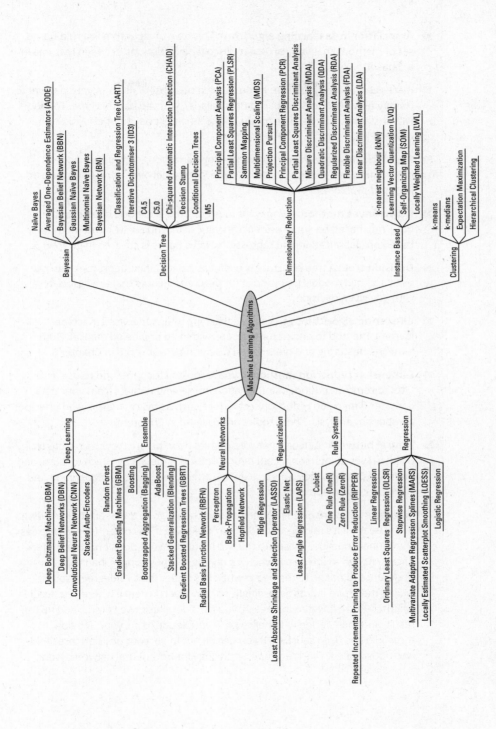

FIGURE 4-2:
Machine learning algorithms can be broken down by function.

>> **Association rule learning algorithm:** This type of algorithm is a rule-based set of methods that you can use to discover associations between features in a dataset.

>> **Instance-based algorithm:** If you want to use observations in your dataset to classify new observations based on similarity, you can use this type. To model with instances, you can use methods like k-nearest neighbor classification, covered in Chapter 7.

>> **Regularizing algorithm:** You can use regularization to introduce added information as a means by which to prevent model overfitting or to solve an ill-posed problem.

>> **Naïve Bayes method:** If you want to predict the likelihood of an event occurring based on some evidence in your data, you can use this method, based on classification and regression. Naïve Bayes is covered in Chapter 5.

>> **Decision tree:** A tree structure is useful as a decision-support tool. You can use it to build models that predict for potential fallouts that are associated with any given decision.

>> **Clustering algorithm:** You can use this type of unsupervised machine learning method to uncover subgroups within an unlabeled dataset. Both k-means clustering and hierarchical clustering are covered in Chapter 6.

>> **Dimension reduction method:** If you're looking for a method to use as a filter to remove redundant information, noise, and outliers from your data, consider dimension reduction techniques such as factor analysis and principal component analysis. These topics are covered in Chapter 5.

>> **Neural network:** A neural network mimics how the brain solves problems, by using a layer of interconnected neural units as a means by which to learn, and infer rules, from observational data. It's often used in image recognition and computer vision applications.

Imagine that you're deciding whether you should go to the beach. You never go to the beach if it's raining, and you don't like going if it's colder than 75 degrees (Fahrenheit) outside. These are the two inputs for your decision. Your preference to not go to the beach when it's raining is a lot stronger than your preference to not go to the beach when it is colder than 75 degrees, so you weight these two inputs accordingly. For any given instance where you decide whether you're going to the beach, you consider these two criteria, add up the result, and then decide whether to go. If you decide to go, your decision threshold has been satisfied. If you decide not to go, your decision threshold was not satisfied. This is a simplistic analogy for how neural networks work.

Now, for a more technical definition. The simplest type of neural network is the *Perceptron*. It accepts more than one input, weights them, adds them up on a processor layer, and then, based on the activation function and the threshold you set for it, outputs a result. An *activation function* is a mathematical function that transforms inputs into an output signal. The processor layer is called a *hidden layer*. A *neural network* is a layer of connected Perceptrons that all work together as a unit to accept inputs and return outputs that signal whether some criteria is met. A key feature of neural nets is that they are *self-learning* — in other words, they adapt, learn, and optimize per changes in input data. Figure 4-3 is a schematic layout that depicts how a Perceptron is structured.

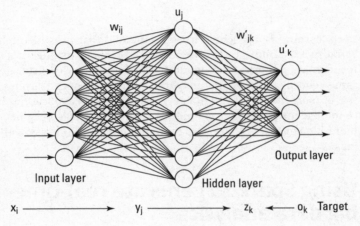

FIGURE 4-3:
Neural networks are connected layers of artificial neural units.

>> **Deep learning method:** This method incorporates traditional neural networks in successive layers to offer deep-layer training for generating predictive outputs. I tell you more about this topic in the next section.

>> **Ensemble algorithm:** You can use ensemble algorithms to combine machine learning approaches to achieve results that are better than would be available from any single machine learning method on its own.

If you use Gmail, you must be enjoying its autoreply functionality. You know — the three 1-line messages from which you can choose an autoreply to a message someone sent you? Well, this autoreply functionality within Gmail is called Smart-Reply, and it is built on deep learning algorithms. Another innovation built on deep learning is Facebook DeepFace, the Facebook feature that automatically recognizes and suggests tags for the people who appear in your Facebook photos. Figure 4-4 is a schematic layout that depicts how a deep learning network is structured.

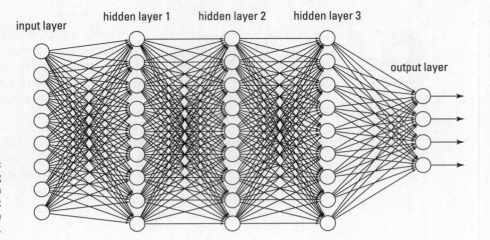

input layer   hidden layer 1   hidden layer 2   hidden layer 3   output layer

FIGURE 4-4:
A deep learning
network is a
neural network
with more than
one hidden layer.

Deep learning is a machine learning method that uses hierarchical neural networks to learn from data in an iterative and adaptive manner. It's an ideal approach for learning patterns from unlabeled and unstructured data. It's essentially the same concept as the neural network, except that deep learning algorithms have two or more hidden layers. In fact, computer vision applications have been known to implement more than 150 hidden layers in a single deep neural network. The more hidden layers there are, the more complex a decision the algorithm can make.

Using Spark to generate real-time big data analytics

Apache Spark is an in-memory distributed computing application that you can use to deploy machine learning algorithms on big data sources in near – real-time, to generate analytics from streaming big data sources. Because it processes data in microbatches, with 3-second cycle times, you can use it to significantly decrease time-to-insight in cases where time is of the essence. It sits on top of the HDFS and acts a secondary processing framework, to be used in parallel with the large-scale batch processing work that's done by MapReduce. Spark is composed of the following submodules:

» **Spark SQL:** You use this module to work with and query structured data using Spark. Within Spark, you can query data using Spark's built-in SQL package: SparkSQL. You can also query structured data using Hive, but then you'd use the HiveQL language and run the queries using the Spark processing engine.

» **GraphX:** The GraphX library is how you store and process network data from within Spark.

>> **Streaming:** The Streaming module is where the big data processing takes place. This module basically breaks a continuously streaming data source into much smaller data streams, called *Dstreams* — or discreet data streams. Because the Dstreams are small, these batch cycles can be completed within three seconds, which is why it's called microbatch processing.

>> **MLlib:** The MLlib submodule is where you analyze data, generate statistics, and deploy machine learning algorithms from within the Spark environment. MLlib has APIs for Java, Scala, Python, and R. The MLlib module allows you to build machine learning models in Python or R but pull data directly from the HDFS (rather than via an intermediary repository). This helps reduce the reliance that data scientists sometimes have on data engineers. Furthermore, computations are known to be 100 times faster when processed in-memory using Spark as opposed to the standard MapReduce framework.

You can deploy Spark on-premise by downloading the open-source framework from the Apache Spark website: `http://spark.apache.org/downloads.html`. Another option is to run Spark on the cloud via the Apache Databricks service `https://databricks.com`.

Chapter 5

Math, Probability, and Statistical Modeling

Math and statistics are not the scary monsters that many people make them out to be. In data science, the need for these quantitative methods is simply a fact of life — and nothing to get alarmed over. Although you must have a handle on the math and statistics that are necessary to solve a problem, you don't need to go study and get a degree in those fields.

Contrary to what many pure statisticians would have you believe, the data science field is not the same as the statistics field. Data scientists have substantive knowledge in one field or several fields, and they use statistics, math, coding, and strong communication skills to help them discover, understand, and communicate data insights that lie within raw datasets related to their field of expertise. Statistics is a vital component of this formula, but not more vital than the others. In this chapter, I introduce you to the basic ideas behind probability, correlation analysis, dimensionality reduction, decision modeling, regression analysis, outlier detection, and time series analysis.

Exploring Probability and Inferential Statistics

Probability is one of the most fundamental concepts in statistics. To even get started in making sense of your data by using statistics, you need to be able to identify something as basic as whether you're looking at *descriptive* or *inferential* statistics. You also need a firm grasp of the basics of probability distribution. The following sections cover these concepts and more.

A *statistic* is a result that's derived from performing a mathematical operation on numerical data. In general, you use statistics in decision making. Statistics come in two flavors:

>> **Descriptive:** Descriptive statistics provide a description that illuminates some characteristic of a numerical dataset, including dataset distribution, central tendency (such as mean, min, or max), and dispersion (as in standard deviation and variance).

>> **Inferential:** Rather than focus on pertinent descriptions of a dataset, inferential statistics carve out a smaller section of the dataset and attempt to deduce significant information about the larger dataset. Use this type of statistics to get information about a real-world measure in which you're interested.

It's true that descriptive statistics describe the characteristics of a numerical dataset, but that doesn't tell you why you should care. In fact, most data scientists are interested in descriptive statistics only because of what they reveal about the real-world measures they describe. For example, a descriptive statistic is often associated with a *degree of accuracy*, indicating the statistic's value as an estimate of the real-world measure.

To better understand this concept, imagine that a business owner wants to estimate the upcoming quarter's profits. The owner might take an average of the past few quarters' profits to use as an estimate of how much he'll make during the next quarter. But if the previous quarters' profits varied widely, a descriptive statistic that estimated the *variation* of this predicted profit value (the amount by which this dollar estimate could differ from the actual profits he will make) would indicate just how far off the predicted value could be from the actual one. (Not bad information to have, right?)

TIP

You can use descriptive statistics in many ways — to detect outliers, for example, or to plan for feature preprocessing requirements or to quickly identify what features you may want, or not want, to use in an analysis.

Like descriptive statistics, *inferential statistics* are used to reveal something about a real-world measure. Inferential statistics do this by providing information about a small data selection, so you can use this information to infer something about the larger dataset from which it was taken. In statistics, this smaller data selection is known as a *sample,* and the larger, complete dataset from which the sample is taken is called the *population.*

If your dataset is too big to analyze in its entirety, pull a smaller sample of this dataset, analyze it, and then make inferences about the entire dataset based on what you learn from analyzing the sample. You can also use inferential statistics in situations where you simply can't afford to collect data for the entire population. In this case, you'd use the data you do have to make inferences about the population at large. At other times, you may find yourself in situations where complete information for the population is not available. In these cases, you can use inferential statistics to estimate values for the missing data based on what you learn from analyzing the data that is available.

WARNING

For an inference to be valid, you must select your sample carefully so that you get a true representation of the population. Even if your sample is representative, the numbers in the sample dataset will always exhibit some *noise* — random variation, in other words — that guarantees the sample statistic is not exactly identical to its corresponding population statistic.

Probability distributions

Imagine that you've just rolled into Las Vegas and settled into your favorite roulette table over at the Bellagio. When the roulette wheel spins off, you intuitively understand that there is an equal chance that the ball will fall into any of the slots of the cylinder on the wheel. The slot where the ball will land is totally random, and the *probability,* or likelihood, of the ball landing in any one slot over another is the same. Because the ball can land in any slot, with equal probability, there is an equal probability distribution, or a *uniform probability distribution* — the ball has an equal probability of landing in any of the slots in the cylinder.

But the slots of the roulette wheel are not all the same — the wheel has 18 black slots and 20 slots that are either red or green. Because of this arrangement, there is 18/38 probability that your ball will land on a black slot. You plan to make successive bets that the ball will land on a black slot.

Your net winnings here can be considered a *random variable,* which is a measure of a trait or value associated with an object, a person, or a place (something in the real world) that is unpredictable. Because this trait or value is unpredictable, however, doesn't mean that you know nothing about it. What's more, you can use what you do know about this thing to help you in your decision making. Here's how . . .

A *weighted average* is an average value of a measure over a very large number of data points. If you take a weighted average of your winnings (your random variable) across the probability distribution, this would yield an *expectation value* — an expected value for your net winnings over a successive number of bets. (An expectation can also be thought of as the best guess, if you had to guess.) To describe it more formally, an *expectation* is a weighted average of some measure associated with a random variable. If your goal is to model an unpredictable variable so that you can make data-informed decisions based on what you know about its probability in a population, you can use random variables and probability distributions to do this.

REMEMBER

When considering the probability of an event, you must know what other events are possible. Always define the set of events as *mutually exclusive* — only one can occur at a time. (Think of the six possible results of rolling a die.) Probability has these two important characteristics:

>> The probability of any single event never goes below 0.0 or exceeds 1.0.

>> The probability of all events always sums to exactly 1.0.

Probability distribution is classified per these two types:

>> **Discrete:** A random variable where values can be counted by groupings

>> **Continuous:** A random variable that assigns probabilities to a range of value

REMEMBER

To understand discrete and continuous distribution, think of two variables from a dataset describing cars. A "color" variable would have a discrete distribution because cars have only a limited range of colors (black, red, or blue, for example). The observations would be countable per the color grouping. A variable describing cars' miles per gallon, or "mpg," would have a continuous distribution because each car could have its own separate value for "mpg."

>> **Normal distributions (numeric continuous):** Represented graphically by a symmetric bell-shaped curve, these distributions model phenomena that tend toward some most-likely observation (at the top of the bell in the bell curve); observations at the two extremes are less likely.

>> **Binomial distributions (numeric discrete):** Model the number of successes that can occur in a certain number of attempts when only two outcomes are possible (the old heads-or-tails coin flip scenario, for example). *Binary* variables — variables that assume only one of two values — have a binomial distribution.

>> **Categorical distributions (non-numeric):** Represents either non-numeric categorical variables or *ordinal variables* (a special case of numeric variable that can be grouped and ranked like a categorical variable).

Conditional probability with Naïve Bayes

You can use the *Naïve Bayes* machine learning method, which was borrowed straight from the statistics field, to predict the likelihood that an event will occur, given evidence defined in your data features — something called *conditional probability*. Naïve Bayes, which is based on classification and regression, is especially useful if you need to classify text data.

To better illustrate this concept, consider the Spambase dataset that's available from UCI's machine learning repository (`https://archive.ics.uci.edu/ml/datasets/Spambase`). That dataset contains 4,601 records of emails and, in its last field, designates whether each email is spam. From this dataset, you can identify common characteristics between spam emails. Once you've defined common features that indicate spam email, you can build a Naïve Bayes classifier that reliably predicts whether an incoming email is spam, based on the empirical evidence supported in its content. In other words, the model predicts whether an email is spam — the *event* — based on features gathered from its content — the *evidence*.

Naïve Bayes comes in these three popular flavors:

>> **MultinomialNB:** Use this version if your variables (categorical or continuous) describe discrete frequency counts, like word counts. This version of Naïve Bayes assumes a multinomial distribution, as is often the case with text data. It does not except negative values.

>> **BernoulliNB:** If your features are binary, you use multinomial Bernoulli Naïve Bayes to make predictions. This version works for classifying text data, but isn't generally known to perform as well as MultinomialNB. If you want to use BernoulliNB to make predictions from continuous variables, that will work, but you first need to sub-divide them into discrete interval groupings (also known as *binning*).

>> **GaussianNB:** Use this version if all predictive features are normally distributed. It's not a good option for classifying text data, but it can be a good choice if your data contains both positive and negative values (and if your features have a normal distribution, of course).

WARNING

Before building a Bayes classifier naïvely, consider that the model holds an *a priori* assumption. Its predictions assume that past conditions still hold true. Predicting future values from historical ones generates incorrect results when present circumstances change.

Quantifying Correlation

Many statistical and machine learning methods assume that your features are independent. To test whether they're independent, though, you need to evaluate their *correlation* — the extent to which variables demonstrate interdependency. In this section, you get a brief introduction to Pearson correlation and Spearman's rank correlation.

TIP

Correlation is quantified per the value of a variable called *r*, which ranges between −1 and 1. The closer the r-value is to 1 or −1, the more correlation there is between two variables. If two variables have an r-value that's close to 0, it could indicate that they're independent variables.

Calculating correlation with Pearson's r

If you want to uncover dependent relationships between continuous variables in a dataset, you'd use statistics to estimate their correlation. The simplest form of correlation analysis is the *Pearson correlation*, which assumes that

>> Your data is normally distributed.

>> You have continuous, numeric variables.

>> Your variables are linearly related.

WARNING

Because the Pearson correlation has so many conditions, *only* use it to determine whether a relationship between two variables exists, but not to rule out possible relationships. If you were to get an r-value that is close to 0, it indicates that there is no linear relationship between the variables, but that a nonlinear relationship between them still could exist.

Ranking variable-pairs using Spearman's rank correlation

The Spearman's rank correlation is a popular test for determining correlation between ordinal variables. By applying Spearman's rank correlation, you're converting numeric variable-pairs into ranks by calculating the strength of the relationship between variables and then ranking them per their correlation.

The Spearman's rank correlation assumes that

>> Your variables are ordinal.

>> Your variables are related non-linearly.

>> Your data is non-normally distributed.

Reducing Data Dimensionality with Linear Algebra

Any intermediate-level data scientist should have a pretty good understanding of linear algebra and how to do math using matrices. Array and matrix objects are the primary data structure in analytical computing. You need them in order to perform mathematical and statistical operations on large and *multidimensional* datasets — datasets with many different features to be tracked simultaneously. In this section, you see exactly what is involved in using linear algebra and machine learning methods to reduce a dataset's dimensionality.

Decomposing data to reduce dimensionality

To start at the very beginning, you need to understand the concept of *eigenvector*. To conceptualize an eigenvector, think of a matrix called A. Now consider a non-zero vector called x and that Ax = λx for a scalar λ. In this scenario, scalar λ is what's called an *eigenvalue* of matrix A. It's permitted to take on a value of 0. Furthermore, x is the eigenvector that corresponds to λ, and again, it's not permitted to be a zero value.

Okay, so what can you do with all this theory? Well, for starters, using a linear algebra method called *singular value decomposition (SVD)*, you can reduce the dimensionality of your dataset — or the number of features that you track when carrying out an analysis. Dimension reduction algorithms are ideal options if you need to compress your dataset while also removing redundant information and noise.

The SVD linear algebra method decomposes the data matrix into the three resultant matrices shown in Figure 5-1. The product of these matrices, when multiplied together, gives you back your original matrix. SVD is handy when you want to remove redundant information by compressing your dataset.

Take a closer look at the figure:

```
A = u * v * S
```

» **A:** This is the matrix that holds all your original data.

» **u:** This is a left-singular vector (an eigenvector) of A, and it holds all the important, non-redundant information about your data's observations.

» **v:** This is a right-singular eigenvector of A. It holds all the important, non-redundant information about columns in your dataset's features.

» **S:** This is the square root of the eigenvalue of A. It contains all the information about the procedures performed during the compression.

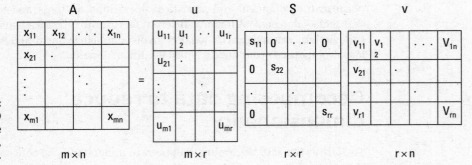

FIGURE 5-1:
You can use SVD to decompose data down to u, S, and V matrices.

Although it might sound complicated, it's pretty simple. Imagine that you've compressed your dataset and it has resulted in a matrix S that sums to 100. If the first value in S is 97 and the second value is 94, this means that the first two columns contain 94 percent of the dataset's information. In other words, the first two columns of the u matrix and the first two rows of the v matrix contain 94 percent of the important information held in your original dataset, A. To isolate only the important, non-redundant information, you'd keep only those two columns and discard the rest.

When you go to reconstruct your matrix by taking the dot product of S, u, and v, you'll probably notice that the resulting matrix is not an exact match to your original dataset. Worry not! That's the data that remains after much of the information redundancy and noise has been filtered out by SVD.

REMEMBER

When deciding the number of rows and columns to keep, it's okay to get rid of rows and columns, as long as you make sure that you retain at least 70 percent of the dataset's original information.

Reducing dimensionality with factor analysis

Factor analysis is along the same lines as SVD in that it's a method you can use for filtering out redundant information and noise from your data. An offspring of the psychometrics field, this method was developed to help you derive a root cause, in cases where a shared root cause results in shared variance — when a variable's variance correlates with the variance of other variables in the dataset.

TECHNICAL STUFF

A variables variability measures how much variance it has around its mean. The greater a variable's variance, the more information that variable contains.

When you find shared variance in your dataset, that means information redundancy is at play. You can use factor analysis or principal component analysis to clear your data of this information redundancy. You see more on principal component analysis in the following section, but for now, focus on factor analysis and the fact that you can use it to compress your dataset's information into a reduced set of meaningful, non–information–redundant *latent variables* — meaningful inferred variables that underlie a dataset but are not directly observable.

Factor analysis makes the following assumptions:

>> Your features are *metric* — numeric variables on which meaningful calculations can be made.

>> Your features should be continuous or ordinal.

>> You have more than 100 observations in your dataset and at least 5 observations per feature.

>> Your sample is homogenous.

>> There is r > 0.3 correlation between the features in your dataset.

In factor analysis, you do a regression on features to uncover underlying latent variables, or factors. You can then use those factors as variables in future analyses, to represent the original dataset from which they're derived. At its core, factor analysis is the process of fitting a model to prepare a dataset for analysis by reducing its dimensionality and information redundancy.

Decreasing dimensionality and removing outliers with PCA

Principal component analysis (PCA) is another dimensionality reduction technique that's closely related to SVD: This unsupervised statistical method finds relationships between features in your dataset and then transforms and reduces them to a set of non-information-redundant *principle components* — uncorrelated features that embody and explain the information that's contained within the dataset (that is, its variance). These components act as a synthetic, refined representation of the dataset, with the information redundancy, noise, and outliers stripped out. You can then take those reduced components and use them as input for your machine learning algorithms, to make predictions based on a compressed representation of your data.

The PCA model makes these two assumptions:

>> Multivariate normality is desirable, but not required.

>> Variables in the dataset should be continuous.

Although PCA is like factor analysis, there are two major differences: One difference is that PCA does not regress to find some underlying cause of shared variance, but instead decomposes a dataset to succinctly represent its most important information in a reduced number of features. The other key difference is that, with PCA, the first time you run the model, you don't specify the number of components to be discovered in the dataset. You let the initial model results tell you how many components to keep, and then you rerun the analysis to extract those features.

REMEMBER

A small amount of information from your original dataset will not be captured by the principal components. Just keep the components that capture at least 95 percent of the dataset's total variance. The remaining components won't be that useful, so you can get rid of them.

When using PCA for outlier detection, simply plot the principal components on an x-y scatter plot and visually inspect for areas that might have outliers. Those data points correspond to potential outliers that are worth investigating.

Modeling Decisions with Multi-Criteria Decision Making

Life is complicated. We're often forced to make decisions where several different criteria come into play, and it often seems unclear what criterion should have priority. Mathematicians, being mathematicians, have come up with quantitative approaches that you can use for decision support when you have several criteria or alternatives on which to base your decision. You see that in Chapter 4, where I talk about neural networks and deep learning, but another method that fulfills this same decision-support purpose is *multi-criteria decision making* (MCDM, for short).

Turning to traditional MCDM

You can use MCDM methods in anything from stock portfolio management to fashion-trend evaluation, from disease outbreak control to land development decision making. Anywhere you have two or more criteria on which you need to base your decision, you can use MCDM methods to help you evaluate alternatives.

To use multi-criteria decision making, the following two assumptions must be satisfied:

>> **Multi-criteria evaluation:** You must have more than one criterion to optimize.

>> **Zero-sum system:** Optimizing with respect to one criterion must come at the sacrifice of at least one other criterion. This means that there must be trade-offs between criteria — to gain with respect to one means losing with respect to at least one other.

The best way to get a solid grasp on MCDM is to see how it's used to solve a real-world problem. MCDM is commonly used in investment portfolio theory. Pricing of individual financial instruments typically reflects the level of risk you incur, but an entire portfolio can be a mixture of virtually riskless investments (U.S. government bonds, for example) and minimum-, moderate-, and high-risk investments. Your level of risk aversion dictates the general character of your investment portfolio. Highly risk-averse investors seek safer and less lucrative investments, and less risk-averse investors choose riskier investments. In the process of evaluating the risk of a potential investment, you'd likely consider the following criteria:

>> **Earnings growth potential:** Here, an investment that falls under an earnings growth potential threshold gets scored as a 0; anything above that threshold gets a 1.

>> **Earnings quality rating:** If an investment falls within a ratings class for earnings quality, it gets scored as a 0; otherwise, it gets scored as a 1.

For you non–Wall Street types out there, *earnings quality* refers to various measures used to determine how kosher a company's reported earnings are; such measures attempt to answer the question, "Do these reported figures pass the smell test?"

» **Dividend performance:** When an investment doesn't reach a set dividend performance threshold, it gets a 0; if it reaches or surpasses that threshold, it gets a 1.

TECHNICAL STUFF

In mathematics, a *set* is a group of numbers that shares some similar characteristic. In traditional set theory, membership is *binary* — in other words, an individual is either a member of a set or it's not. If the individual is a member, it is represented with the number 1. If it is not a member, it is represented by the number 0. Traditional MCDM is characterized by binary membership.

Imagine that you're evaluating 20 different potential investments. In this evaluation, you'd score each criterion for each of the investments. To eliminate poor investment choices, simply sum the criteria scores for each of the alternatives and then dismiss any investments that do not get a total score of 3 — leaving you with the investments that fall within a certain threshold of earning growth potential, that have good earnings quality, and whose dividends perform at a level that's acceptable to you.

Focusing on fuzzy MCDM

If you prefer to evaluate suitability within a range, instead of using binary membership terms of 0 or 1, you can use *fuzzy multi-criteria decision making (FMCDM)* to do that. With FMCDM you can evaluate all the same types of problems as you would with MCDM. The term *fuzzy* refers to the fact that the criteria being used to evaluate alternatives offer a range of acceptability — instead of the binary, crisp set criteria associated with traditional MCDM. Evaluations based on fuzzy criteria lead to a range of potential outcomes, each with its own level of suitability as a solution.

TIP

One important feature of FMCDM: You're likely to have a list of several fuzzy criteria, but these criteria might not all hold the same importance in your evaluation. To correct for this, simply assign weights to criteria to quantify their relative importance.

Introducing Regression Methods

Machine learning algorithms of the regression variety were adopted from the statistics field, to provide data scientists with a set of methods for describing and quantifying the relationships between variables in a dataset. Use regression techniques if you want to determine the strength of correlation between variables in your data. You can use regression to predict future values from historical values, but be careful: Regression methods assume a cause-and-effect relationship between variables, but present circumstances are always subject to flux. Predicting future values from historical ones will generate incorrect results when present circumstances change. In this section, I tell you all about linear regression, logistic regression, and the ordinary least squares method.

Linear regression

Linear regression is a machine learning method you can use to describe and quantify the relationship between your target variable, y — the *predictant*, in statistics lingo — and the dataset features you've chosen to use as predictor variables (commonly designated as dataset X in machine learning). When you use just one variable as your predictor, linear regression is as simple as the middle school algebra formula y=mx+b. But you can also use linear regression to quantify correlations between several variables in a dataset — called *multiple linear regression*. Before getting too excited about using linear regression, though, make sure you've considered its limitations:

>> Linear regression only works with numerical variables, not categorical ones.

>> If your dataset has missing values, it will cause problems. Be sure to address your missing values before attempting to build a linear regression model.

>> If your data has outliers present, your model will produce inaccurate results. Check for outliers before proceeding.

>> The linear regression assumes that there is a linear relationship between dataset features and the target variable. Test to make sure this is the case, and if it's not, try using a log transformation to compensate.

>> The linear regression model assumes that all features are independent of each other.

>> Prediction errors, or *residuals,* should be normally distributed.

TIP

Don't forget dataset size! A good rule of thumb is that you should have at least 20 observations per predictive feature if you expect to generate reliable results using linear regression.

Logistic regression

Logistic regression is a machine learning method you can use to estimate values for a categorical target variable based on your selected features. Your target variable should be numeric, and contain values that describe the target's class — or category. One cool thing about logistic regression is that, in addition to predicting the class of observations in your target variable, it indicates the probability for each of its estimates. Though logistic regression is like linear regression, it's requirements are simpler, in that:

>> There does not need to be a linear relationship between the features and target variable.

>> Residuals don't have to be normally distributed.

>> Predictive features are not required to have a normal distribution.

When deciding whether logistic regression is a good choice for you, make sure to consider the following limitations:

>> Missing values should be treated or removed.

>> Your target variable must be binary or ordinal.

>> Predictive features should be independent of each other.

Logistic regression requires a greater number of observations (than linear regression) to produce a reliable result. The rule of thumb is that you should have at least 50 observations per predictive feature if you expect to generate reliable results.

Ordinary least squares (OLS) regression methods

Ordinary least squares (OLS) is a statistical method that fits a linear regression line to a dataset. With OLS, you do this by squaring the vertical distance values that describe the distances between the data points and the best-fit line, adding up those squared distances, and then adjusting the placement of the best-fit line so that the summed squared distance value is minimized. Use OLS if you want to construct a function that's a close approximation to your data.

REMEMBER

As always, don't expect the actual value to be identical to the value predicted by the regression. Values predicted by the regression are simply estimates that are most similar to the actual values in the model.

OLS is particularly useful for fitting a regression line to models containing more than one independent variable. In this way, you can use OLS to estimate the target from dataset features.

WARNING

When using OLS regression methods to fit a regression line that has more than one independent variable, two or more of the IVs may be interrelated. When two or more IVs are strongly correlated with each other, this is called *multicollinearity*. Multicollinearity tends to adversely affect the reliability of the IVs as predictors when they're examined apart from one another. Luckily, however, multicollinearity doesn't decrease the overall predictive reliability of the model when it's considered collectively.

Detecting Outliers

Many statistical and machine learning approaches assume that there are no outliers in your data. Outlier removal is an important part of preparing your data for analysis. In this section, you see a variety of methods you can use to discover outliers in your data.

Analyzing extreme values

Outliers are data points with values that are significantly different than the majority of data points comprising a variable. It is important to find and remove outliers, because, left untreated, they skew variable distribution, make variance appear falsely high, and cause a misrepresentation of intervariable correlations.

Most machine learning and statistical models assume that your data is free of outliers, so spotting and removing them is a critical part of preparing your data for analysis. Not only that, you can use outlier detection to spot anomalies that represent fraud, equipment failure, or cybersecurity attacks. In other words, outlier detection is a data preparation method and an analytical method in its own right.

Outliers fall into the following three categories:

>> **Point:** Point outliers are data points with anomalous values compared to the normal range of values in a feature.

>> **Contextual:** Contextual outliers are data points that are anomalous only within a specific context. To illustrate, if you are inspecting weather station data from January in Orlando, Florida, and you see a temperature reading of 23 degrees F, this would be quite anomalous because the average temperature there is 70 degrees F in January. But consider if you were looking at data from January at a weather station in Anchorage, Alaska — a temperature reading of 23 degrees F in this context is not anomalous at all.

>> **Collective:** These outliers appear nearby to one another, all having similar values that are anomalous to the majority of values in the feature.

You can detect outliers using either a univariate or multivariate approach.

Detecting outliers with univariate analysis

Univariate outlier detection is where you look at features in your dataset, and inspect them individually for anomalous values. There are two simple methods for doing this:

>> Tukey outlier labeling

>> Tukey boxplot

It is cumbersome to detect outliers using Tukey outlier labeling, but if you want to do it, the trick here is to see how far the minimum and maximum values are from the 25 and 75 percentiles. The distance between the *1st quartile* (at 25 percent) and the *3rd quartile* (at 75 percent) is called the *inter-quartile range (IQR)*, and it describes the data's spread. When you look at a variable, consider its spread, its Q1 / Q3 values, and its minimum and maximum values to decide whether the variable is suspect for outliers.

TIP

Here's a good rule of thumb: a = Q1 − 1.5*IQR and b = Q3 + 1.5*IQR. If your minimum value is less than a, or your maximum value is greater than b, the variable probably has outliers.

In comparison, a Tukey boxplot is a pretty easy way to spot outliers. Each boxplot has whiskers that are set at 1.5*IQR. Any values that lie beyond these whiskers are outliers. Figure 5-2 shows outliers as they appear within a Tukey boxplot.

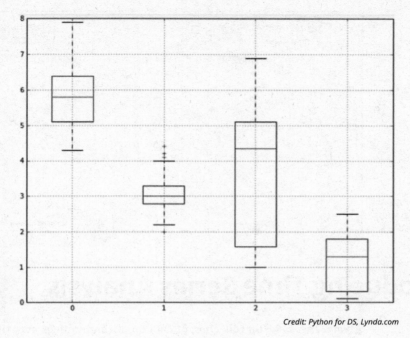

Credit: Python for DS, Lynda.com

FIGURE 5-2: Spotting outliers with a Tukey boxplot.

Detecting outliers with multivariate analysis

Sometimes outliers only show up within combinations of data points from disparate variables. These outliers really wreak havoc on machine learning algorithms, so it's important to detect and remove them. You can use multivariate analysis of outliers to do this. A multivariate approach to outlier detection involves considering two or more variables at a time and inspecting them together for outliers. There are several methods you can use, including

>> Scatter-plot matrix

>> Boxplot

>> Density-based spatial clustering of applications with noise (DBScan) — as discussed in Chapter 6

>> Principal component analysis (shown in Figure 5-3)

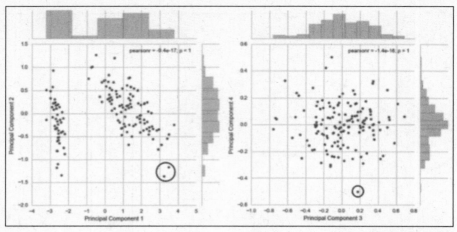

Credit: Python for DS, Lynda.com

FIGURE 5-3:
Using PCA to spot
outliers.

Introducing Time Series Analysis

A *time series* is just a collection of data on attribute values over time. Time series analysis is performed to predict future instances of the measure based on the past observational data. To forecast or predict future values from data in your dataset, use time series techniques.

Identifying patterns in time series

Time series exhibit specific patterns. Take a look at Figure 5-4 to get a better understanding of what these patterns are all about. *Constant* time series remain at roughly the same level over time, but are subject to some random error. In contrast, *trended* series show a stable linear movement up or down. Whether constant or trended, time series may also sometimes exhibit *seasonality* — predictable, cyclical fluctuations that reoccur seasonally throughout a year. As an example of seasonal time series, consider how many businesses show increased sales during the holiday season.

If you're including seasonality in your model, incorporate it in the quarter, month, or even 6-month period — wherever it's appropriate. Time series may show *nonstationary processes* — or, unpredictable cyclical behavior that is not related to seasonality and that results from economic or industry-wide conditions instead. Because they're not predictable, nonstationary processes can't be forecasted. You must transform nonstationary data to stationary data before moving forward with an evaluation.

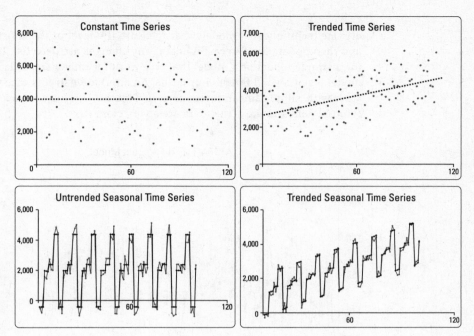

FIGURE 5-4:
A comparison of patterns exhibited by time series.

Take a look at the solid lines in Figure 5-4. These represent the mathematical models used to forecast points in the time series. The mathematical models shown represent very good, precise forecasts because they're a very close fit to the actual data. The actual data contains some random error, thus making it impossible to forecast perfectly.

Modeling univariate time series data

Similar to how multivariate analysis is the analysis of relationships between multiple variables, *univariate analysis* is the quantitative analysis of only one variable at a time. When you model univariate time series, you are modeling time series changes that represent changes in a single variable over time.

Autoregressive moving average (ARMA) is a class of forecasting methods that you can use to predict future values from current and historical data. As its name implies, the family of ARMA models combines *autoregression* techniques (analyses that assume that previous observations are good predictors of future values and perform an autoregression analysis to forecast for those future values) and *moving average* techniques — models that measure the level of the constant time series and then update the forecast model if any changes are detected. If you're looking for a simple model or a model that will work for only a small dataset, the ARMA model is not a good fit for your needs. An alternative in this case might be to just stick with simple linear regression. In Figure 5-5, you can see that the model forecast data and the actual data are a very close fit.

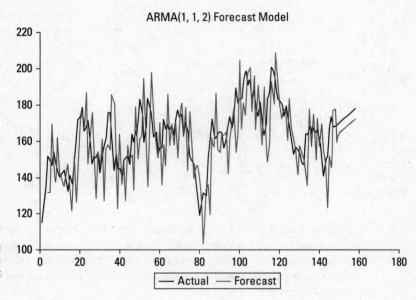

FIGURE 5-5:
An example of an ARMA forecast model.

To use the ARMA model for reliable results, you need to have at least 50 observations.

REMEMBER

» Clustering your data with the k-means algorithm and kernel density estimation

» Getting to know hierarchical and neighborhood clustering algorithms

» Checking out decision tree and random forest algorithms

Chapter **6**

Using Clustering to Subdivide Data

D ata scientists use clustering to help them divide their unlabeled data into subsets. The basics behind clustering are relatively easy to understand, but things get tricky fast when you get into using some of the more advanced algorithms. In this chapter, I introduce the basics behind clustering. I follow that by introducing several nuanced algorithms that offer clustering solutions to meet your requirements, based on the specific characteristics of your feature dataset.

Introducing Clustering Basics

To grasp advanced methods for use in clustering your data, you should first take a few moments to make sure you have a firm understanding of the basics that underlie all forms of clustering. Clustering is a form of *machine learning* — the machine in this case is your computer, and *learning* refers to an algorithm that's repeated over and over until a certain set of predetermined conditions is met. Learning algorithms are generally run until the point that the final analysis results will not change, no matter how many additional times the algorithm is passed over the data.

Clustering is one of the two main types of machine learning: In *unsupervised* machine learning, the data in the dataset is unlabeled. Because the data is unlabeled, the algorithms must use inferential methods to discover patterns, relationships, and correlations within the raw dataset. To put clustering through its paces, I want to use a readily available sample dataset from the World Bank's open datasets on country income and education. This data shows the percentage of income earned by the bottom 10 percent of the population in each country and the percentage of children who complete primary school in each country.

TECHNICAL STUFF

For this chapter's discussion, I'm isolating the median reported statistic from the years 2000 to 2003. (Some countries report on these statistics only every few years, and during 2000 to 2003, this data was fully reported by 81 of 227 countries.)

WARNING

In datasets about the percentage of children who complete primary school, some are reported at over 100 percent. That's because some countries count this statistic at different ages, but the data was *normalized* so that the percentage distribution is proportionally scaled across the range of countries represented in the dataset. In other words, although the total scale exceeds 100 percent, the values have been normalized so that they're proportional to one another and you're getting an apples-to-apples comparison. Thus, the fact that some countries report completion rates greater than 100 percent has no adverse effect on the analysis you make in this chapter.

Getting to know clustering algorithms

You use clustering algorithms to subdivide unlabeled datasets into clusters of observations that are most similar for a predefined feature. If you have a dataset that describes multiple features about a set of observations and you want to group your observations by their feature similarities, use clustering algorithms. There are different clustering methods, depending on how you want your dataset to be divided. The two main types of clustering algorithms are

>> **Partitional:** Algorithms that create only a single set of clusters

>> **Hierarchical:** Algorithms that create separate sets of nested clusters, each in its own hierarchal level

You can read about both approaches later in this chapter, but for now, start by looking at Figure 6-1, a simple scatter plot of the Country Income and Education datasets.

In unsupervised clustering, you start with this data and then proceed to divide it into subsets. These subsets, called *clusters,* are composed of observations that are most similar to one another. In Figure 6-1, it appears that there are at least two clusters, probably three — one at the bottom with low income and education, and then the high-education countries look like they might be split between low and high incomes.

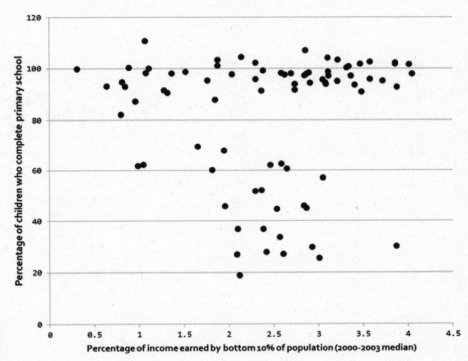

FIGURE 6-1:
A simple
scatter plot.

Figure 6-2 shows the result of *eyeballing,* or making a visual estimate of, clusters in this dataset.

TIP

Although you can generate visual estimates of clusters, you can achieve much more accurate results when dealing with much larger datasets by using algorithms to generate clusters for you. Visual estimation is a rough method that's useful only on smaller datasets of minimal complexity. Algorithms produce exact, repeatable results, and you can use algorithms to generate clusters from multiple dimensions of data within your dataset.

Clustering algorithms are appropriate in situations where the following characteristics are true:

>> You know and understand the dataset you're analyzing.

>> Before running the clustering algorithm, you don't have an exact idea of the nature of the subsets (clusters). Often, you don't even know how many subsets are in the dataset before you run the algorithm.

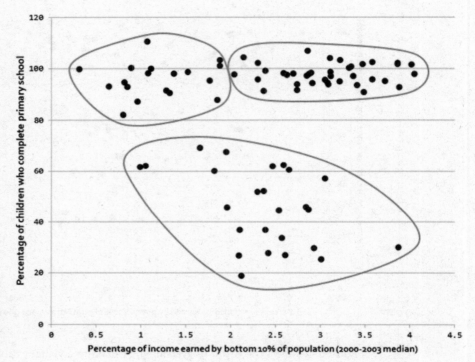

>> The subsets (clusters) are determined by only the single dataset you're analyzing.

>> Your goal is to determine a model that describes the subsets in a single dataset and only this dataset.

If you add more data to your dataset after you've already built the model, be sure to rebuild the model from scratch to get more complete and accurate model results.

Looking at clustering similarity metrics

Classification methods are based on calculating the similarity or difference between two observations. If your dataset is *numeric* — composed of only numerical features — and can be portrayed on an n-dimensional plot, you can use various geometric metrics to scale your multidimensional data.

REMEMBER

An *n-dimensional plot* is a multidimensional scatter plot that you can use to plot *n* number of dimensions of data.

Some popular geometric metrics used for calculating distances between observations are simply different geometric functions that are useful for modeling distances between points:

» **Euclidean metric:** A measure of the distance between points plotted on a Euclidean plane.

» **Manhattan metric:** A measure of the distance between points where distance is calculated as the sum of the absolute value of the differences between two points' Cartesian coordinates.

» **Minkowski distance metric:** A generalization of the Euclidean and Manhattan distance metrics. Quite often, these metrics can be used interchangeably.

» **Cosine similarity metric:** The cosine metric measures the similarity of two data points based on their orientation, as determined by taking the cosine of the angle between them.

Lastly, for non-numeric data, you can use metrics like the *Jaccard distance metric*, an index that compares the number of features that two observations have in common. For example, to illustrate a Jaccard distance, look at these two text strings:

Saint Louis de Ha-ha, Quebec

St-Louis de Ha!Ha!, QC

What features do these text strings have in common? And what features are different between them? The Jaccard metric generates a numerical index value that quantifies the similarity between text strings.

Identifying Clusters in Your Data

You can use many different algorithms for clustering, but the speed and robustness of the k-means algorithm makes it a popular choice among experienced data scientists. As alternatives, kernel density estimation methods, hierarchical algorithms, and neighborhood algorithms are also available to help you identify clusters in your dataset.

Clustering with the k-means algorithm

The *k-means* clustering algorithm is a simple, fast, unsupervised learning algorithm that you can use to predict groupings within a dataset. The model makes its prediction based on the *number of centroids present* — represented by *k,* a model parameter that you must define — and the nearest mean values, measured by the Euclidean distance between observations. Because the features of a dataset are usually on different scales, the difference of scales can distort the results of this distance calculation. To avoid this problem, scale your variables before using k-means to predict data groupings.

The quality of the clusters is heavily dependent on the correctness of the *k* value you specify. If your data is 2- or 3-dimensional, a plausible range of *k* values may be visually determinable. In the eyeballed approximation of clustering from the World Bank Income and Education data scatter plot (refer to Figure 6-2), a visual estimation of the *k* value would equate to three clusters, or *k* = 3.

TIP

When defining the *k* value, it may be possible to choose the number of centroids by looking at a scatter plot (if your dataset is 2- or 3-dimensional) or by looking for obvious, significant groupings within your dataset's variables. You can pick the number of centroids based on the number of groupings that you know exist in the dataset, or by the number of groupings that you want to exist in the dataset. Whatever the case, use your subjective knowledge about the dataset when choosing the number of clusters to be modeled.

If your dataset has more than three dimensions, however, you can use computational methods to generate a good value for *k.* One such method is the *silhouette coefficient* — a method that calculates the average distance of each point from all other points in a cluster and then compares that value with the average distance to every point in every other cluster. Luckily, because the k-means algorithm is efficient, it does not require much computer processing power, and you can easily calculate this coefficient for a wide range of *k* values.

The k-means algorithm works by placing sample cluster centers on an *n*-dimensional plot and then evaluating whether moving them in any single direction would result in a new center with higher *density* — with more observations closer to it, in other words. The centers are moved from regions of lower density to regions of higher density until all centers are within a region of *local maximum density* — a true center of the cluster, where each cluster gets a maximum number of points closest to its cluster center. Whenever possible, you should try to place the centers yourself, manually. If that's not possible, simply place the centers randomly and run the algorithm several times to see how often you end up with the same clusters.

One weakness of the k-means algorithm is that it may produce incorrect results by placing cluster centers in areas of *local minimum density*. This happens when centers get lost in *low-density regions* (in other words, regions of the plot that have relatively few points plotted in them) and the algorithm-driven *directional movement* (the movement that's meant to increase point density) starts to bounce and oscillate between faraway clusters. In these cases, the center gets caught in a low-density space that's located between two high-point density zones. This results in erroneous clusters based around centers that converge in areas of low, local minimum density. Ironically, this happens most often when the underlying data is very well-clustered, with tight, dense regions that are separated by wide, sparse areas.

TIP

To try things out for yourself, start clustering your data with the k-means methods by using either R's cluster package or Python's Scikit-learn library. For more on R's cluster package, check out

```
http://cran.r-project.org/web/packages/cluster/cluster.pdf;
        for more on Scikit-learn, check out
        http://scikit-learn.org
```

Estimating clusters with kernel density estimation (KDE)

If the k-means algorithm doesn't appeal to you, one alternative way to identify clusters in your data is to use a density smoothing function instead. *Kernel density estimation* (KDE) is that smoothing method; it works by placing a *kernel* — a weighting function that is useful for quantifying density — on each data point in the dataset and then summing the kernels to generate a kernel density estimate for the overall region. Areas of greater point density will sum out with greater kernel density, and areas of lower point density will sum out with less kernel density.

Because kernel smoothing methods don't rely on cluster center placement and clustering techniques to estimate clusters, they don't exhibit a risk of generating erroneous clusters by placing centers in areas of local minimum density. Where k-means algorithms generate hard-lined definitions between points in different clusters, KDE generates a plot of gradual density change between observations. For this reason, it's a helpful aid when eyeballing clusters. Figure 6-3 shows what the World Bank Income and Education scatter plot looks like after a KDE has been applied.

In Figure 6-3, you can see that the white spaces between clusters have been reduced. When you look at the figure, it's fairly obvious that there are at least three clusters, and possibly more, if you want to allow for small clusters.

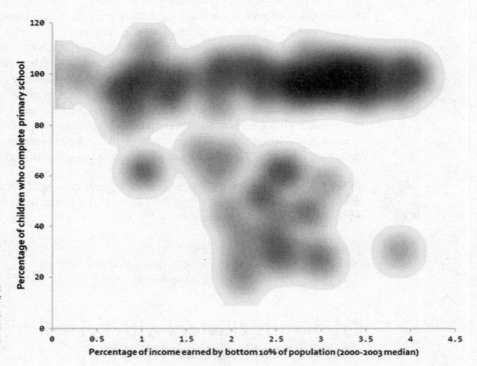

FIGURE 6-3:
KDE smoothing of the World Bank's Income and Education data scatter plot.

Clustering with hierarchical algorithms

A hierarchical clustering algorithm is yet another alternative to k-means clustering. In comparison to k-means clustering, the hierarchical clustering algorithm is a slower, clunkier unsupervised clustering algorithm. It predicts groupings within a dataset by calculating the distance and generating a link between each singular observation and its nearest neighbor. It then uses those distances to predict subgroups within a dataset. If you're carrying out a statistical study or analyzing biological or environmental data, hierarchical clustering might be your ideal machine learning solution.

To visually inspect the results of your hierarchical clustering, generate a *dendrogram* — a visualization tool that depicts the similarities and branching between groups in a data cluster. You can use several different algorithms to build a dendrogram, and the algorithm you choose dictates where and how branching occurs within the clusters. Additionally, dendrograms can be built either *bottom-up* (by assembling pairs of points and then aggregating them into larger and larger groups) or *top-down* (by starting with the full dataset and splitting it into smaller and smaller groups). Looking at the dendrogram results makes it easier to decide the appropriate number of clusters for your dataset. In the dendrogram example shown in Figure 6-4, the underlying dataset appears to have either three or four clusters.

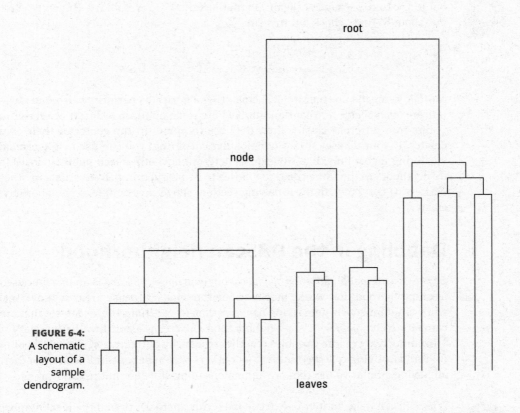

FIGURE 6-4:
A schematic
layout of a
sample
dendrogram.

In hierarchical clustering, the distance between observations is measured in three different ways: Euclidean, Manhattan, or Cosine. Additionally, linkage is formed by three different methods: Ward, Complete, and Average. When deciding what distance and linkage parameters to use, trial-and-error is an easy approach. Just try each combination and then compare all your model results. Go with the model that produces the most accurate prediction.

Hierarchical clustering algorithms are more computationally expensive than k-means algorithms because with each iteration of hierarchical clustering, many observations must be compared to many other observations. The benefit, however, is that hierarchical clustering algorithms are not subject to errors caused by center convergence at areas of local minimum density (as exhibited with the k-means clustering algorithms).

WARNING

If you're working with a large dataset, watch out! Hierarchical clustering will probably be *way* too slow.

TIP

If you want to get started working with hierarchical clustering algorithms, check out R's hclust package or (again) Python's Scikit-learn library. (If you're curious about hclust, check out this site:

```
https://stat.ethz.ch/R-manual/R-
            patched/library/stats/html/hclust.html
```

Neither k-means nor hierarchical clustering algorithms perform well when clusters are *nonglobular* — a configuration where some points in a cluster are closer to points in a different cluster than they are to points in the center of their own cluster. If your dataset shows nonglobular clustering, you can use neighborhood clustering algorithms, like DBScan, to determine whether each point is closer to its neighbors in the same cluster or closer to its neighboring observations in other clusters. (Figure 6-5, in the following section, shows an example of neighborhood clustering.)

Dabbling in the DBScan neighborhood

Density-based spatial clustering of applications with noise (DBScan) is an unsupervised learning method that works by clustering *core samples* (dense areas of a dataset) while simultaneously demarking *non-core samples* (portions of the dataset that are comparatively sparse). It's a neighborhood clustering algorithm that's ideal for examining two or more variables together to identify outliers. It's particularly useful for identifying *collective* outliers — outliers that appear nearby to one another, all having similar values that are anomalous to most values in the variable.

TIP

With DBScan, take an iterative, trial-and-error approach to find the ideal number of outliers for inspection. When experimenting with the DBScan model, outliers should comprise 5 percent or less of the dataset's observations. You must adjust the model parameters until you've isolated this small select group of observations.

Neighborhood clustering algorithms are generally effective, but they are subject to these two weaknesses:

» **Neighborhood clustering can be computationally expensive.** With every iteration of this method, every data point might have to be compared to every other data point in the dataset.

FIGURE 6-5: Sample output from a neighborhood clustering algorithm.

» **With neighborhood clustering, you might have to provide the model with empirical parameter values for expected cluster size and cluster density.** If you guess either of these parameters incorrectly, the algorithm misidentifies clusters, and you must start the whole long process over again to fix the problem. If you choose to use the DBScan method, you're required to specify these parameters. (As an alternative, you could try the average nearest neighbor and k-nearest neighbor algorithms, which are discussed in Chapter 7.)

TIP

To avoid making poor guesses for the cluster size and cluster density parameters, you can first use a quick k–means algorithm to determine plausible values.

Categorizing Data with Decision Tree and Random Forest Algorithms

In cases where clustering algorithms fail, decision tree and random forest algorithms might just offer you a perfect alternative machine learning solution.

At certain times, you can get stuck trying to cluster and classify data from a non-numerical dataset. It's times like these that you can use a decision tree model to help cluster and classify your data correctly.

A *decision tree* algorithm works by developing a set of yes-or-no rules that you can follow for new data to see exactly how it will be characterized by the model. But you must be careful when using decision tree models, because they run the high risk of *error propagation,* which occurs whenever one of the model rules is incorrect. Errors are generated in the results of decisions that are made based on that incorrect rule, and then propagated through every other subsequent decision made along that branch of the tree.

To illustrate this type of algorithm, consider a dataset that's often used in machine learning demonstrations — the list of passenger names from the *Titanic.* Using a simple decision tree model, you can predict that if a passenger was female or was a male child with a large family, he or she probably survived the catastrophe. Figure 6-6 illustrates this determination.

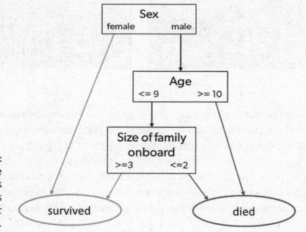

FIGURE 6-6: A decision tree model predicts survival rates from the *Titanic* catastrophe.

Lastly, random forest algorithms are a slower but more powerful alternative. Instead of building a tree from the data, the algorithm creates random trees and then determines which one best classifies the testing data. This method eliminates the risk of error propagation that is inherent in decision tree models.

Chapter **7**

Modeling with Instances

ata scientists use classification methods to help them build predictive models that they can then use to forecast the classification of future observations. Classification is a form of *supervised machine learning:* The classification algorithm learns from labeled data. Data labels make it easier for your models to make decisions based on the logic rules you've defined. Your plain-vanilla clustering algorithm, like the k-means method, can help you predict subgroups from within unlabeled datasets. But there's more to life than plain vanilla. I think it's about time to take things one step further, by exploring the instance-based family of machine learning algorithms.

Instance-based learning classifiers are supervised, *lazy learners* — they have no training phase, and they simply memorize training data, in-memory, to predict classifications for new data points. This type of classifier looks at instances — observations within a dataset — and, for each new observation, the classifier searches the training data for observations that are most similar, and then classifies the new observation based on its similarity to instances in the training set. Instance–based classifiers include

>> k-nearest neighbor (kNN)

>> Self-organizing maps

>> Locally weighted learning

If you're unsure about your dataset's distribution, instance-based classifiers might be a good option, but first make sure that you know their limitations. These classifiers are not well-suited for

>> Noisy data (data with unexplainable random variation)

>> Datasets with unimportant or irrelevant features

>> Datasets with missing values

To keep this chapter as simple as possible, I stick to explaining the k-nearest neighbor classification algorithm (known affectionately as kNN). The concepts involved in kNN are a bit tricky, though, so first I introduce you to the simpler average nearest neighbor methods before into the kNN approach.

Recognizing the Difference between Clustering and Classification

The purpose of both clustering and classification algorithms is to make sense of, and extract value from, large sets of structured and unstructured data. If you're working with huge volumes of unstructured data, it only makes sense to try to partition the data into some sort of logical groupings before attempting to analyze it. Both clustering and classification methods allow you to take a sweeping glance of your data en masse and then form some logical structures based on what you find there, before going deeper into the nuts-and-bolts analysis.

Reintroducing clustering concepts

In their simplest form, *clusters* are sets of unlabeled data points that share similar attribute values, and *clustering algorithms* are the methods that group these data points into different clusters based on their similarities. You'll see clustering algorithms used for disease classification in medical science, but you'll also see them used for customer classification in marketing research and for environmental health risk assessment in environmental engineering.

Getting to know classification algorithms

You might have heard of classification and thought that it's the same concept as clustering. Many people do, but this is not the case. In *classification,* your data is *labeled,* so before you analyze it, you already know the number of classes into which it should be grouped. You also already know what class you want assigned to each data point. In contrast, with *clustering* methods, your data is *unlabeled,* so you have no predefined concept of how many clusters are appropriate. You must rely on the clustering algorithms to sort and cluster the data in the most appropriate way.

With classification algorithms, you use what you know about an existing labeled dataset to generate a predictive model for classifying future observations. If your goal is to use your dataset and its known subsets to build a model for predicting the categorization of future observations, you'll want to use classification algorithms. When implementing supervised classification, you already know your dataset's *labels* — these labels are used to subset observations into *classes.* Classification helps you see how well your data fits into the dataset's predefined classes so that you can then build a predictive model for classifying future observations.

Figure 7-1 illustrates how it looks to classify the World Bank's Income and Education datasets according to the Continent feature.

In Figure 7-1, you can see that, in some cases, the subsets you might identify with a clustering technique do correspond to the Continents category, but in other cases, they don't. For example, look at the lone Asian country in the middle of the African observations. That's Bhutan. You could use the data in this dataset to build a model that would predict a continent class for incoming observations. But if you introduced a data point for a new country that showed statistics similar to those of Bhutan, the new country could be categorized as being part of either the Asian continent or the African continent, depending on how you define your model.

Now imagine a situation in which your original data doesn't include Bhutan and you use the model to predict Bhutan's continent as a new data point. In this scenario, the model would incorrectly predict that Bhutan is part of the African continent. This is an example of *model overfitting* — a situation in which a model is so tightly fit to its underlying dataset, as well as its noise or random error, that the model performs poorly as a predictor for new observations.

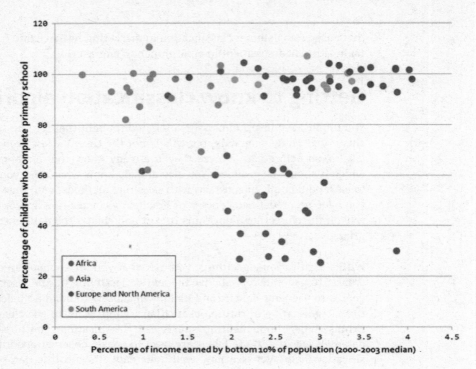

FIGURE 7-1:
A classification of
World Bank data,
according to the
Continent
category.

To avoid overfitting your models, divide your data into a training set and a test set. A typical ratio is to assign 70 percent of the data to the training set and the remaining 30 percent to the test set. Build your model with the training set, and then use the test set to evaluate the model by pretending that the test set observations are unknown. You can evaluate the accuracy of your model by comparing the classes assigned to the test set observations to the true classes of these observations.

Model overgeneralization can also be a problem. *Overgeneralization* is the opposite of overfitting: It happens when a data scientist tries to avoid misclassification due to overfitting by making a model extremely general. Models that are too general end up assigning every class a low degree of confidence. To illustrate model overgeneralization, consider again the World Bank Income and Education datasets. If the model used the presence of Bhutan to cast doubt on every new data point in its nearby vicinity, you end up with a wishy-washy model that treats all nearby points as African, but with a low probability. This model would be a poor predictive performer.

I can illustrate a good metaphor for overfitting and overgeneralization by using this well-known maxim: "If it walks like a duck and talks like a duck, then it's a duck." Overfitting would turn this statement into this: "It's a duck if, and only if, it walks and quacks exactly in the ways that I have personally observed a duck to walk and quack. Since I've never observed the way an Australian spotted duck walks and quacks, an Australian spotted duck must not really be a duck at all." In contrast, overgeneralization would say, "If it moves around on two legs and emits any high-pitched, nasal sound, it's a duck. Therefore, Fran Fine, Fran Drescher's character in the 1990s American sitcom *The Nanny*, must be a duck."

REMEMBER

Be aware of the constant danger of overfitting and overgeneralization. Find a happy medium between the two.

When classifying data, keep these two points in mind:

» **Model predictions are only as good as the model's underlying data.** In the World Bank data example, it could be the case that, if other factors such as life expectancy or energy use per capita were added to the model, its predictive strength might increase.

» **Model predictions are only as good as the categorization of the underlying dataset.** For example, what do you do with countries, like Russia, that span two continents? Do you distinguish North Africa from sub-Saharan Africa? Do you lump North America in with Europe because they tend to share similar features? Do you consider Central America to be part of North America or South America?

Making Sense of Data with Nearest Neighbor Analysis

At their core, nearest neighbor methods work by taking an observation's attribute value and then locating another observation whose attribute value is numerically nearest to it. Because the nearest neighbor technique is a classification method, you can use it to perform tasks as scientifically oriented as deducing the molecular structure of a vital human protein or uncovering key biological evolutionary relationships or as business-driven as designing recommendation engines for e-commerce sites or building predictive models for consumer transactions. The applications are limitless.

A good analogy for the nearest neighbor concept is illustrated in GPS technology. Imagine that you're in desperate need of a Starbucks iced latte, but you have no idea where the nearest store is located. What to do? One easy solution is simply to ask your smartphone where the nearest one is located.

When you do that, the system looks for businesses named Starbucks within a reasonable proximity of your current location. After generating a results listing, the system reports back to you with the address of the Starbucks coffeehouse closest to your current location — the one that is your nearest neighbor, in other words.

As the term *nearest neighbor* implies, the primary purpose of a nearest neighbor analysis is to examine your dataset and find the observation that's quantitatively most similar to your observation. Note that similarity comparisons can be based on any quantitative attribute, whether that is distance, age, income, weight, or any other factor that can describe the observation you're investigating. The simplest comparative attribute is distance.

In my Starbucks analogy, the x, y, z coordinates of the store reported to you by your smartphone are the most similar to the x, y, z coordinates of your current location. In other words, its location is closest in actual physical distance. The quantitative *attribute* being compared is distance, your current location is the *observation,* and the reported Starbucks coffeehouse is the *most similar observation.*

REMEMBER

Modern nearest neighbor analyses are almost always performed using computational algorithms. The nearest neighbor algorithm is known as a *single-link algorithm* — an algorithm that merges clusters if the clusters share between them at least one *connective edge* (a shared boundary line, in other words). In the following sections, you can learn the basics of the average nearest neighbor algorithm and the k-nearest neighbor algorithm.

Classifying Data with Average Nearest Neighbor Algorithms

Average nearest neighbor algorithms are basic yet powerful classification algorithms. They're useful for finding and classifying observations that are most similar on average. Average nearest neighbor algorithms are used in pattern recognition, in chemical and biological structural analysis, and in spatial data modeling. They're most often used in biology, chemistry, engineering, and geosciences.

In this section, you can find out how to use average nearest neighbor algorithms to compare multiple attributes between observations and, subsequently, identify which of your observations are most similar. You can also find out how to use average nearest neighbor algorithms to identify significant patterns in your dataset.

The purpose of using an average nearest neighbor algorithm is to classify observations based on the average of the arithmetic distances between them. If your goal is to identify and group observations by average similarity, the average nearest neighbor algorithm is a great way to do that.

With respect to nearest neighbor classifiers, a dataset is composed of observations, each which has an x- and y-variable. An x-variable represents the input value, or *feature,* and the y-variable represents the data label, or target variable. To keep all these terms straight, consider the following example.

Suppose that your friendly neighborhood business analyst, Business Analyst Stu, is using average nearest neighbor algorithms to perform a classification analysis of datasets in his organization's database. He's comparing employees based on the following four features:

>> Age

>> Number of children

>> Annual income

>> Seniority

In his dataset, however (shown in Table 7-1), each employee in Stu's organization is represented by a 5-dimensional *tuple* — or a set of five features.

>> Employee Mike: (34, 1, 120000, 9, 0)

>> Employee Liz: (42, 0, 90000, 5, 0)

>> Employee Jin: (22, 0, 60000, 2, 0)

>> Employee Mary: (53, 3, 180000, 30, 1)

Using the variables Age, Number of Children, Annual Income, and Seniority as predictive features, Business Analyst Stu calculates the average arithmetic differences between each of the employees. Figure 7-2 shows the calculated distances between each of the employees.

TABLE 7-1

Business Analyst Stu's Employee Data

Employee Name	Age	Number of Children	Annual Income	Seniority	Eligible to Retire
Mike	34	1	$120,000	9	0
Liz	42	0	$90,000	5	0
Jin	22	0	$60,000	2	0
Mary	53	3	$180,000	30	1

Mike	34	1	120000	9
Liz	42	0	90000	5
Distance between employees	**8**	**1**	**30000**	**4**
Mike	34	1	120000	9
Jin	22	0	60000	2
Distance between employees	**12**	**1**	**60000**	**7**
Mike	34	1	120000	9
Mary	53	3	180000	30
Distance between employees	**19**	**2**	**60000**	**21**
Liz	42	0	90000	5
Jin	22	0	60000	2
Distance between employees	**20**	**0**	**30000**	**3**
Liz	42	0	90000	5
Mary	53	3	180000	30
Distance between employees	**11**	**3**	**90000**	**25**
Jin	22	0	60000	2
Mary	53	3	180000	30
Distance between employees	**31**	**3**	**120000**	**28**

FIGURE 7-2: The distances between the employees' tuples.

After Business Analyst Stu has this arithmetic measure of distance between the employees, he finds the *average nearest neighbor* by taking an average of these separation distances. Figure 7-3 shows that average similarity.

Stu then groups the employees by the average separation distance between them. Because the average separation distance values between Mike, Liz, and Jin are the smallest, they're grouped into class 0. Mary's average separation distances are quite unlike the others, so she is put into her own class — class 1.

But does this make sense? Well, you're working with a labeled dataset and you can see that the attribute Eligible to Retire assumes only one of two possible values. So, yes. If the algorithm predicts two classifications within the data, that's a reasonable prediction. Furthermore, if Stu gets new incoming data points that are unlabeled with respect to a person's eligibility to retire, he could probably use this algorithm to predict for that eligibility, based on the other four features.

Finding Average Similarities	
Average Distance (Mike - Liz)	
Average Distance Value - (Average of 8, 1, 30000, 4)	7503.25
Average Distance (Mike - Jin)	
Average Distance Value - (Average of 12, 1, 60000, 7)	15005
Average Distance (Mike - Mary)	
Average Distance Value - (Average of 19, 2, 60000, 21)	15010.5
Average Distance (Liz - Jin)	
Average Distance Value - (Average of 20, 0, 30000, 3)	7505.75
Average Distance (Liz - Mary)	
Average Distance Value - (Average of 11, 3, 90000, 25)	22509.75
Average Distance (Jin - Mary)	
Average Distance Value - (Average of)	30015.5

FIGURE 7-3:
Finding the average similarity between employees.

Classifying with K-Nearest Neighbor Algorithms

k-nearest neighbor is a supervised machine learning classifier that uses the observations it memorizes from within a test dataset to predict classifications for new, unlabeled observations. kNN makes its predictions based on *similarity* — the more similar the training observations are to the new, incoming observations, the more likely it is that the classifier will assign them both the same class. kNN works best if your dataset is

>> Low on noise

>> Free of outliers

>> Labeled

>> Composed only of relevant selected features

>> Composed of distinguishable groups

WARNING

If you're working with a large dataset, you may want to avoid using kNN, because it will probably take way too long to make predictions from larger datasets.

In the larger context of machine learning, kNN is known as a *lazy* machine learning algorithm — in other words, it has little to no training phase. It simply memorizes training data and then uses that information as the basis on which to classify new observations. The goal of the kNN is to estimate the class of the query point P based on the classes of its k-nearest neighbors. In this way, kNN works in ways quite similar to how the human brain works.

The kNN algorithm is a generalization of the nearest neighbor algorithm. Rather than consider the nearest neighbor, you consider k numbers of nearest neighbors from within a dataset that contains n number of data points — k defines how many nearest neighbors will have an influence on the classification process. In kNN, the classifier classifies the query point P per the classification labels found in a majority of k-nearest points surrounding the query point.

kNN is a good classification method for you to use if you know little about the distribution of your dataset. What's more, if you do have a solid idea about your dataset's distribution and *feature selection criteria* — criteria for identifying and removing noise in the dataset — you can leverage this information to create significant enhancements in the algorithm's performance.

REMEMBER

kNN is among the simplest and most easy-to-implement classification methods, yet it yields competitive results when compared to some of the more sophisticated machine learning methods. Probably because of its simplicity and the competitive results it provides, the kNN algorithm has been ranked among the top ten most influential data mining algorithms by the academic research community.

Understanding how the k-nearest neighbor algorithm works

To use kNN, you simply need to pick a query point — usually called P — in the sample dataset and then compute the k-nearest neighbors to this point. The query point P is classified with a label that's the same as the label of most k-nearest points that surround it. (Figure 7-4 gives a bird's-eye view of the process.)

REMEMBER

K-nearest neighbors are quantified by either distance or similarity based on another quantitative attribute.

Consider the following example: A dataset is given by [1, 1, 4, 3, 5, 2, 6, 2, 4], and point P is equal to 5. Figure 7-4 shows how kNN would be applied to this dataset.

Now, if you were to specify that k is equal to 3, there are, based on distance, three nearest neighbors to the point 5. Those neighbors are 4, 4, and 6. So, based on the kNN algorithm, query point P will be classified as 4 because 4 is the majority number in the k number of points nearest to it. Similarly, kNN continues defining other query points using the same majority principle.

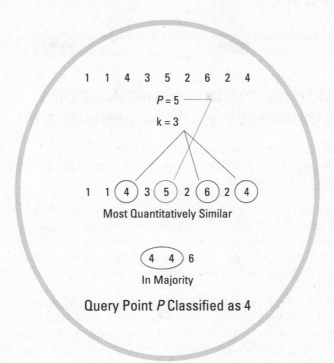

1 1 4 3 5 2 6 2 4

$P = 5$

$k = 3$

1 1 ④ 3 ⑤ 2 ⑥ 2 ④

Most Quantitatively Similar

④ 4 6

In Majority

Query Point *P* Classified as 4

FIGURE 7-4:
How kNN works.

REMEMBER

When using kNN, it's crucial to choose a *k* value that minimizes *noise* — unexplainable random variation, in other words. At the same time, you must choose a *k* value that includes sufficient data points in the selection process. If the data points aren't uniformly distributed, it's generally harder to predetermine a good *k* value. Be careful to select an optimum *k* value for each dataset you're analyzing.

TIP

Large *k* values tend to produce less noise and more *boundary smoothing* — clearer definition and less overlap — between classes than small *k* values do.

Knowing when to use the k-nearest neighbor algorithm

kNN is particularly useful for *multi-label learning* — supervised learning where the algorithm is applied so that it automatically *learns from* (detects patterns in) multiple sets of instances. Each of these sets could potentially have several classes of their own. With multi-label learning, the algorithm learns to predict multiple class labels for each new instance it encounters.

The problem with kNN is that it takes a lot longer than other classification methods to classify a sample. Nearest neighbor classifier performance depends on calculating the distance function and on the value of the neighborhood parameter k. You can try to speed things up by specifying optimal values for k and n.

Exploring common applications of k-nearest neighbor algorithms

kNN is often used for internet database management purposes. In this capacity, kNN is useful for website categorization, web page ranking, and other user dynamics across the web.

kNN classification techniques are also quite beneficial in *customer relationship management (CRM)*, a set of processes that ensure a business sustains improved relationships with its clients while simultaneously experiencing increased business revenues. Most CRMs get tremendous benefit from using kNN to data-mine customer information to find patterns that are useful in boosting customer retention.

The method is so versatile that even if you're a small-business owner or a marketing department manager, you can easily use kNN to boost your own marketing return on investment. Simply use kNN to analyze your customer data for purchasing patterns, and then use those findings to customize marketing initiatives so that they're more exactly targeted for your customer base.

Solving Real-World Problems with Nearest Neighbor Algorithms

Nearest neighbor methods are used extensively to understand and create value from patterns in retail business data. In the following sections, I present two powerful cases where kNN and average-NN algorithms are being used to simplify management and security in daily retail operations.

Seeing k-nearest neighbor algorithms in action

K-nearest neighbor techniques for pattern recognition are often used for theft prevention in the modern retail business. Of course, you're accustomed to seeing CCTV cameras around almost every store you visit, but most people have no idea how the data gathered from these devices is being used.

You might imagine that someone in the back room, monitoring these cameras for suspicious activity, and perhaps that is how things were done in the past. But now a modern surveillance system is intelligent enough to analyze and interpret video data on its own, without the need for human assistance. The modern systems can now use k-nearest neighbor for visual pattern recognition to scan and detect hidden packages in the bottom bin of a shopping cart at checkout. If an object is detected that is an exact match for an object listed in the database, the price of the spotted product could even automatically be added to the customer's bill. Though this automated billing practice is not used extensively now, the technology has been developed and is available for use.

K-nearest neighbor is also used in retail to detect patterns in credit card usage. Many new transaction-scrutinizing software applications use kNN algorithms to analyze register data and spot unusual patterns that indicate suspicious activity. For example, if register data indicates that a lot of customer information is being entered manually rather than through automated scanning and swiping, this could indicate that the employee who's using that register is in fact stealing a customer's personal information. Or, if register data indicates that a particular good is being returned or exchanged multiple times, this could indicate that employees are misusing the return policy or trying to make money from making fake returns.

Seeing average nearest neighbor algorithms in action

Average nearest neighbor algorithm classification and point pattern detection can be used in grocery retail to identify key patterns in customer purchasing behavior, and subsequently increase sales and customer satisfaction by anticipating customer behavior. Consider the following story:

> As with other grocery stores, buyer behavior at (the fictional) Waldorf Food Co-op tends to follow fixed patterns. Managers have even commented on the odd fact that members of a particular age group tend to visit the store during the same particular time window, and they even tend to buy the same types of products. One day, Manager Mike got extremely proactive and decided to hire a data scientist to analyze his customer data and provide exact details about these odd trends he'd been noticing. When Data Scientist Dan got in there, he quickly uncovered a pattern among working middle-aged male adults — they tended to visit the grocery store only during the weekends or at the end of the day on weekdays, and if they came into the store on a Thursday, they almost always bought beer.

Armed with these facts, Manager Mike quickly used this information to maximize beer sales on Thursday evenings by offering discounts, bundles, and specials. Not only was the store owner happy with the increased revenues, but Waldorf Food Co-op's male customers were also happy, because they got more of what they wanted, when they wanted it.

» Seeing how data science supports the IoT

» Grasping the powerful combination of and IoT

Chapter **8**

Building Models That Operate Internet-of-Things Devices

The *Internet of things (IoT)* is a network of connected devices that use the Internet to communicate amongst each other. That sounds sort of scary, right — like the movie *Her,* where machine–machine communications allow machines to begin thinking and acting autonomously? But actually, IoT represents the next level of insight, efficiency, and virtual assistance — the stuff we modern humans love and crave.

The rise of IoT has been facilitated by three major factors:

» An increased adoption of machine learning practices

» Increased deployment of sensor technologies

» Improved real-time data processing capabilities

The good news for data scientists is that data science is at the root of each of these three factors, making the IoT an ideal area for data scientists to develop expertise.

Just like data science, IoT itself is not the endgame. What's most inspiring and impressive about IoT is how it's deployed within different *vertical markets* — niche areas of commercial and industrial application (for example, manufacturing, oil and gas, retail, banking, and so on). For some examples, consider the following types of emerging technologies:

>> **Industrial processing:** Early detection of equipment failure is accessible via real-time processing of vibration sensor data.

>> **Environmental:** Sensor-enabled urban monitoring and recommendations that are constructed from real-time readings from devices that measure urban air quality, visibility, traffic patterns, water quality, fire hazards, and noise pollution (ambient or otherwise).

>> **Fitness:** Real-time fitness tracking and exercise recommendations are accessible via real-time processing and analysis of 3-dimensional motion sensor data.

Read on to learn how IoT works, the technologies that support it, and the advancements it promises to foster.

Overviewing the Vocabulary and Technologies

The Internet of things is its own class of technology. It has its own vocabulary and its own set of underlying technologies. Before getting into IoT data science, take a moment to familiarize yourself with them in the next four sections.

Learning the lingo

Before delving into the data science and innovation that's related to IoT, you need a grasp of the fundamental vocabulary. The *fog* — or *IoT cloud* — is a network of cloud services that connect to IoT-enabled devices. Cloud-based big data processing and analytics requirements are supported by these IoT cloud services. They use cloud-based data processing and analytics to support the IoT by facilitating intelligent, adaptive, and autonomous device operations.

Edge devices are the IoT-enabled devices that are connected to the IoT cloud. Besides being connected to the fog, these devices all share one thing in common: They generate data through any number of appliances, including sensors, odometers, cameras, contact sensors, pressure sensors, laser scanners, thermometers, smoke detectors, microphones, electric meters, gas meters, water flow meters, and much more.

WARNING

IoT-connected devices generate too much data! Some estimates put data generation by these devices at more than 2.5 million terabytes per day. Without proper filtering and treatment, the volume and velocity of this data could render it useless. To optimize device operations using the data that these devices generate, data storage and processing must be strategic.

The good news is that not all the data that's produced on edge devices needs to be moved to the cloud for processing, storage, and analytics. In fact, most edge devices come equipped with *device-embedded applications* that are capable of processing and deriving insights locally, using the data that's created by device appliances in real-time. Local data processing and analytic deployment is called *edge processing,* and it helps save resources by

>> **Detecting data that is useful to the analytics operations running on the device and discarding the rest:** This lowers the data transfer and storage overhead.

>> **Handling analytic deployments locally, doing away with the need to transfer data to and from the cloud:** A side benefit of these device-embedded analytics applications is that they return results faster than if the data is processed in the cloud.

Whether processing happens locally or on the cloud, IoT analytic applications that implement adaptive machine learning algorithms are called *adaptive IoT applications.* These adaptive IoT applications enable devices to adjust and adapt to the local conditions in which the device is operating. Later in this chapter, you can see an overview of popular machine learning methods for data science in IoT. Figure 8-1 illustrates some of these components to help pull them together into a conceptual schematic.

Like most other things related to the IoT, IoT professionals are a breed of their own. *IoT cloud application developers* are data scientists and engineers who focus exclusively on building adaptive IoT applications for deployment on local devices. The more general *IoT developer,* on the other hand, is responsible for building products and systems that serve the greater needs of the IoT cloud at-large, including all its connected IoT devices, data sources, and cloud computing environments.

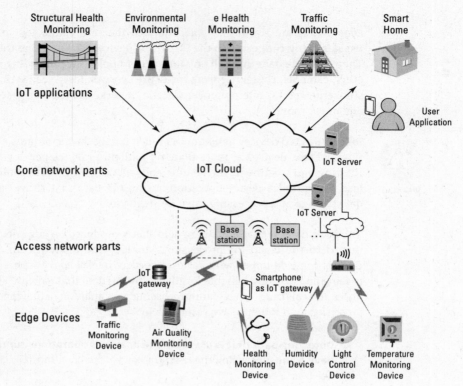

Structural Health Monitoring   Environmental Monitoring   e Health Monitoring   Traffic Monitoring   Smart Home

IoT applications

User Application

Core network parts   IoT Cloud   IoT Server

IoT Server

Access network parts   Base station   Base station   ...

Edge Devices

IoT gateway

Smartphone as IoT gateway

Traffic Monitoring Device   Air Quality Monitoring Device   Health Monitoring Device   Humidity Device   Light Control Device   Temperature Monitoring Device

FIGURE 8-1: Conceptual schematic of the IoT network.

Procuring IoT platforms

IoT platforms are broken into hardware platforms and software platforms. *IoT hardware platforms* are hardware components that you can use to connect devices to the IoT cloud, to stream data, and to manage device operations locally. Each platform offers its own set of core features, so you'll need to do some research into which meets your specific needs; some popular IoT hardware platforms are Raspberry Pi, Intel Edison, and Arduino products. *IoT software platforms* offer services such as device management, integration, security, data collection protocols, analytics, and limited data visualization. Again, each solution offers its own, unique blend of features, so do the research; major vendors are AWS IoT platform and IBM IoT Foundation Device Cloud.

Spark streaming for the IoT

Spark is an ideal framework for integrated real-time big data processing and analysis. With respect to the IoT, each IoT sensor stream can be transformed into Spark *DStreams* — discreet data streams that are the fundamental data abstraction in the Spark *Streaming module* (the module where data processing is carried out).

After you have your data in DStreams, it's then quite simple to construct automated analytical operations that filter, process, and detect based on DStream content. Depending on what's detected, real-time notifications and alerts are issued back to IoT applications regarding mission-critical insights. You can use the Spark Streaming *window operations* on DStream sources to quickly and easily aggregate processing and alerting to any regular time intervals of your choosing. Lastly, for comparative analytics, you can use Spark's Resilient Distributed Datasets (RDD) — an immutable collection of objects, and a fundamental Spark data structure — to store any relevant historical datasets in-memory.

WARNING

Edge devices often experience data transmission delays due to things like network congestion and intermittent network connectivity. High latency is not uncommon. To get around this, make sure to analyze data by the timestamp from when the machine data was generated, not from when it arrives back at the IoT cloud.

Getting context-aware with sensor fusion

Major IoT advancements are being made in *contextual-awareness* — where sensors are generating data that can be used for real-time context-aware services rendered by the device that's generating the data. This context awareness is facilitated by a technology called *sensor fusion* — where data from several different sensors is fused by a microcontroller to produce a broader, more detailed view on what's happening in a local environment. Technologies that support sensor fusion include EM Microelectronic, NXP, and even Apache Flink.

Digging into the Data Science Approaches

If you want to build predictive IoT models and applications, you need to know Python and SQL, covered in Chapter 14 and Chapter 16, respectively. You can use Python for data wrangling, visualization, time series analysis, and machine learning. Knowing SQL is useful for querying data from traditional databases or from the Hadoop Distributed File System. (I tell you more about this topic in Chapter 2.) Read on to learn more about specific analytical methods as they relate to IoT data science.

WARNING

An issue with IoT data, and sensor data specifically, is that it's often *sparse* — most of its values are empty, or "NaN" — "not a number." Be prepared to do a lot of *imputing* missing values — replacing missing values with approximations — when you're preprocessing data for analysis.

Taking on time series

Most IoT sensor data is composed of time series, so you should be adept at building and using time series models. One way that time series models are useful in the IoT is for decreasing the data transmission overhead for a wireless sensor network. (You'll understand why after you read the following list.) These two time series models are important for IoT data science:

>> **Moving average models:** Moving average models make forecasts based on the average of past observations. These models update the forecast whenever any significant deviations from predicted values are detected. Moving average models are important in IoT because of their automated model update feature, as explained further in the following bullet.

>> **Autoregressive integrated moving average models (ARIMA):** ARIMA combines the autoregressive moving average (ARMA) class of forecasting methods (which I tell you about in Chapter 5) with the process of *differencing* — making a time series stationary by calculating the difference between consecutive observations. By deploying the ARIMA model on a sensor node, you can significantly decrease the amount of data that is transmitted back to the IoT cloud for analysis. That's because only the data that falls outside of the prediction error range will get sent, and because the model continually updates with significant changes in the sensor readings.

Geospatial analysis

Just as sensor nodes create data that's labeled with a timestamp, they also produce data that's labeled with a geospatial location stamp. Each observation occurs at its given time — and place — so location is a big deal when it comes to the IoT. Many IoT applications consider an edge device's location, and nearness, with respect to other connected devices. All of this requires multidimensional geospatial data processing and analytics capabilities, which only a GIS application — a *geographic information system* application — is designed to offer. GIS, coupled with IoT network and data technologies, facilitate real-time geo-space-time analytics, enabling geo-insights to be delivered at the right time and place, precisely when these insights are actionable. Real-time geospatial analytics generate serious, sometimes life-saving, results when you use them to do things like this:

>> Identify and engage local customers while they are in your vicinity.

>> Monitor field assets for early-warning signs of equipment failure.

>> Evoke real-time situationally aware emergency response.

Dabbling in deep learning

Deep learning is an exciting development within IoT. That's because deep learning enables adaptive autonomous operations of the machine network. As you may recall from Chapter 4, *deep learning* is a machine learning algorithm that deploys layers of hierarchical neural networks to learn from data in an iterative and adaptive way. Similar to how the moving average and ARIMA models update on their own, deep learning models are able to adjust to and learn from data, despite changes and irregularities present in incoming sensor data.

I've listed some of the requirements that a deep learning model will face when deployed in the IoT environment:

>> The model must autonomously handle sparse dataset pre-processing requirements.

>> The model must learn from unlabeled data.

>> The model should self-evaluate its results and optimize parameters, if necessary.

>> The model should not be prone to overfitting.

TECHNICAL STUFF

Reinforcement learning can also be useful in generating analytics from IoT data. *Reinforcement learning* — or semisupervised machine learning — is an up-and-coming method that trains models via a reward system logic that closely resembles how humans learn. A reinforcement learning agent self-learns by interacting with its environment and choosing actions that will reap it as many rewards as possible. You set the rules for how rewards are given out, and the agent learns to take the actions that maximize the number of rewards it receives.

Advancing Artificial Intelligence Innovation

To understand artificial intelligence and its place in the IoT, you first need to grasp some key differences between the terms *artificial intelligence, machine learning,* and *IoT.* The term *artificial intelligence (AI)* refers to built-systems that mimic human behavior by making insightful decisions that are derived from artificial neural network model outputs. Many AI technologies implement deep learning or reinforcement learning, but, traditionally, the driving intelligence behind AI was artificial neural networks. As I explain in Chapter 4, neural nets are one type of machine learning method, among many. So, to be clear, machine learning is not

AI, but it encompasses a few methods that drive the decisions that are made by AI technologies. In itself, *machine learning* is simply the practice of applying algorithmic models to data in order to discover hidden patterns or trends that you can use to make predictions.

The IoT is a network of connected, smart devices, many of which depend on output from machine learning models to direct and manage device operations. In this sense, some IoT devices are considered a form of artificial intelligence. But not all devices that are connected to the IoT are AI technologies. Some connected devices are managed by traditional control systems that don't include machine learning or advanced analytics, like SCADA — Supervisory Control and Data Acquisition. These devices would still be IoT devices, but they would not be considered AI-driven technologies.

Artificial intelligence has been around awhile — since the 1940s, in fact. Some of the more recent AI-driven innovations include these objects:

>> **Self-driving cars:** These cars deploy machine learning to make the decisions that are required in order to operate and drive themselves. Human supervision is still required in order to ensure passenger safety.

>> **Military robotics:** These armed military robots deploy machine learning to act autonomously in hostile conflict environments.

>> **AlphaGo:** The Google gaming application used deep learning to win $1 million, by beating Lee Sedol at the Chinese game called Go.

IoT is ushering in its own breed of AI advancements, though. One type of innovation that is already available is the smart home. To understand how IoT combines with AI to produce a smart home, imagine that it's summertime and it's very hot outside. When you leave for work, your air conditioning is always turned off, and then when you get home at 5 p.m., it takes a long time to cool the house. Well, with IoT and AI advancements, you can connect your phone's GPS, an outdoor temperature sensor, and the air conditioner. The network can learn what features indicate your impending arrival — like departure from work, time of departure, and directionality of travel — to predict that you will arrive by a certain time. The network can use the outdoor temperature reading to learn how long the air conditioner should run and at what temperature, to bring the room temperature down to the temperature setting you've selected. So, when you arrive home, your house will be the perfect temperature without you having had to wait or to turn the systems on or off. They could act autonomously, based on what they've learned from the various connected devices, and based on the parameters you set for them.

3

Creating Data Visualizations That Clearly Communicate Meaning

Chapter **9**

Following the Principles of Data Visualization Design

Any standard definition of data science will specify that its purpose is to help you extract meaning and value from raw data. Finding and deriving insights from raw data is at the crux of data science, but these insights mean nothing if you don't know how to communicate your findings to others. Data visualization is an excellent means by which you can visually communicate your data's meaning. To design visualizations well, however, you must know and truly understand the target audience and the core purpose for which you're designing. You must also understand the main types of data graphics that are available to you, as well as the significant benefits and drawbacks of each. In this chapter, I present you with the core principles in data visualization design.

A *data visualization* is a visual representation that's designed for the purpose of conveying the meaning and significance of data and data insights. Since data visualizations are designed for a whole spectrum of different audiences, different purposes, and different skill levels, the first step to designing a great data visualization is to *know your audience*. Audiences come in all shapes, forms, and sizes. You could be designing for the young and edgy readers of *Rolling Stone* magazine or to convey scientific findings to a research group. Your audience might consist of board members and organizational decision makers or a local grassroots organization.

Data Visualizations: The Big Three

Every audience is composed of a unique class of consumers, each with unique data visualization needs, so you have to clarify for whom you're designing. I first introduce the three main types of data visualizations, and then I explain how to pick the one that best meets the needs of your audience.

Data storytelling for organizational decision makers

Sometimes you have to design data visualizations for a less technical-minded audience, perhaps in order to help members of this audience make better-informed business decisions. The purpose of this type of visualization is to tell your audience the story behind the data. In data storytelling, the audience depends on you to make sense of the data behind the visualization and then turn useful insights into visual stories that they can understand.

With *data storytelling*, your goal should be to create a clutter-free, highly focused visualization so that members of your audience can quickly extract meaning without having to make much effort. These visualizations are best delivered in the form of static images, but more adept decision makers may prefer to have an interactive dashboard that they can use to do a bit of exploration and what-if modeling.

Data showcasing for analysts

If you're designing for a crowd of logical, calculating analysts, you can create data visualizations that are rather open-ended. The purpose of this type of visualization is to help audience members visually explore the data and draw their own conclusions.

When using *data showcasing* techniques, your goal should be to display a lot of contextual information that supports audience members in making their own interpretations. These visualizations should include more contextual data and less conclusive focus so that people can get in and analyze the data for themselves, and then draw their own conclusions. These visualizations are best delivered as static images or dynamic, interactive dashboards.

Designing data art for activists

You could be designing for an audience of idealists, dreamers, and change-makers. When designing for this audience, you want your data visualization to make a point! You can assume that typical audience members aren't overly analytical. What they lack in math skills, however, they more than compensate for in solid convictions.

These people look to your data visualization as a vehicle by which to make a statement. When designing for this audience, data art is the way to go. The main goal in using *data art* is to entertain, to provoke, to annoy, or to do whatever it takes to make a loud, clear, attention-demanding statement. Data art has little to no narrative and offers no room for viewers to form their own interpretations.

REMEMBER

Data scientists have an ethical responsibility to always represent data accurately. A data scientist should never distort the message of the data to fit what the audience wants to hear — not even for data art! Nontechnical audiences don't even recognize, let alone see, the possible issues. They rely on the data scientist to provide honest and accurate representations, thus amplifying the level of ethical responsibility that the data scientist must assume.

Designing to Meet the Needs of Your Target Audience

To make a functional data visualization, you must get to know your target audience and then design precisely for their needs. But to make every design decision with your target audience in mind, you need to take a few steps to make sure that you truly understand your data visualization's target consumers.

To gain the insights you need about your audience and your purpose, follow this process:

1. Brainstorm.

   Think about a specific member of your visualization's audience, and make as many educated guesses as you can about that person's motivations.

Give this (imaginary) audience member a name and a few other identifying characteristics. I always imagine a 45-year-old divorced mother of two named Brenda.

2. Define the purpose of your visualization.

Narrow the purpose of the visualization by deciding exactly what action or outcome you want audience members to make as a result of the visualization.

3. Choose a functional design.

Review the three main data visualization types (discussed earlier in this chapter) and decide which type can best help you achieve your intended outcome.

The following sections spell out this process in detail.

Step 1: Brainstorm (about Brenda)

To brainstorm properly, pull out a sheet of paper and think about your imaginary audience member (Brenda) so that you can create a more functional and effective data visualization. Answer the following questions to help you better understand her, and thus better understand and design for your target audience.

Form a picture of what Brenda's average day looks like — what she does when she gets out of bed in the morning, what she does over her lunch hour, and what her workplace is like. Also consider how Brenda will use your visualization.

To form a comprehensive view of who Brenda is and how you can best meet her needs, ask these questions:

>> Where does Brenda work? What does she do for a living?

>> What kind of technical education or experience, if any, does she have?

>> How old is Brenda? Is she married? Does she have children? What does she look like? Where does she live?

>> What social, political, caused-based, or professional issues are important to Brenda? What does she think of herself?

>> What problems and issues does Brenda have to deal with every day?

>> How does your data visualization help solve Brenda's work problems or her family problems? How does it improve her self-esteem?

>> Through what avenue will you present the visualization to Brenda — for example, over the Internet or in a staff meeting?

>> What does Brenda need to be able to do with your data visualization?

Say that Brenda is the manager of the zoning department in Irvine County. She is 45 years old and a single divorcee with two children who are about to start college. She is deeply interested in local politics and eventually wants to be on the county's board of commissioners. To achieve that position, she has to get some major "oomph" on her county management résumé. Brenda derives most of her feelings of self-worth from her job and her keen ability to make good management decisions for her department.

Until now, Brenda has been forced to manage her department according to her gut-feel intuition, backed by a few disparate business systems reports. She is not extraordinarily analytical, but she knows enough to understand what she sees. The problem is that Brenda hasn't had the visualization tools that are necessary to display all the relevant data she should be considering. Because she has neither the time nor the skill to code something herself, she's been waiting in the lurch. Brenda is excited that you'll be attending next Monday's staff meeting to present the data visualization alternatives available to help her get under way in making data-driven management decisions.

Step 2: Define the purpose

After you brainstorm about the typical audience member (see the preceding section), you can much more easily pinpoint exactly what you're trying to achieve with the data visualization. Are you attempting to get consumers to feel a certain way about themselves or the world around them? Are you trying to make a statement? Are you seeking to influence organizational decision makers to make good business decisions? Or do you simply want to lay all the data out there, for all viewers to make sense of, and deduce from what they will?

Return to the hypothetical Brenda: What decisions or processes are you trying to help her achieve? Well, you need to make sense of her data, and then you need to present it to her in a way that she can clearly understand. What's happening within the inner mechanics of her department? Using your visualization, you seek to guide Brenda into making the most prudent and effective management choices.

Step 3: Choose the most functional visualization type for your purpose

Keep in in mind that you have three main types of visualization from which to choose: data storytelling, data art, and data showcasing. If you're designing for organizational decision makers, you'll most likely use data storytelling to directly tell your audience what their data means with respect to their line of business. If you're designing for a social justice organization or a political campaign, data art can best make a dramatic and effective statement with your data. Lastly, if you're designing for engineers, scientists, or statisticians, stick with data showcasing so that these analytical types have plenty of room to figure things out on their own.

Back to Brenda — because she's not extraordinarily analytical and because she's depending on you to help her make excellent data-driven decisions, you need to employ *data storytelling* techniques. Create either a static or interactive data visualization with some, but not too much, context. The visual elements of the design should tell a clear story so that Brenda doesn't have to work through tons of complexities to get the point of what you're trying to tell her about her data and her line of business.

Picking the Most Appropriate Design Style

Analytical types might say that the only purpose of a data visualization is to convey numbers and facts via charts and graphs — no beauty or design is needed. But more artistic-minded folks may insist that they have to *feel* something in order to truly understand it. Truth be told, a good data visualization is neither artless and dry nor completely abstract in its artistry. Rather, its beauty and design lie somewhere on the spectrum between these two extremes.

To choose the most appropriate design style, you must first consider your audience (discussed earlier in this chapter) and then decide how you want them to respond to your visualization. If you're looking to entice the audience into taking a deeper, more analytical dive into the visualization, employ a design style that induces a calculating and exacting response in its viewers. But if you want your data visualization to fuel your audience's passion, use an emotionally compelling design style instead.

Inducing a calculating, exacting response

If you're designing a data visualization for corporate types, engineers, scientists, or organizational decision makers, keep the design simple and sleek, using the data showcasing or data storytelling visualization. To induce a logical, calculating feel in your audience, include a lot of bar charts, scatter plots, and line charts. Color choices here should be rather traditional and conservative. The look and feel should scream "corporate chic." (See Figure 9-1.) Visualizations of this style are meant to quickly and clearly communicate what's happening in the data — direct, concise, and to the point. The best data visualizations of this style convey an elegant look and feel.

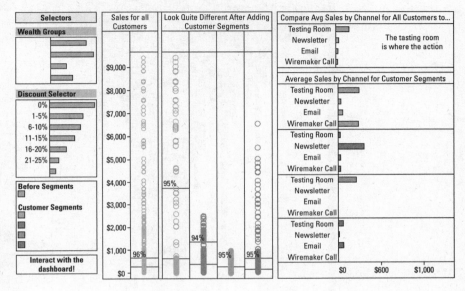

FIGURE 9-1: This design style conveys a calculating and exacting feel.

Eliciting a strong emotional response

If you're designing a data visualization to influence or persuade people, incorporate design artistry that invokes an emotional response in your target audience. These visualizations usually fall under the data art category, but an extremely creative data storytelling piece could also inspire this sort of strong emotional response. Emotionally provocative data visualizations often support the stance of one side of a social, political, or environmental issue. These data visualizations include fluid, artistic design elements that flow and meander, as shown in Figure 9-2. Additionally, rich, dramatic color choices can influence the emotions of the viewer. This style of data visualization leaves a lot of room for artistic creativity and experimentation.

TIP

Keep artistic elements relevant — and recognize when they're likely to detract from the impression you want to make, particularly when you're designing for analytical types.

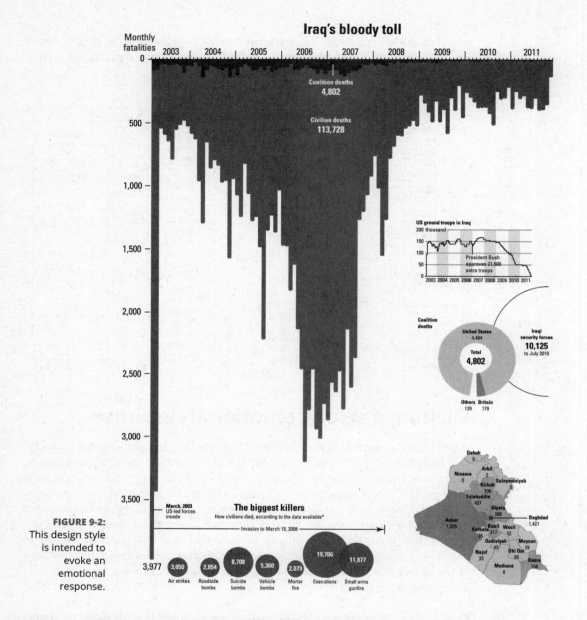

Iraq's bloody toll

FIGURE 9-2: This design style is intended to evoke an emotional response.

Choosing How to Add Context

Adding context helps people understand the value and relative significance of the information your data visualization conveys. Adding context to calculating, exacting data visualization styles helps to create a sense of relative perspective. In pure data art, you should omit context because, with data art, you're only trying to make a single point and you don't want to add information that would distract from that point.

Creating context with data

In data showcasing, you should include relevant contextual data for the key metrics shown in your data visualization — for example, in a situation where you're creating a data visualization that describes conversion rates for e-commerce sales. The key metric would be represented by the percentage of users who convert to customers by making a purchase. Contextual data that's relevant to this metric might include shopping cart abandonment rates, average number of sessions before a user makes a purchase, average number of pages visited before making a purchase, or specific pages that are visited before a customer decides to convert. This sort of contextual information helps viewers understand the "why and how" behind sales conversions.

Adding contextual data tends to decentralize the focus of a data visualization, so add this data only in visualizations that are intended for an analytical audience. These folks are in a better position to assimilate the extra information and use it to draw their own conclusions; with other types of audiences, context is only a distraction.

Creating context with annotations

Sometimes you can more appropriately create context by including annotations that provide a header and a small description of the context of the data that's shown. (See Figure 9-3.) This method of creating context is most appropriate for data storytelling or data showcasing. Good annotation is helpful to both analytical and non-analytical audiences alike.

Creating context with graphical elements

Another effective way to create context in a data visualization is to include graphical elements that convey the relative significance of the data. Such graphical elements include moving average trend lines, single-value alerts, target trend lines (as shown in Figure 9-4), or predictive benchmarks.

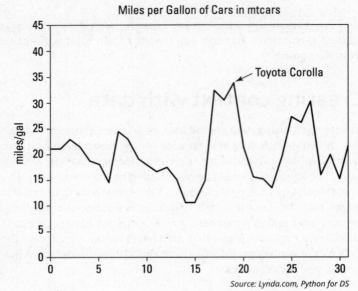

FIGURE 9-3:
Using annotation
to create context.

Source: Lynda.com, Python for DS

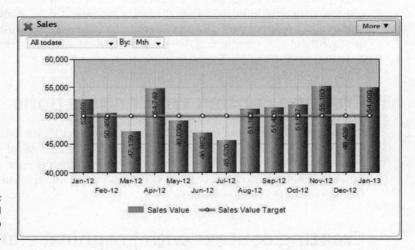

FIGURE 9-4:
Using graphical
elements to
create context.

Selecting the Appropriate Data Graphic Type

Your choice of data graphic type can make or break a data visualization. Because you probably need to represent many different facets of your data, you can mix and match among the different graphical classes and types. Even among the same class, certain graphic types perform better than others; therefore, create test representations to see which graphic type conveys the clearest and most obvious message.

WARNING

This book introduces only the most commonly used graphic types (among hundreds that are available). Don't wander too far off the beaten path. The further you stray from familiar graphics, the harder it becomes for people to understand the information you're trying to convey.

REMEMBER

Pick the graphic type that most dramatically displays the data trends you're seeking to reveal. You can display the same data trend in many ways, but some methods deliver a visual message more effectively than others. The point is to deliver a clear, comprehensive visual message to your audience so that people can use the visualization to help them make sense of the data presented.

Among the most useful types of data graphics are standard chart graphics, comparative graphics, statistical plots, topology structures, and spatial plots and maps. The next few sections take a look at each type in turn.

Standard chart graphics

When making data visualizations for an audience of non-analytical people, stick to standard chart graphics. The more foreign and complex your graphics, the harder it is for non-analytical people to understand them. And not all standard chart types are boring — you have quite a variety to choose from, as the following list makes clear:

» **Area:** Area charts (see Figure 9-5) are a fun yet simple way to visually compare and contrast attribute values. You can use them to effectively tell a visual story when you've chosen data storytelling and data showcasing.

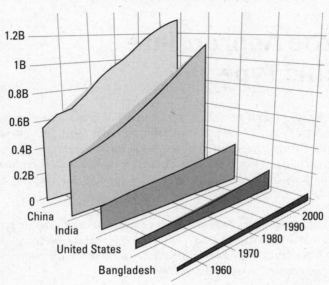

FIGURE 9-5:
An area chart in three dimensions.

Source: Lynda.com, Python for DS

» **Bar:** Bar charts (see Figure 9-6) are a simple way to visually compare and contrast values of parameters in the same category. Bar charts are best for data storytelling and data showcasing.

» **Line:** Line charts (see Figure 9-7) most commonly show changes in time-series data, but they can also plot relationships between two, or even three, parameters. Line charts are so versatile that you can use them in all data visualization design types.

» **Pie:** Pie chart graphics (see Figure 9-8), which are among the most commonly used, provide a simple way to compare values of parameters in the same category. Their simplicity, however, can be a double-edged sword; deeply analytical people tend to scoff at them, precisely because they seem so simple, so you may want to consider omitting them from data-showcasing visualizations.

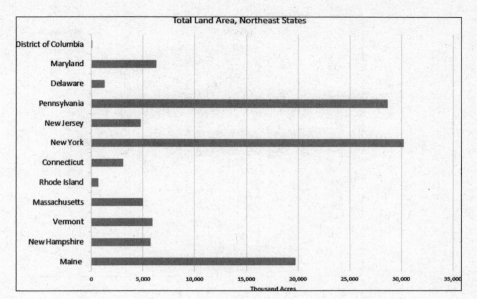

FIGURE 9-6:
A bar chart.

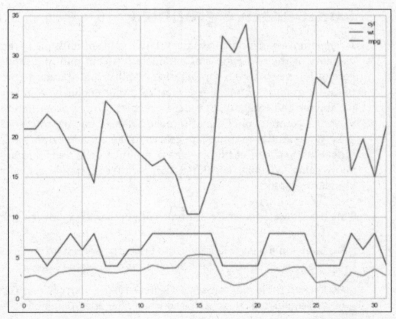

FIGURE 9-7:
A line chart.

Source: Lynda.com, Python for DS

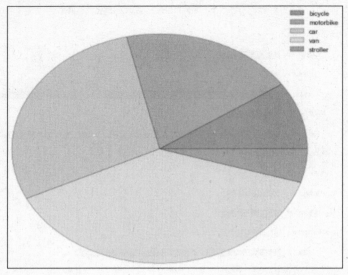

FIGURE 9-8:
A pie chart.

Source: Lynda.com, Python for DS

Comparative graphics

A *comparative graphic* displays the relative value of multiple parameters in a shared category or the relatedness of parameters within multiple shared categories. The core difference between comparative graphics and standard graphics is that comparative graphics offer you a way to simultaneously compare more than one parameter and category. Standard graphics, on the other hand, provide a way to view and compare only the difference between one parameter of any single category. Comparative graphics are geared for an audience that's at least slightly analytical, so you can easily use these graphics in either data storytelling or data showcasing. Visually speaking, comparative graphics are more complex than standard graphics.

This list shows a few different types of popular comparative graphics:

>> **Bubble plots** (see Figure 9-9) use bubble size and color to demonstrate the relationship between three parameters of the same category.

>> **Packed circle diagrams** (see Figure 9-10) use both circle size and clustering to visualize the relationships between categories, parameters, and relative parameter values.

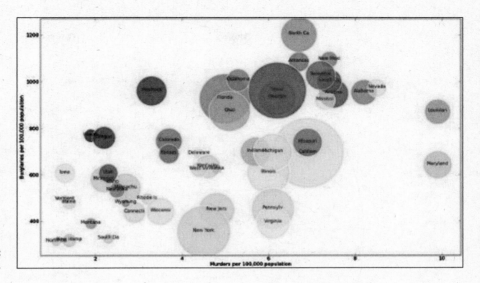

FIGURE 9-9:
A bubble chart.

>> **Gantt charts** (see Figure 9-11) are bar charts that use horizontal bars to visualize scheduling requirements for project management purposes. This type of chart is useful when you're developing a plan for project delivery. It's also helpful in determining the sequence in which tasks must be completed in order to meet delivery timelines.

Choose Gantt charts for project management and scheduling.

>> **Stacked charts** (see Figure 9-12) are used to compare multiple attributes of parameters in the same category. To ensure that it doesn't become difficult to make a visual comparison, resist the urge to include too many parameters.

>> **Tree maps** aggregate parameters of like categories and then use area to show the relative size of each category compared to the whole, as shown in Figure 9-13.

>> **Word clouds** use size and color to show the relative difference in frequency of words used in a body of text, as shown in Figure 9-14. Colors are generally employed to indicate classifications of words by usage type.

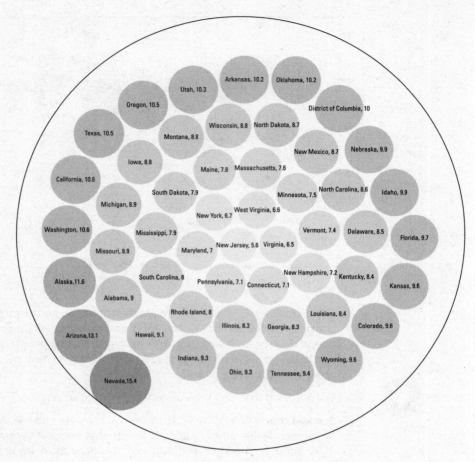

FIGURE 9-10:
A packed circle
diagram.

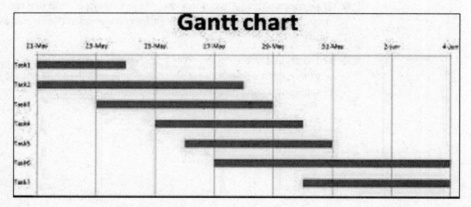

FIGURE 9-11:
A Gantt chart.

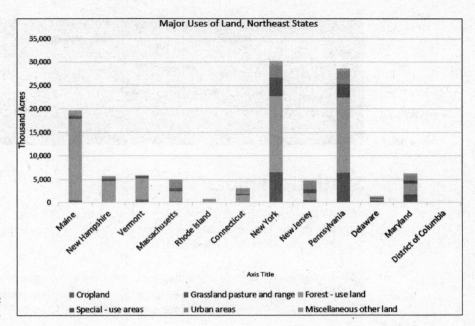

FIGURE 9-12:
A stacked chart.

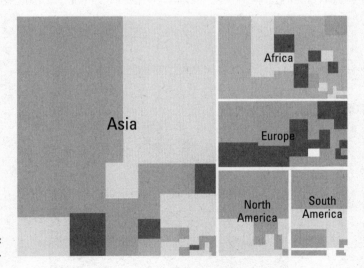

FIGURE 9-13:
A tree map.

FIGURE 9-14:
A simple
word cloud.

Statistical plots

Statistical plots, which show the results of statistical analyses, are usually useful only to a deeply analytical audience (and aren't useful for making data art). Your statistical-plot choices are described in this list:

>> **Histogram:** A diagram that plots a variable's frequency and distribution as rectangles on a chart, a histogram (see Figure 9-15) can help you quickly get a handle on the distribution and frequency of data in a dataset.

TIP

Get comfortable with histograms. You'll see a lot of them in the course of making statistical analyses.

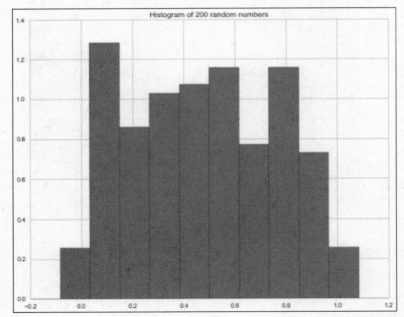

FIGURE 9-15:
A histogram.

Source: Lynda.com, Python for DS

» **Scatter plot:** A terrific way to quickly uncover significant trends and outliers in a dataset, a scatter plot plots data points according to its x- and y- values in order to visually reveal any significant patterns. (See Figure 9-16.) If you use data storytelling or data showcasing, start by generating a quick scatter plot to get a feel for areas in the dataset that may be interesting — areas that could potentially uncover significant relationships or yield persuasive stories.

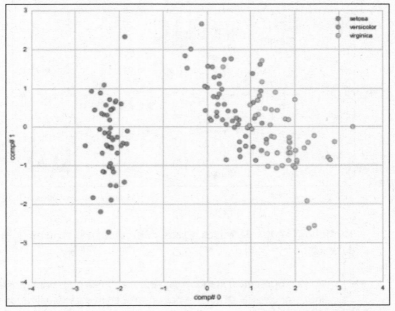

FIGURE 9-16: A scatter plot.

Source: Lynda.com, Python for DS

» **Scatter plot matrix:** A good choice when you want to explore the relationships between several variables, a scatter plot matrix places its scatter plots in a visual series that shows correlations between multiple variables, as shown in Figure 9-17. Discovering and verifying relationships between variables can help you to identify clusters among variables and identify oddball outliers in your dataset.

Topology structures

Topology is the practice of using geometric structures to describe and model the relationships and connectedness between entities and variables in a dataset. You need to understand basic topology structures so that you can accurately structure your visual display to match the fundamental underlying structure of the concepts you're representing.

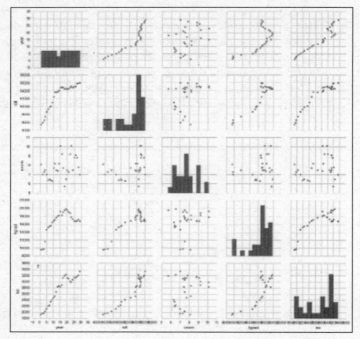

FIGURE 9-17:
A scatter plot
matrix.

Source: Lynda.com, Python for DS

The following list describes a series of topological structures that are popular in data science:

>> **Linear topological structures:** Representing a pure one-to-one relationship, linear topological structures are often used in data visualizations that depict time-series flow patterns. Any process that can occur only by way of a sequential series of dependent events is linear (see Figure 9-18), and you can effectively represent it by using this underlying topological structure.

FIGURE 9-18:
A linear topology.

>> **Graph models:** These kinds of models underlie group communication networks and traffic flow patterns. You can use graph topology to represent many-to-many relationships (see Figure 9-19), like those that form the basis of social media platforms.

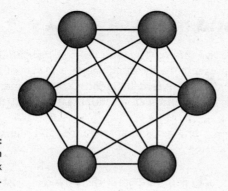

FIGURE 9-19:
A graph mesh
network
topology.

REMEMBER

In a *many-to-many* relationship structure, each variable or entity has more than one link to the other variables or entities in that same dataset.

» **Tree network topology:** This topology represents a *hierarchical* classification, where a network is distributed in a top-down order — nodes act as receivers and distributors of connections, and lines represent the connections between nodes. End nodes act only as receivers and not as distributors. (See Figure 9-20.) Hierarchical classification underlies clustering and machine learning methodologies in data science. Tree network structures can represent one-to-many relationships, such as the ones that underlie a family tree or a taxonomy structure.

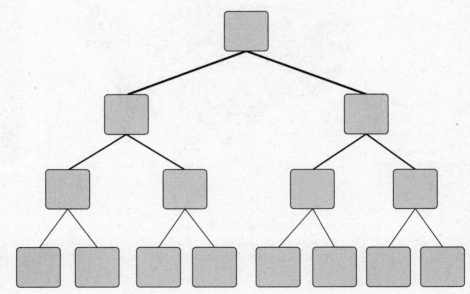

FIGURE 9-20:
A hierarchical
tree topology.

Spatial plots and maps

Spatial plots and maps are two different ways of visualizing spatial data. A *map* is just a plain figure that represents the location, shape, and size of features on the face of the earth. A *spatial plot,* which is visually more complex than a map, shows the values for, and location distribution of, a spatial feature's attributes.

The following list describes a few types of spatial plots and maps that are commonly used in data visualization:

>> **Cloropleth:** Despite its fancy name, a Cloropleth map is really just spatial data plotted out according to area boundary polygons rather than by point, line, or raster coverage. To better understand what I mean, look at Figure 9-21. In this map, each state boundary represents an *area boundary* polygon. The color and shade of the area within each boundary represents the relative value of the attribute for that state — where red areas have a higher attribute value and blue areas have a smaller attribute value.

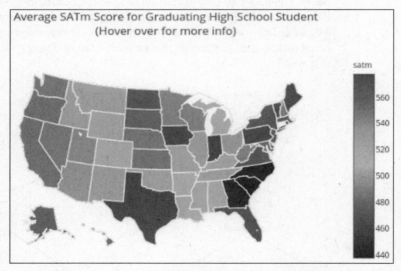

FIGURE 9-21:
A Cloropleth map.

Source: Lynda.com, Python for DS

>> **Point:** Composed of spatial data that is plotted out according to specific point locations, a point map presents data in a graphical point form (see Figure 9-22) rather than in a polygon, line, or raster surface format.

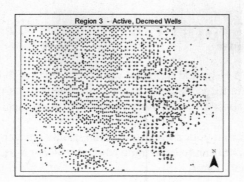

FIGURE 9-22:
A point map.

>> **Raster surface:** This spatial map can be anything from a satellite image map to a surface coverage with values that have been interpolated from underlying spatial data points. (See Figure 9-23.)

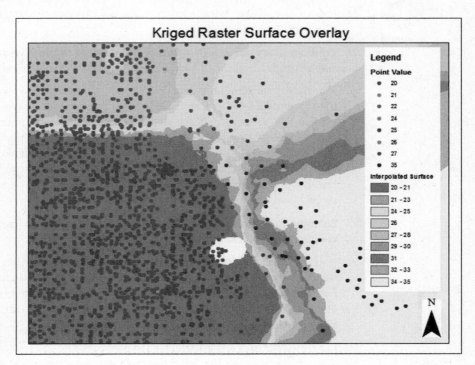

FIGURE 9-23:
A raster
surface map.

REMEMBER

Whether you're a data visualization designer or a consumer, be aware of some common pitfalls in data visualization. Simply put, a data visualization can be misleading if it isn't constructed correctly. Common problems include pie charts that don't add up to 100 percent, bar charts with a scale that starts in a strange place, and multicolumn bar charts with vertical axes that don't match.

Choosing a Data Graphic

When you want to craft clear and powerful visual messages with the appropriate data graphic, follow the three steps in this section to experiment and determine whether the one you choose can effectively communicate the meaning of the data:

1. **Ask the questions that your data visualization should answer, and then examine the visualization to determine whether the answers to those questions jump out at you.**

   Before thinking about what graphics to use, first consider the questions you want to answer for your audience. In a marketing setting, the audience may want to know why their overall conversion rates are low. Or, if you're designing for business managers, they may want to know why service times are slower in certain customer service areas than in others.

   REMEMBER

   Though many data graphic types can fulfill the same purpose, whatever you choose, ensure that your choices clearly answer the exact and intended questions.

2. **Consider users and media in determining where the data visualization will be used.**

   Ask who will consume your data visualization, and using which medium, and then determine whether your choice of data graphics makes sense in that context. Will an audience of scientists consume it, or will you use it for content marketing to generate Internet traffic? Do you want to use it to prove a point in a boardroom? Or do you want to support a story in an upcoming newspaper publication? Pick data graphic types that are appropriate for the intended consumers and for the medium through which they'll consume the visualization.

3. **Examine the data visualization a final time to ensure that its message is clearly conveyed using only the data graphic.**

   If viewers have to stretch their minds to make a visual comparison of data trends, you probably need to use a different graphic type. If they have to read numbers or annotations to get the gist of what's happening, that's not good enough. Try out some other graphic forms to see whether you can convey the visual message more effectively.

   Just close your eyes and ask yourself the questions that you seek to answer through your data visualization. Then open your eyes and look at your visualization again. Do the answers jump out at you? If not, try another graphic type.

Chapter **10**

Using D3.js for Data Visualization

The truth of the matter is, you can come up with the perfect data visualization you need to meet the exact needs of your target audience gathered in that meeting room down the hall, but what works in the physical meeting room may not work in that virtual meeting room out on the World Wide Web. In this chapter, I show you how you can use D3.js technology to build custom web-based visualizations — the type of visualizations you need if you're showcasing your work online. The power of programming in D3.js is that it enables you to create absolutely stunning, dynamic data visualizations with which your audience can interact and explore, straight from their browsers, with no add-ons required.

TIP

D3.js is not the only option available for constructing dynamic, web-based data visualizations — it's just an excellent one. Other options include jQuery Javascript library (http://jquery.com), JpGraph PHP library (http://jpgraph.net), High-Charts (www.highcharts.com), and iCharts (http://icharts.net).

Introducing the D3.js Library

D3.js is an open-source JavaScript library that's taken the data visualization world by storm since its first release in 2011. It was created (and is maintained) by Mike Bostock — famous data visualization guru and graphics editor of the

New York Times. You can use this library to create high-quality, Data-Driven Documents (D3) in a fraction of the usual time and with a fraction of the effort required to code in plain (a.k.a. vanilla) JavaScript.

In its essence, *D3.js* is a collection of classes and functions that, when you apply just a little coding, you can use to execute much longer strings of lower-level JavaScript. D3.js calls on only a special class of commands in the JavaScript library — the ones that are typically used in data visualization. You use these commands to do things like draw axes, plot elements, and recalculate positions when resizing graphs.

If your goal is to create *dynamic* web-based data visualizations — visualizations that change in response to user interactions — D3.js is the perfect JavaScript library to use.

REMEMBER

If you want users to be able to interact with your data visualization and choose what data to display, you need to create a dynamic visualization.

With dynamic data visualizations, your users can

» Interact with the visualization to choose what data to display

» See additional data when they hover the mouse cursor over the visualization or click parts of it

» Drill down into deeper levels of related data to see more detailed views on interesting parts of the data

» Explore animated visualizations that show changes over time

» Choose from a variety of different transitions between views

The D3.js library is still being developed. With Mike Bostock and countless other users contributing new types of visualizations, the library's capabilities are expanding daily. The D3.js design philosophy is rather open-ended. It doesn't limit you to using predefined, cookie-cutter data visualizations. Rather, this library can accommodate the individual creativity and imagination of each unique user.

Knowing When to Use D3.js (and When Not To)

The main purpose of D3.js in the data visualization world is to make creative, interactive, web-based visualizations using only a small bit of code. Because D3.js is so powerful and open-ended, it's also more complex than some other JavaScript libraries, web applications, and software packages. D3.js has the same basic syntax as JavaScript, so you need a basic working knowledge of JavaScript in order to code in D3.js. Beyond using a bit of JavaScript, you need to know a whole vocabulary and programming style before getting started. This chapter covers the basics of getting started in D3.js, but if you want more extensive training, work through the tutorials that Mike Bostock has developed, and hosts, at his GitHub repository: https://github.com/mbostock/d3/wiki/Tutorials.

With the help of a few D3.js learning resources, you might be able to learn both JavaScript and D3.js at the same time. But many online tutorials presuppose a level of programming experience that you might not have.

TIP

Because you have to face a significant learning curve in mastering even the basic concepts of D3.js, use this library only if you want to create unique, interactive, scalable web-based visualizations. Otherwise, just stick with static data visualizations. In this case, the simpler, less open-ended frameworks available for creating static data visualizations are easier and can provide everything you might need.

If you choose to go with D3.js, however, you can find thousands of online open-source examples from which to learn and create. In addition to Mike Bostock's tutorials, another good place to start is with the Dashing D3.js Tutorials at www.dashingd3js.com/table-of-contents.

These tutorials will get you started in learning how to build visualizations with data. From there, you can get into more advanced topics, such as building drillable sunburst diagrams and adjustable, force-directed network graphs. You can even use D3.js to make a heat map calendar, to visualize time-series trends in your data. The options and alternatives expand almost daily.

Getting Started in D3.js

I want to introduce you to the underlying concepts you need to master in order to create dynamic, web-based data visualizations using D3.js. In the following sections, I cover the basics of JavaScript, HTML, CSS, and PHP as they pertain to creating visualizations using D3.js. Also, I tell you how you can maximize the portion of client-side work that's done by the JavaScript language. (*Client-side* work is the portion that's done on your computer, rather than on the network server.) If you're not content with stopping there, you can find out about JavaScript's Document Object Model (DOM) and how it interacts with HyperText Markup Language (HTML) to produce dynamic changes in a web page's HTML.

In the section "Bringing in the JavaScript and SVG," later in this chapter, I talk about how you can use D3.js to efficiently display and change *Scalable Vector Graphics (SVG)* — an XML-based image format that's useful for serving images to interactive visualization designs and animation applications — in your data visualization. You can find out how to make sweeping style changes across a web page by using Cascading Style Sheets (CSS), in the section "Bringing in the Cascading Style Sheets (CSS)," later in this chapter. And lastly, this chapter's section "Bringing in the web servers and PHP" explains how to minimize the amount of client-side work that's required by deploying PHP programs across a web server.

Bringing in the HTML and DOM

HyperText Markup Language (HTML) is the backbone of a web page. It delivers the static content you see on many websites, especially older ones. HTML is recognizable by its plain text and limited interactivity. The only interactive features you get with plain-HTML websites are perhaps some hyperlinks that lead you to other boring static pages throughout the site.

You can use HTML to display plain text with a series of tags that give instructions to the client's browser. The following HTML code is pretty basic, but at least it gives you an idea of what's involved:

```
<html>
    <head>
        <title>This is a simple HTML page</title>
    </head>
    <body>
    <p>This is a paragraph.</p>
    </body>
</html>
```

TIP

Just in case you're not aware, HTML relies on start tags and end tags. The preceding sample has a couple nice examples, like <p> </p> and <body> </body>.

JavaScript uses the HTML Document Object Model (DOM). Through the HTML DOM, JavaScript can interact with HTML tags and their content. DOM treats tags as hierarchical layers, just like objects in an object-oriented programming language (like JavaScript). For example, the <body> tag in the preceding HTML is a child of the top-level <html> tag; it has one sibling, <head>, and one child, <p>. In the DOM, that <p> tag is fully defined by its path while you traverse from the top of the model (html > body > p, for example). DOM allows you to control object selections based on object attribute properties.

In D3.js, the purpose of HTML is to provide a bare scaffold of static tags and web page content that can be interacted with via JavaScript's DOM to produce dynamic, changeable HTML pages. D3.js is built on top of a bare backbone of HTML. Although HTML is static, it becomes dynamic in D3.js if a programmer or user interaction causes predetermined scripts to make on-the-fly changes to the underlying HTML code. The HTML that is displayed is then often dynamic and different from that which was originally sent to the browser.

Bringing in the JavaScript and SVG

Using the JavaScript language gives you a simple way to get work done *client-side* (on the user's machine). The slowest part of any interaction between a user and a website is in sending data from the server to the client's computer over the Internet. That interaction can be vastly accelerated if, instead of sending all the information needed for a browser display, you send a much shorter, simpler chain of instructions that the client's web browser can use to re-create that information and then create the web page using the client computer's own processing speed. This is how client-side work is carried out.

TECHNICAL STUFF

If your goal is to retain a decent level of security, without needing plug-ins or special permissions to run code on your browser, JavaScript offers you a terrific solution. What's more, JavaScript is *fast!* Because it's a programming language intended for browsers, JavaScript is unencumbered by the advanced features that make other languages more versatile but less speedy.

A note about Microsoft Internet Explorer: Different versions of Internet Explorer are compatible with different versions of JavaScript. It's a complex problem that can sometimes cause even experienced JavaScript programmers to pull their hair out. As a rule of thumb, JavaScript doesn't run on IE versions that are older than IE8.

In JavaScript, graphics rendering is based on Scalable Vector Graphics (SVG) — a vector image format that delivers images to interactive visualizations and web-based animations. In D3.js, SVG functions as a file format that stores vector graphics for use in 2-dimensional, interactive, web-based data visualizations. Vector graphics require a lot less bandwidth than images because vector graphics contain only instructions for how to draw them, as opposed to the final pixel-by-pixel raster renderings of images. If your goal is to rapidly deploy web-based graphics that also provide you lossless scaling capabilities, then SVG is a perfect solution. SVG is optimal for use in creating graphical elements such as bars, lines, and markers.

REMEMBER

You can use D3.js to select, add, modify, or remove SVG elements on a page, in just the same way you do with HTML elements. Since D3.js is most useful for working with web-based graphical elements, most of your D3.js scripting will interact with SVG elements.

Bringing in the Cascading Style Sheets (CSS)

The purpose of using Cascading Style Sheets (CSS) is to define the look of repeated visual elements, such as fonts, line widths, and colors. You can use CSS to specify the visual characteristics of page elements all at one time and then efficiently apply these characteristics to an entire HTML document (or to only the parts of the document defined in the DOM, if you wish). If you want to make sweeping, all-at-once changes to the look and feel of your web page elements, use CSS.

TECHNICAL STUFF

If you're building visualizations on several pages of a website, you can create a separate document .css file, and then call that document instead of putting CSS in each page. If you do this, then when you make a change to this .css document, it will be applied to the pages collectively.

As an example, the basic CSS for a simple web page might include the following:

```
<style type="text/css">
    p {
    font-family: arial, verdana, sans-serif;
font-size: 12 pt;
color: black;
    }
.highlighted {
    color: red;
}
</style>
```

The preceding example would render the text in this HTML example:

```
<p>This text is black and <span class="highlighted">this text is
        red.</span></p>
```

The preceding CSS and HTML code generates text in the `<p>` tag that has a default value of black, whereas the inner object is designated as a `highlighted` class and generates a red-colored text.

D3.js leverages CSS for drawing and styling text elements and drawn elements so that you can define and change the overall look of your visualization in one compact, easy-to-read block of code.

Bringing in the web servers and PHP

Though one of the main purposes behind using JavaScript and D3.js is to maximize the portion of work that's carried out on the client's machine, some work is just better carried out on the web server. (In case you aren't familiar with the term, a *web server* can be thought of as a server-based computer that sends information over the Internet to users when they visit a website.)

In web programming, the words *client* and *user* can be used interchangeably. Both words refer to either the end user or the end user's computer.

As an example of how web servers work, think of a sales site that has millions of products available for purchase. When you go to search for a type of product, of course the website doesn't send the company's entire product catalog to your computer and expect your PC to do the work of paring down the product information. Instead, the site's web server processes the search parameters you've defined and then sends only the information that's relevant to answer your particular search questions.

REMEMBER

In web programming, you commonly have a SQL database set up as a main information source and also a PHP program that defines the HTML code to be sent to the client's computer. You use PHP programs to query the SQL database and determine what information to send over to the client. PHP is a scripting language that's run on a server and produces on-the-fly HTML code in response to user interactions.

In pre-D3.js days, you'd have had to use a lot more time and bandwidth constructing web-based, interactive data visualizations. Due to the effectiveness of the PHP/D3.js combination, things are simpler now. In response to a request from the user, PHP selects information from the server and sends it to the client's computer, in the form of HTML with embedded CSS, JavaScript, and D3.js code. At this point, the D3.js can take over and expand the HTML. If necessary, D3.js can even make on-the-fly HTML expansions in response to additional user interactions. This process uses only a fraction of the bandwidth and time that would have been required in a PHP-only or JavaScript-only setup.

Implementing More Advanced Concepts and Practices in D3.js

In this section, you can see the ways that more advanced D3.js features can help you become more efficient in using the library to create dynamic data visualizations. In the following section, I explain how to use so-called *chain syntax* — syntax that chains together functions and methods into a single line of code — to minimize your coding requirements. You can also find out how to use the scale and axis functions to automatically define or change the proportions and elements for graphic outputs in the section "Getting to know scales," later in this chapter. In the section "Getting to know transitions and interactions," later in this chapter, you see how to use transitions and interactions to maximize audience exploration, analysis, and learning from your end-product data visualization.

For the rest of this chapter, refer to Listing 10-1 (a complete HTML file that contains CSS, JavaScript, and D3.js elements) when working through the examples. Don't get too stressed out by the listing itself. I know it's lengthy, but simply look through it, and then focus on the snippets I pull from it for later discussion.

And for future reference, the code shown in Listing 10-1 produces the interactive bar chart that's shown in Figure 10-1.

LISTING 10-1: **An HTML File with CSS, JavaScript, and D3.js Elements**

```
<!DOCTYPE html>
<html>
<head>
  <meta http-equiv="content-type" content="text/html;
        charset=UTF-8">
  <title>D3.js example</title>
      <script type='text/javascript'
            src="http://d3js.org/d3.v3.min.js"></script>
  <style type='text/css'>
    rect:hover {
    fill: brown;
}
  </style>

<script type='text/javascript'>//<![CDATA[
window.onload=function(){
var column_data = [{
    position: 0,
    quantity: 5
}, {
    position: 1,
    quantity: 20
}, {
    position: 2,
    quantity: 15
}, {
    position: 3,
    quantity: 25
}, {
    position: 4,
    quantity: 10
}];
```

```
var total_width = 400;
var total_height = 200;

var scale_y = d3.scale.linear()
    .domain([0, d3.max(column_data, function (d) {
    return d.quantity;
})])
    .range([0, total_height]);

var scale_x = d3.scale.ordinal()
    .domain(d3.range(column_data.length))
    .rangeRoundBands([0, total_width], 0.05);

var position = function (d) {
    return d.position;
};

var svg_container = d3.select("body")
    .append("svg")
    .attr("width", total_width)
    .attr("height", total_height);

svg_container.selectAll("rect")
    .data(column_data, position)
    .enter()
    .append("rect")
    .attr("x", function (d, i) {
    return scale_x(i);
})
    .attr("y", function (d) {
    return total_height - scale_y(d.quantity);
})
    .attr("width", scale_x.rangeBand())
    .attr("height", function (d) {
    return scale_y(d.quantity);
})
    .attr("fill", "teal");

var sort = function () {
    bars_to_sort = function (a, b) {
        return b.quantity - a.quantity;
    };
```

(continued)

LISTING 10-1: *(continued)*

```
        svg_container.selectAll("rect")
            .sort(bars_to_sort)
            .transition()
            .delay(0)
            .duration(300)
            .attr("x", function (d, n) {
            return scale_x(n);
        });
    };

    d3.select("#sort").on("click", sort);
    d3.select("#unsort").on("click", unsort);

    function unsort() {
        svg_container.selectAll("rect")
            .sort(function (a, b) {
            return a.position - b.position;
        })
            .transition()
            .delay(0)
            .duration(1200)
            .attr("x", function (d, i) {
            return scale_x(i);
        });

    };
}//]]>

</script>

</head>

<body>
    <button id="sort" onclick="sortBars()">Sort</button>
    <button id="unsort" onclick="unsort()">Unsort</button>
    <p>
</body>

</html>
```

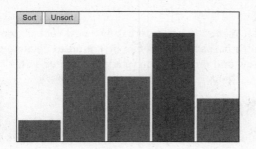

FIGURE 10-1:
An interactive,
web-based
bar chart made
in D3.js.

Getting to know chain syntax

As I mention in the section "Bringing in the HTML and DOM," earlier in this chapter, you can use D3.js to turn a bare scaffold of HTML into a complex visualization by modifying page elements. The D3.js library uses an efficient operator syntax called *chain syntax.* The purpose of chain syntax is to chain together several methods, thereby allowing you to perform multiple actions using only a single line of code. Instead of name–value pair syntax (like what you would see in CSS), D3.js chains together multiple expressions, each one creating a new object and selection for the next.

The fundamental concept behind D3.js is the Append, Enter, and Exit selections. These methods select, add, or remove HTML tags that are *bound,* or assigned, to your data. The Append selection refers to existing data elements that are paired with existing HTML tags. When there are more data elements than tags, the Enter selection adds tags paired with the surplus data elements. When there are more tags than data elements, you can use the Exit selection to remove those tags.

Taking another look at a section of Listing 10-1, notice the code block that draws the bars of the graph:

```
svg_container.selectAll("rect")
    .data(column_data, position)
    .enter()
    .append("rect")
    .attr("x", function (d, i) {
    return scale_x(i);
```

This D3.js script defines an object `svg_container`. The first element, `selectAll("rect")`, defines the container to be all the "rect" elements in the document. To this container, the script then goes through the data in `column_data` and `position`, and binds each data item to one of the `rects` in the container. To handle data items that don't (yet) have a `rect` in the container, the `enter` expression creates new placeholder elements that can be turned into real document elements by further expressions. And, in fact, this is just what the next expression — append("rect") — does, creating a new rect element for each new data item. The key idea is that datasets can be bound to document elements and used to create, destroy, and modify them in a variety of very flexible ways.

Getting to know scales

In D3.js, the scale function plots input domains to output ranges so that the output data visualization graphics are drawn at appropriate, to-scale proportions. Looking at the following section of Listing 10-1, notice how scale variables are defined using D3.js:

```
var scale_y = d3.scale.linear()
    .domain([0, d3.max(column_data, function (d) {
    return d.quantity;
})])
    .range([0, total_height]);

var scale_x = d3.scale.ordinal()
    .domain(d3.range(column_data.length))
    .rangeRoundBands([0, total_width], 0.05);
```

One of the main features of D3.js is its ability to do difficult and tedious calculations under the hood. A key part of this work is done in scaling plots. If you want to automatically map the range of your data to actual pixel dimensions in your graph, you can use the scale function to change either or both parameters without having to do any manual recalculations.

From this snippet, you can see that the total height of the graph has been specified as a .range. This means you no longer need to calculate margins or positions or how the values map to fixed positions.

The following section from Listing 10-1 shows that the greatest quantity value in the total height range is 25:

```
var column_data = [{
    position: 0,
    quantity: 5
}, {
    position: 1,
    quantity: 20
}, {
```

```
    position: 2,
    quantity: 15
}, {
    position: 3,
    quantity: 25
}, {
    position: 4,
    quantity: 10
}];

var total_width = 400;
var total_height = 200;
```

By automatically mapping the range of your data (0[nd]25) to the actual pixel height of your graph, you can change either or both parameters without having to do any manual recalculations.

Although you can use D3.js to automatically handle the placement of axis labels and tick marks, the library can also handle all calculations involved in date ranges. This functionality leaves you free to concentrate on the overall look and feel of the visualization, instead of having to tinker with its mechanics.

Getting to know transitions and interactions

The true beauty of D3.js lies in how you can use it to easily incorporate dynamic elements into your web-based data visualization. If you want to encourage users to explore and analyze the data in your dynamic visualization, create features that offer a lot of user interactivity. Also, incorporating transitions into your dynamic visualization can help you capture the interest of your audience. Transitions in D3.js build the aesthetic appeal of a data visualization by incorporating elements of motion into the design.

As a prime example of D3.js interactivity, take a look at the following code from Listing 10-1:

```
<style type='text/css'>
    rect:hover {
    fill: brown;
}
    </style>
```

Here, a single piece of CSS code changes the color of the bars whenever the user hovers the cursor over them.

And, looking at another snippet taken from Listing 10-1 (shown next), you can see code that defines a sort function and then creates buttons to transition the bars between sorted and unsorted states (if you tried for the same effect using vanilla JavaScript, it would be more tedious and time-consuming):

```
var sort = function () {
    bars_to_sort = function (a, b) {
        return b.quantity - a.quantity;
    };
    svg_container.selectAll("rect")
        .sort(bars_to_sort)
        .transition()
        .delay(0)
        .duration(300)
        .attr("x", function (d, n) {
        return scale_x(n);
    });
};

d3.select("#sort").on("click", sort);
d3.select("#unsort").on("click", unsort);

function unsort() {
    svg_container.selectAll("rect")
        .sort(function (a, b) {
        return a.position - b.position;
    })
        .transition()
        .delay(0)
        .duration(1200)
        .attr("x", function (d, i) {
        return scale_x(i);
    });

};
}//]]>
```

```
</script>
</head>
<body>
    <button id="sort" onclick="sortBars()">Sort</button>
    <button id="unsort" onclick="unsort()">Unsort</button>
    <p>
</body>
</html>
```

The D3.js wiki has a gallery of visualizations that give you an idea of this library's enormous potential (https://github.com/d3/d3/wiki/Gallery). Across the web, people are finding new ways to use the library or adding to it for improved usability in specialized applications. As a modern interactive data visualization designer, you can use skills in D3.js to create almost anything you can imagine.

Chapter **11**

Web-Based Applications for Visualization Design

In recent years, the World Wide Web has seen an impressive rise in the number of easy-to-use online tools available for data visualization and infographic design. So you no longer need to purchase, download, install, and maintain proprietary software packages to help you do this type of work. Instead, you can choose from a seemingly limitless number of open-source, web-based solutions that are available to help you achieve practically any visualization goal you're after. In this chapter, I bring you up to speed on the best options available to help you reach your specific goals.

Don't worry if you're not overly technical. With many of these web-based applications, you simply need to upload your data (often using a simple copy-and-paste operation), format it, and then quickly experiment with different chart-type offerings. Usually, the hardest part of this work involves finding answers to the following (quite agreeable) questions:

>> Does my data look better in a bar chart or a line plot?

>> Does my data look better in a map or a bubble chart?

>> Should I go with something a bit more creative, like a text cloud or a heat map?

Get ready to be introduced to some of the web's most popular and effective visualization tools. For each service, I give you a description of the platform, some examples of chart types offered by the application, and some links you can use to find and explore visualizations for yourself.

For sample data, I've used a dataset from the U.S. Census Bureau's American Communities Survey (www.census.gov/programs-surveys/acs) that shows the number of people per state who, during the year 2011, changed addresses but remained within the same county. (Intriguingly, these nearby moves are three times more common in Nevada than in New Jersey.)

Designing Data Visualizations for Collaboration

Collaborative data visualization platforms are web-based platforms through which you can design data visualizations and then share those visualizations with other platform users to get their feedback on design or on the data insights conveyed.

Collaborative data visualization platforms have been described as the YouTube of data visualization, but actually, these platforms are far more interactive than YouTube. Collaborative data visualization platforms are like a version of YouTube that lets you instantly copy and edit every video using your own software tools and then republish the video through your own social channels.

Collaborative platforms are quite efficient and effective for working in teams. Instead of having to email versions back and forth, or (heaven forbid) learn a dedicated version-control system like GitHub, you and your teammates can use the platform's sharing features to work on visualizations as a team.

Even if you don't need or want to work with collaborators, collaborative platforms still have much to offer in the way of useful data analysis and visualization tools. These tools are often as powerful as (and sometimes even more powerful than) comparable desktop packages — just keep in mind that they often require users to publicly share their data and results so that others can view, modify, or use those results for their specific needs.

TIP

Many sites offer *freemium* plans that allow you to keep your work private if you purchase a paid account.

Visualizing and collaborating with Plotly

The Plotly collaborative platform aims to accommodate the data collaboration needs of professionals and nonprofessionals alike. This powerful tool doesn't stop at data visualization; it goes one step further by providing you with the tools you need to make sense of your data through advanced statistical analysis. Plotly even offers seamless integration with dedicated programming environments like Python, MATLAB, and R.

If you want a quick and easy way to create interesting and attractive data visualizations, Plotly offers a great solution. Although Plotly focuses on traditional data chart types, you can much more easily portray variables by size or color in Plotly than in most other web applications. If you work in one of the STEM fields, Plotly may be particularly well-suited for your needs. In addition to standard bubble plots, line charts, bar charts, and area graphs, Plotly offers histograms, 2-dimensional histograms, heat maps, scatter charts, boxplots, 3-dimensional scatter charts, 3-dimensional surface charts, and polar plots.

As far as collaborative functionality goes, Plotly provides you with features for social media sharing, user commenting, visualization modification and sharing, data sharing, and embed code usage so that you can embed and display your visualization directly on your website if you want.

TECHNICAL STUFF

For all you techies out there, a cool collaborative feature of Plotly is its code-sharing feature. Each visualization hosted on Plotly offers you an option to see and copy the data visualization's source code.

To use Plotly, you need to sign up for an account first. To do that, start by clicking the Sign-Up button in the upper-right corner of Plotly's home page (at `https:// plot.ly`). Luckily, the Plotly platform has a large user base and is in active development, with new features being added all the time. If you get stuck, you can find a lot of answers, either in its extensive online documentation (at `http://help. plot.ly`) or at the Plotly corner of the popular technical Q&A website Stack Overflow (`http://stackoverflow.com/questions/tagged/plotly`).

Figures 11-1 and 11-2 show two visualizations created with Plotly — a set of interactive boxplots that show the distribution of some variables from the `mtcars` dataset (a dataset that you can get from the GitHub repository for this book, `https://github.com/BigDataGal/Data-Science-for-Dummies`), and a 3D scatter plot that shows the ground-truth classification of observations in the iris dataset (also available from this book's GitHub repository). (*Note:* You can also get these datasets, and tons of other ones, for free in the R datasets package, located on CRAN at `https://stat.ethz.ch/R-manual/R-devel/library/datasets/html/00Index.html`.) Lastly, to see all sorts of new visualizations as they're published, check out Plotly's Graphing News Feed (at `https://plot.ly/feed`).

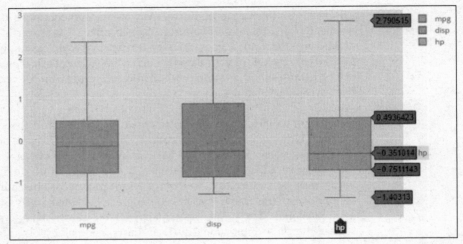

FIGURE 11-1:
Interactive boxplots in Plotly.

Source: Lynda.com, Python for DS

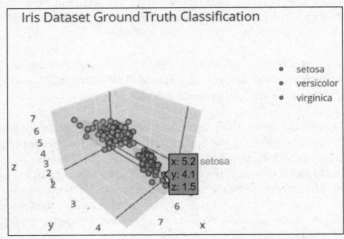

FIGURE 11-2:
Three-dimensional scatterplot in Plotly.

Source: Lynda.com, Python for DS

Talking about Tableau Public

Tableau Public (www.tableausoftware.com/public) is a free desktop application that aims to be a complete package for chart-making. If its name sounds familiar, it may be because Tableau Public is the free version of the popular Tableau Desktop program. As part of the freeware limitation, the application doesn't let you save files locally to your computer. All of your work must be uploaded to Tableau Public's cloud server, unless you purchase the software.

Tableau Public creates three levels of document: the worksheet, the dashboard, and the story. In the worksheet, you can create individual charts from data you've imported from Access, Excel, or a text-format .csv file. You can then use Tableau to easily do things such as choose between different data graphic types or drag columns to different axes or subgroups.

WARNING

You have to deal with a bit of a learning curve when working with the flow of the application and its nomenclature — for example, *dimensions* are categorical data and *measures* are numeric data.

Tableau offers many different default chart types: bar charts, scatter plots, line charts, bubble charts, Gantt charts, and even geographical maps. Tableau Public can even look at the type of data you have and suggest types of charts that you can use to best represent it. For example, imagine that you have two dimensions and one measure. In this situation, a bar chart is a popular choice because you have two categories of data and only one numeric measure for those two categories. But if you have two dimensions and two measures, a scatter plot might be a good option because the scatter plot data graphic allows you to visualize two sets of numerical data for two categories of data.

You can use a Tableau dashboard to combine charts with text annotations or with other data charts. You can also use the dashboard to add interactive filters, such as check boxes or sliders, so that users can interact with your data to visualize only certain time series or categories. With a Tableau story, you can combine several dashboards into a sort of slide show presentation that shows a linear story revealed through your data.

And at last, you can use Tableau Public's online gallery to collaborate and share all the worksheets, dashboards, and stories that you generate within the application. You can also embed them into websites that link back to the Tableau Public cloud server.

Visualizing Spatial Data with Online Geographic Tools

With the advent of online Geographic Information Systems (GIS, for short) like Google Maps, Open Street Map, and Bing Maps, geographic data visualization is no longer solely reserved for cartographers and GIS gurus. Web-based mapping applications have now made it possible for data enthusiasts from a wide range of backgrounds to quickly and easily analyze and map spatial data.

The purpose behind all web-based geographic applications is to visually present *geographic data* — quantitative and qualitative data that's associated with particular locations. This area of data science intersects heavily with cartography and spatial statistics. You can learn more about GIS in Chapter 13.

Newbies often get confused about one important aspect of geographic data visualization: Geographic data is always presented as a point, a line, or a polygon area on a map.

If you need to define an area within particular boundaries, as would be the case with a county boundary, country border, sales district, or political focus area, use a polygon. Because polygons include boundary lines as well as the entire area that lies within those boundary lines, they're the best way of representing areas on a map.

In web-based geographic data visualization, you're likely to represent areas using either a categorical fill or a choropleth map. A *categorical fill* is a way to visually represent qualitative attributes of your spatial dataset. For example, when you're looking at a map that shows an election outcome, states with a majority of Democrat votes are colored blue, and states with a majority of Republican votes are colored red. The categorical attribute is "Political Party," and the fill color is determined by whether the value of that categorical attribute is "Republican" or "Democrat." On the other hand, a *choropleth* is a map representation where spatial areas are filled with a particular hue or intensity of color to represent the comparative distribution of your data quantities across space.

If you want to represent your data as single markers plotted by latitude and longitude, you plot point data. The red, inverted droplet of Google Maps is a prime example of point data on a web-based mapping application. You can represent spatial data with line features as well. A line feature consists of a start node, an end node, and a connective line between them. Lines are commonly used to represent streets, highways, and rivers.

Lastly, you can also create heat maps from point data. To illustrate this concept, imagine that you want to show the density of coffee shops in Seattle. Rather than display thousands (and thousands) of markers on a map, it would be far more effective to aggregate your data into bands of color that correspond to coffee shop density per unit area. So, in this example, if you have 30 coffee shops in a 1-square-mile area, you cover this area in a hot red color on the map; but if you have only three coffee shops in 1 square mile, you cover that area of the map in a cool blue color.

WARNING

The area and marker display type can change with the zoom level, depending on what web application you use and how it renders markers. For example, in a view of the entire Earth, New York City may appear as a marker; but if you zoom in to the state of New York, the city is represented as an area.

Web-based geographic data visualizations depend heavily on *geocoding* — the automatic association of data points with geographic points, based on the location information you provide. If you have a column of state names, or even street addresses, web applications generally can automap that data for you.

WARNING

Web-based geographic applications can sometimes be quite finicky with their data standards. For geocoding functions to work effectively, you may need to reformat some data so that it better meets those standards. For example, a web-application that recognizes **District of Columbia** might not recognize **Washington, D.C.** Format your data accordingly. Because each application has its own requirements, you have to check those on an application-by-application basis.

Making pretty maps with OpenHeatMap

OpenHeatMap is a user-friendly service that allows you to upload and geocode spatial data. OpenHeatMap can automatically geocode spatial identifiers, requiring only minimal user oversight. It's not as versatile as Google Fusion Tables or CartoDB, but it's so easy to use that many people consider it their favorite web-based mapping application. A unique feature of OpenHeatMap is that it doesn't offer user accounts. Anyone and everyone can upload data and use the service anonymously. To learn more, just go over and check out the OpenHeatMap home page (at www.openheatmap.com).

If your goal is to quickly create a choropleth or marker-based heat map, OpenHeatMap is the easiest solution on the Internet. "How easy?" you ask? Figure 11-3 shows a choropleth of the in-county moving dataset created in OpenHeatMap, which I managed to put together in a matter of seconds. Not bad, right?

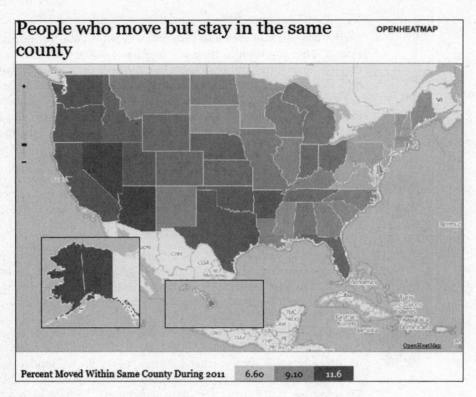

People who move but stay in the same county

OPENHEATMAP

Percent Moved Within Same County During 2011   6.60   9.10   11.6

OpenHeatMap

Mapmaking and spatial data analytics with CartoDB

If you're not a professional programmer or cartographer, CartoDB is about the most powerful online mapping solution that's available. People in information services, software engineering, media and entertainment, and urban development industries often use CartoDB for digital visual communications.

By using CartoDB, you can create a heat map simply by uploading or linking to a list of spatial coordinates. Likewise, if you want to create a choropleth map to show values for quantitative attributes, simply upload or link to a set of spatial coordinates that includes attribute data.

CartoDB allows you to overlay markers and shapes on all sorts of interesting base maps. You can use it to make anything from simple outline maps of geographic regions to stylish, antiqued, magazine-style maps. You can even use it to generate street maps from satellite imagery. CartoDB's geocoding functionality is so well implemented that you can drill down to a location using individual addresses, postal codes, or even IP addresses.

To get going in CartoDB, you need to first set up a user account. You can do that via the CartoDB home page (at http://cartodb.com).

For more advanced users, CartoDB offers these options:

>> Link to SQL databases.

>> Customize Cascading Style Sheets (CSS).

>> Incorporate other chart types in the form of superimposed graphs, outlines, and 3-dimensional surface plots.

Figure 11-4 shows CartoDB's version of the sample choropleth map of the in-county moving dataset, and Figure 11-5 shows a bubble map of the same dataset. CartoDB is interactive: It allows you to click features to see attribute information and turn map layers on and off in the same map interface.

FIGURE 11-4:
An interactive choropleth map in CartoDB.

TECHNICAL
STUFF

Map layers are spatial datasets that represent different features on a map. In shared areas, layers often overlap one another in the same spatial region. To better understand this concept, think again about a map that shows an election outcome. This type of map has a States layer and a Political Party layer. The States layer shows you the name and spatial boundary of the state. The Political Party layer, geographically overlaid on top of the States layer, tells you, state by state, how the majority of voters voted in the election. Although the layers overlap in physical location, both the states layer and the political party layer are based on separate, individual datasets. This is how layers work in mapping applications.

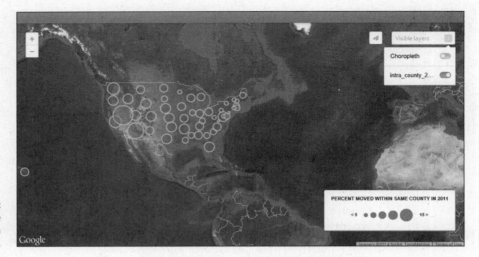

Visualizing with Open Source: Web-Based Data Visualization Platforms

The sole purpose of a noncollaborative, open-source, web-based data visualization platform is to help you quickly and easily create data visualizations without the need to invest tons of time and money learning how to code them up from scratch. These services do away with the need for specialized or bloated proprietary software packages and let you simply upload your data to get the results you need. Most of these platforms aim to help you create visualizations that you can subsequently use offsite. Some services don't even provide you with any storage capacity, so you have to store your data and visualizations on a hard drive, on the cloud, or on another remote data storage device.

Making pretty data graphics with Google Fusion Tables

Google Fusion Tables is an extension of *Google Drive* — the service for storing and editing office-type documents in the cloud. Google Fusion Tables can create visual communications in a wide range of industries, from information publishing to civil and environmental engineering, sustainable development, and real estate. Even human resource management can use it.

Because Fusion Tables only runs off data that's stored in *Google Sheets* — Google Drive's spreadsheet application — you must have a Google account with Google

Drive (at www.google.com/drive) and Google Fusion Tables (at https://support.google.com/fusiontables/answer/2571232) activated. To easily create data visualizations with Fusion Tables, simply link your Google Sheets to the Google Fusion Tables application and then let the application do all the work. You can use Google Fusion Tables to create pie charts, bar charts, line charts, scatter charts, timelines, and geographic maps. You can also automatically geotag columns with place names that associate your data with single geographic points. Data that's queried from Google Fusion Tables can even be mapped as points on a Google Map.

TECHNICAL STUFF

You can also use Google Fusion Tables to plot polygon data on top of Google Maps, but this task is a bit more challenging because Google Maps doesn't play well with polygon mapping.

For all the benefits it offers, Fusion Tables has one major drawback: It has a steep learning curve. If you're truly committed to using the application, though, Google offers a free online code lab (at https://developers.google.com/fusiontables/docs/v1/getting_started) from which you can figure out Fusion Tables at your own pace. If you become a more advanced user of Fusion Tables, you can bolster Fusion Tables' capabilities with a powerful API — an application-programmer interface that tells software applications how they should interact with one another.

Using iCharts for web-based data visualization

iCharts offers a web-based visual analytics platform that allows everyone to create, embed, and share interactive charts. The product provides cloud-based, fully interactive analytics that can be connected to live data using a variety of connectors, including an iCharts API, Google Sheets, Google Big Query, and NetSuite. iCharts' visual analytics are fully embeddable and have built-in SEO optimization and social sharing features. You can use iCharts to visualize your data through a variety of built-in chart types, including bar charts, column charts, pie charts, line charts, and free-form charts.

In addition to the free offering targeted to individuals (such as bloggers), the company offers paid plans focused on the following scenarios:

>> **Visual content marketing:** Media companies and publishers can create, publish, and share interactive visualizations that allow them to offer a richer experience to their audiences and expand their brand reach.

>> **Embedded visual analytics:** Companies of any size can embed iCharts within their enterprise systems to quickly visualize their data in real-time, with no IT support or data extraction or aggregation.

To get started using iCharts, first create an account (at www.icharts.net). To see what iCharts can do, check out Figure 11-6, which shows an iCharts version of a bar chart.

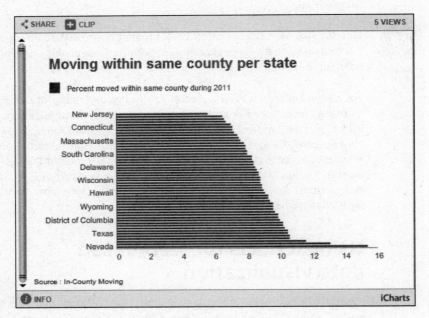

Moving within same county per state

Percent moved within same county during 2011

Source : In-County Moving

INFO   iCharts

FIGURE 11-6:
A bar chart in
iCharts.

Using RAW for web-based data visualization

You can use the unique and unusual web application *RAW* to make artistic and creative visualizations from your dataset. RAW's layout provides you with a simple drag-and-drop interface that you can use to make unique and interesting styles of data visualizations with just a few clicks of the mouse. If you want to get funky and cool with your data visualization, but you don't have the time or money it takes to learn how to code this sort of thing for yourself, RAW is the perfect data visualization alternative.

REMEMBER

Like I said, RAW is funky. It doesn't even offer standard bar chart visualizations. It does, however, offer clustered force diagrams, Voronoi tessellations, Reingold-Tilford trees, and other, less-well-known chart types.

To use RAW, first go to the RAW home page (at http://raw.densitydesign.org) and then navigate to the USE IT NOW! button. You don't even need to create an account to use the application — just copy and paste your raw data into the application and then choose the optimal chart types for that data. RAW makes it easy to choose between chart types by telling you the precise number of quantitative attributes, categorical attributes, and labels that are required to generate each plot.

This service wasn't designed for novices, but its simple, straightforward interface makes it a fun, user-friendly application for playing with your data and figuring out how to generate unique chart types. Even if you don't know a convex hull from a hexagonal bin, you can play around with settings, drag columns from place to place, and view how those changes affect the overall visualization. With enough practice, you may even end up using some of the visualization strategies that you learn from RAW in other contexts.

REMEMBER

You can have fun getting cool and funky with visualization design, but always make sure that your visual result is easy to understand for the average viewer.

Figure 11-7 shows a circle packing diagram of the in-county moving dataset I created in RAW. (*Note:* This is just about the only type of visualization RAW offers that would work with such a simple dataset!)

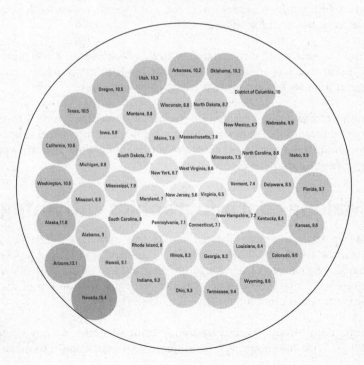

FIGURE 11-7:
A circle packing
diagram.

Knowing When to Stick with Infographics

Although the contextual difference between an infographic and a data visualization is often clear, even data visualization professionals can sometimes have a hard time distinguishing between the two. A good rule of thumb is that if the data graphics are primarily produced in an automated fashion using a data-graphing application, it's a data visualization. But if you use a custom graphic-design tool, such as Photoshop or Illustrator, to produce the final product, it's an infographic.

This categorization gets a bit more complicated, though. An infographic often incorporates one or more charts, making it more difficult to determine the manner in which the visualization was produced. Complicating the issue, online infographic design applications, such as Piktochart and Infogr.am, have dual functionality that allows for automated data graphing and customizable, artistic graphic design.

REMEMBER

An even broader rule of thumb is that if the visualization looks artfully designed, it's an infographic, but if it looks rather plain and analytical, it's a data visualization.

Although infographics can be dynamic or static, when you're designing a graphic for print, a slide for PowerPoint, or an image for social media syndication, just stick with static infographics. If you want to tell a story with your data or create data art, use an infographic.

TIP

You can easily and directly embed static graphics into a social media post. Social content that has an embedded graphic tends to get more attention and engagement than social content that is posted as text-only.

Applications used to create infographics provide many more creative alternatives than do traditional data visualization applications. In fact, this is as good a time as any to introduce you to a few of the better applications that are available for infographic design. Read on for all the details.

Making cool infographics with Infogr.am

Infogr.am is an online tool that you can use to make aesthetically appealing, vertically stacked card infographics — a visualization that's composed of a series of cards, stacked vertically on top of one another, each with its own set of data graphics. Since the cards are stacked vertically, one on top of the other, the end infographic is often longer than it is wide.

Infogr.am offers a variety of trendy color schemes, design schemes, and chart types. With Infogr.am, you can import your own images to make an infographic that much more personalized. Infogr.am also provides you with sharing capabilities so that you can spread your infographic quickly and easily across social channels or via private email.

You can use Infogr.am to create stylish infographics that display bar charts, column charts, pie charts, line charts, area charts, scatter charts, bubble charts, pictorials, hierarchical charts, tables, progress displays, word clouds, tree maps, or even financial charts. To get started using Infogr.am, just head over to the home page (at `https://infogr.am`) and register for an account. Its freemium plan is robust enough to supply all your more basic infographic-making needs.

Figure 11-8 shows a bar chart of the (by now familiar) in-county moving dataset in Infogr.am.

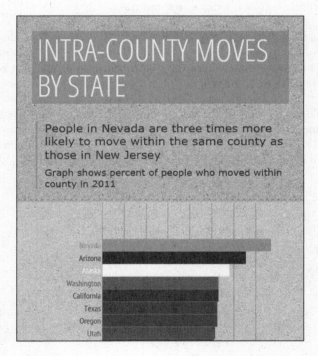

FIGURE 11-8:
A bar chart in Infogr.am.

TIP

If you want to check out some great Infogr.am examples before you get started, you can view a live feed of featured infographics at Infogr.am's Featured Infographics page (`http://infogr.am/featured`).

Making cool infographics with Piktochart

The Piktochart web application provides an easy-to-use interface that people like you and me can use to quickly create beautiful infographics. Piktochart offers a large selection of attractive templates, but be warned that only members who have paying accounts can access most of these templates. These templates are a great option if you want to save time and money on design but need to produce documents in an infographic format. Piktochart offers more creative flexibility than other comparable web applications, which makes Piktochart useful in a wide range of industries, from nonprofit grassroots to media and entertainment.

You can use Piktochart to make either static or dynamic infographics, and you can also link your infographics to Google Sheets for live updating. Piktochart offers the usual array of chart types, in addition to more infographic-oriented types, such as Venn diagrams, gauges, and matrixes.

If you use the free version of Piktochart to create your infographic, be warned that your infographic will be made available to the public. If you sign up for a paid account, however, you have the option of keeping your work private. You can register for Piktochart on the application's home page at http://piktochart.com.

Using Piktochart, you can create infographics that display bar charts, triangle charts, line charts, area charts, scatter charts, pie charts, Venn diagrams, matrixes, pyramids, gauges, donuts, swatches, and icons. Figure 11-9 shows a Piktochart version of a bar chart of the in-county moving dataset example.

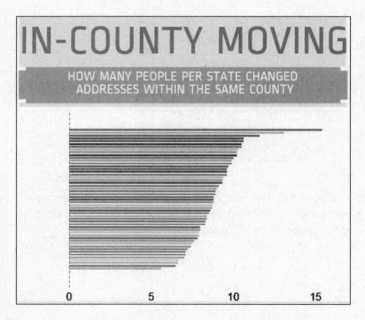

FIGURE 11-9: A bar chart in Piktochart.

Chapter **12**

Exploring Best Practices in Dashboard Design

B ig data, data engineering, and data science are revolutionizing business. While more and more data is collected at faster and faster rates, the demand for clear and meaningful data insights increases. Organizational decision-makers need information delivered quickly, and in a concise and easy-to-understand format.

In this context, data analytics dashboards are one of the more popular methods for delivering such information. Acting as (you hope!) a user-friendly software interface, such dashboards can provide a single-page, easy-to-understand summary of information that's vital to organizational and managerial decision making. A dashboard can also serve as a portal through which users can drill down to obtain more detailed information when needed.

Although dashboards have the potential to be highly effective communication mediums, their usefulness is heavily dependent on the designers' implementation of strategic and thoughtful design principles. In this chapter, I introduce you to the best practices of dashboard design, and explain why those practices are important.

As with any type of design, you can find a lot of good and bad dashboard examples out there. Bad design is usually the direct result of a poorly scoped purpose. Dashboards, like all visualizations, have to be designed for a specific audience to serve a specific function. If you don't define the audience and function clearly in advance, the dashboard probably can't succeed.

The term *dashboard* was adopted from the automobile panel. Don't let the metaphorical title "dashboard" shape your image of the analytics dashboard, though. Dashboards that incorporate illustrations of gauges and odometers are now considered old-fashioned and clunky. These design elements consume a lot of screen space, deliver sparse information, and create needless visual clutter on a layout that should be clear, concise, and to the point. Use cleaner, more compact elements instead.

Focusing on the Audience

Dashboards are all about communication, and the golden rule in communication is *know your audience.* One of the most common errors in dashboard design happens when a designer tries to make a dashboard be all things to all people. This designer inevitably uses every type of doodad and gewgaw to visualize every possible item of interest, thus creating a dashboard that's so cluttered and unfocused that it's nearly impossible to use.

A business intelligence dashboard for upper management should have an entirely different focus than that of a small-business e-commerce dashboard. Focus less attention on what your audience *might want* to know and more attention on what your audience *needs* to know. Focus on what's useful to your audience in an at-a-glance resource. Set up your dashboard in such a way that users keep coming back precisely because your dashboard is the one that delivers actionable, timely insights that they can turn to for quick and easy decision support. If the insights aren't actionable, or if they're too hard to understand, your target audience won't adopt the dashboard as a decision-support instrument. This is generally just how things turn out.

One important, yet often overlooked, best practice in dashboard design is to plan your dashboard as though every user is seeing it for the first time. To secure the comfort of your users, your dashboard must be self-explanatory and intuitive. For this reason, you need to keep your dashboards simple. Use icons, as well as text; label everything; use tooltips, where appropriate; and never expect a user to read a Help file before getting started.

Starting with the Big Picture

In design, there are large-scale issues and smaller, more detail-oriented issues. The space limitations implicit in dashboard design require that you hold strong focus on purpose and carefully integrate and harmonize both large-scale and detail elements to fulfill that purpose. Most industry standard best practices for dashboard design have been established through trial-and-error procedures. When conceptualizing your dashboard's design, it also helps to study what clients and managers have found most useful and helpful in their previous dashboards.

Here are a few best practices to keep in mind when designing the overall, big-picture layout of your dashboard (in the next section, I drill down to the detail level):

>> **Keep it on a single page.** Dashboards are supposed to be an at-a-glance resource, and you can glance at only one page at a time. Therefore, when designing a dashboard, find a way to fit everything on that one page. Also, don't get sucked into the trap of thinking that you need to fit tons of stuff on that page — leave out everything except the most important information.

>> **Let it breathe.** *White space* — the blank white space on a screen where no text or images are placed — is vital in design. If you pack everything in closely, the eye has trouble focusing on anything. Carefully chosen white space can guide your users to focus on only the most important parts of the dashboard.

>> **Give the layout a natural flow.** Your dashboard should flow from top to bottom and from left to right. This logical progression intuitively makes sense to users. The progression can be from more specific to more general, it can follow a workflow pathway, or it can simply follow some path of dependencies between one concept and another.

TIP

Of course, reading from top to bottom, and from left to right, is the standard practice of western cultures. If you're Japanese, you'd read from right to left, and you should design a visualization that naturally flows in that direction. What's important is that you design your dashboard so that it makes the most intuitive sense for your particular audience, according to their specific cultural norms.

>> **Provide a method to drill down to more specific information.** The dashboard should function as an overall summary of the desired information, but if you're including something of particular interest to your audience, users probably want to explore that area more fully. A good dashboard makes getting more information a near-effortless process. Unlike a static snapshot, a dashboard can provide an interactive experience where users can *drill down* — click different parts of the data graphics in order to be presented with a more detailed version. For example, a dashboard shows a Sales Stats by

Region section and, when you click any given region, a Sales Stats by County pop-up window appears, to provide you with the more detailed information.

>> **Choose alerts wisely.** Get feedback from end users to determine what's important enough to warrant an alert function. For example, for dashboards that track stock valuations, having a stock price fall below a certain value threshold for an allotted period should trigger a dashboard alert. Because no two users' needs are the same, alerts can be a difficult balancing act. If you flag everything, you're really flagging nothing because people will quickly begin to ignore all the constant alerts. On the other hand, you don't want to let important situations slide by unnoticed. Prepare for a lot of tweaking when configuring alert functionalities.

>> **Less is more.** The dashboard should be attractive and aesthetically appealing, but it mustn't be overdesigned. In every design decision, make sure to focus on utility and usefulness as the top criteria. Let the dashboard's form naturally follow from a simple and functional approach.

Getting the Details Right

After you have conceptualized your dashboard — you know who your audience is, of what they need to be informed, and what elements need to go where on the page — you need to get into the nitty-gritty details. Even if everything was perfect until this point, your dashboard can still fail to deliver if you haven't taken time to think about the look and feel of the individual elements that comprise it. The following list describes a set of best practices that are helpful when planning the details of your design:

>> **Less is more.** Even though this was the last bullet point in the preceding section, I'm reusing it here because it's vitally important in designing dashboard details, as well as in overall dashboard design. Real estate on the dashboard is at a premium, and user time and attention aren't guaranteed. Make it as easy as possible for users to get what they need, by presenting everything as simply as possible. Although green, yellow, and red traffic lights or thermometer bulbs might work in an infographic, they're much too distracting on a dashboard. Use simple bars and dots instead.

>> **Stay current.** *Flat design* — a modern minimalistic design approach that restricts designers to using only 2-dimensional elements, and to placing those elements in an exceptionally clean and clutterfree visual layout — is all the rage these days. The greatest advantage of this style is that it makes user interaction simple and easy. If a flat design approach works with your data, you can increase your hipness factor by making use of it.

Keeping your source data current is also extremely important. When you're designing a dashboard to support other people's decision making, timeliness is everything — if you haven't equipped your dashboards with real-time updating, they must at least be based on current, up-to-date sources.

>> **Use color sparingly.** Choose a simple, muted color palette that's easy on the eyes without being monotone and boring. Reserve vibrant colors for alerts and notifications — you need them to stand out from the background.

>> **Stay horizontal.** Since most people from western cultures read words horizontally, our eyes can better follow representations of data when they're laid out horizontally as well. Make bar charts progress from left to right instead of up and down, and arrange items in lines instead of vertical stacks. These two data graphic innovations are quite useful for designing effective dashboards:

● *Sparkline:* Invented by data visualization pioneer Edward Tufte, sparklines consist of tiny line or bar charts that are presented in the same space and at the same size as words, either in a table or a paragraph. Sparklines offer a compact and effective way to present trends on a dashboard. (See Figure 12-1 for an example.)

● *Bullet graph:* A simple and elegant alternative to the old-fashioned thermometers and progress bars of yesteryear. Figure 12-2 shows a bullet graph that represents a danger zone, where the number of new customers in a period is fewer than 250. In this graphic, the acceptable zone is 250 to 400, and the good zone is above 400. Instead of using gaudy red, yellow, and green colors, this graphic nicely presents the information by using subtle shades of gray. In this graphic, the current status shows 300 new customers, with a goal of 450.

FIGURE 12-1:
Sparklines are an effective way to communicate data insights.

Revenues
Expenses

FIGURE 12-2:
Bullet graphs offer an aesthetically appealing alternative to progress bars.

New customers

0   100   200   300   400   500

Testing Your Design

No matter how careful and strategic your dashboard design, you're bound to come up against trouble when the product goes live. Developing and releasing a preliminary version of the dashboard is just the first step. Dashboard designers must be prepared to see it through until they're certain that the product works, and works well.

You can't please everyone, and you may have to juggle and prioritize a list of complaints, but true testing comes from observing how the dashboard works in action. Because dashboards are almost always web-based nowadays, you can easily get some hard statistics about their performance and usability. Log files can tell you about visitor counts, session durations, and user click patterns. You can even incorporate A/B testing by shuffling items around to see which layout is most effective.

You can't prepare for all potential scenarios in advance, and with a topic as complex and subjective as dashboard design, you're better off adopting a flexible design approach. That way, you have a better chance of designing a product that end users will actually use, and isn't that the point?

Chapter **13**

Making Maps from Spatial Data

A dvanced statistical methods are great tools when you need to make predictions from spatial datasets, and everyone knows that data visualization design can help you present your findings in the most effective way possible. That's all fine and dandy, but wouldn't it be great if you could combine the two approaches?

I'm here to tell you that it can be done. The key to putting the two together involves envisioning how one could map spatial data — *spatial data visualization,* in other words. Whether you choose to use a proprietary or open-source application, the simplest way to make maps from spatial datasets is to use Geographic Information Systems (GIS) software to help you do the job. This chapter introduces the basics of GIS and how you can use it to analyze and manipulate spatial datasets.

TIP

The proprietary GIS software, ESRI ArcGIS for Desktop, is the most widely used mapmaking application. It can be purchased from the ESRI website (at www.esri. com/software/arcgis/arcgis-for-desktop). But if you don't have the money to invest in this solution, you can use open-source QGIS (at www.qgis.org) to accomplish the same goals. GRASS GIS (at http://grass.osgeo.org) is another good open-source alternative to proprietary ESRI products. In practice, all these software applications are simply referred to as *GIS*.

Getting into the Basics of GIS

People use GIS for all sorts of purposes. Some simply want to make beautiful maps, and others could not care less about aesthetics and are primarily interested in using GIS to help them make sense of significant patterns in their spatial data. Whether you're a cartographer or a statistician, GIS offers a little bit for everyone. In the following sections, I cover all the basic concepts you need to know about GIS so that you can get started making maps from your spatial data.

To get a handle on some basic concepts, imagine that you have a dataset that captures information on snow events. When most people think of snow events, they may think of making a snowman, or of scary avalanches, or of snowskiing. When a GIS person thinks of a snow event, however, she more likely thinks about snowfall rates, snow accumulation, or in what city it snowed the most. A spatial dataset about snow might provide just this kind of information.

Check out the simple snow dataset shown in Figure 13-1. Although this table provides only a small amount of information, you can use the data in this table to make a simple map that shows what cities have snow and what cities don't.

ID	Snow	Location
1	No	Valley City
2	Yes	Grand Forks
3	Yes	Jamestown
4	No	Aberdeen

FIGURE 13-1: A sample of basic spatial data.

Although you can use this data to make a simple map, you need to have your location data in a numerical format if you want to go deeper into GIS analysis. Imagine that you go back to the table from Figure 13-1 and add three columns of data — one column for latitudinal coordinates, one column for longitudinal coordinates, and one column for number of road accidents that occur at the locations where these coordinates intersect. Figure 13-2 shows what I have in mind.

When you have spatial data coordinates that specify position and location, you can use GIS to store, manipulate, and perform analysis on large volumes of data. For the snow example, you could use GIS to calculate how much snow has fallen and accumulated in each city or to determine the cities where it's particularly dangerous to drive during snow events.

ID	Snow (mm)	City	Latitude	Longitude	Road accidents (last 24 h)
1	0	Valley City	46.96	-98.01	2
2	120	Grand Forks	47.95	-97.01	5
3	140	Jamestown	46.92	-98.23	6
4	0	Aberdeen	45.98	-98.47	3
5	150	Miles City	45.74	-98.71	6
6	80	Dickinson	45.79	-96.98	6
7	0	Minot	49.16	-97.76	2
8	20	Bismark	46.91	-98.01	2

FIGURE 13-2: Spatial data described through coordinates and additional attributes.

To do all that neat stuff, you need to bone up on some core GIS concepts that are central to helping you understand spatial databases, GIS file formats, map projections, and coordinate systems. The following sections help you accomplish that task.

Spatial databases

The main purpose of a spatial database is to store, manage, and manipulate attribute, location, and geometric data for all records in a feature's database. With respect to GIS, an *attribute* is a class of fact that describes a feature, *location* describes the feature's location on Earth, and *geometric data* describes the feature's *geometry type* — either a point, a line, or a polygon.

Imagine that you want to make a map of all Dunkin' Donuts restaurants that also sell Baskin-Robbins ice cream. The feature you're mapping is "Dunkin' Donuts restaurants," the attribute is "Baskin-Robbins Vendor? (Y/N)," the location fields tell you where these restaurants are located, each store is represented by its own *record* in the database, and the geometric data tells you that these restaurants must be represented by points on the map.

REMEMBER

A spatial database is similar to a plain relational database, but in addition to storing data on qualitative and quantitative attributes, spatial databases store data about physical location and feature geometry type. Every record in a spatial database is stored with numeric coordinates that represent where that record occurs on a map and each feature is represented by only one of these three geometry types:

>> Point

>> Line

>> Polygon

Whether you want to calculate the distance between two places on a map or determine the area of a particular piece of land, you can use spatial database querying to quickly and easily make automated spatial calculations on entire sets of records at one time. Going one step further, you can use spatial databases to perform almost all the same types of calculations on — and manipulations of — attribute data that you can in a plain relational database system.

File formats in GIS

To facilitate different types of analysis and outputs, GIS accommodates two main file formats: raster and vector. Since these are the main two file format types used in GIS, both proprietary and open-source GIS applications have been specifically designed to support each.

Raster data is broken up and plotted out along a 2-dimensional grid structure so that each grid cell gets its own attribute value. (See Figure 13-3.) Although most people know that rasters are used to store image data in digital photographs, few people know that the raster file format is useful for storing spatial data as well.

FIGURE 13-3:
Raster and vector representations of different geometric features used in GIS.

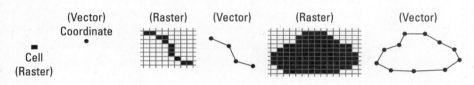

REMEMBER Raster files can be used to store data for only one attribute at a time. In GIS, data for a single attribute is stored and plotted in a 2-dimensional grid, where the horizontal dimension represents longitude and the vertical dimension represents latitude. Digital photographs and Doppler weather radar maps are two common examples of raster files in the modern world.

Vector format files, on the other hand, store data as either points, lines, or polygons on a map. (Refer to Figure 13-3.) Point features are stored as single point records plotted in geographic space, whereas line and polygon features are stored as a series of vertices that comprise each record plotted in geographic space. For data in vector format, GIS can easily handle tens of attributes for each record stored in the spatial database. Google Maps, modern digital graphics, and engineering computer-aided design (CAD) drawings are some prime examples of vector graphics at use in the real world.

To conceptualize the raster versus vector idea, imagine that you have some graphing paper and a pencil and you want to draw a map of a street cul-de-sac that's in your neighborhood. You can draw it as a series of polygons — one representing the area covered by the street and the others representing the parcels that abut the street. Or, you can fill in the squares of the graph paper, one after the other, until you cover all the areas with one, single multicolored surface.

Vector format data is like drawing the street and parcels as a set of separate *polygons*. Raster data format is like making one *surface* by coloring the entire area around the cul-de-sac so that all street areas and the adjoining parcel areas are covered in their own, representative color. The difference between the two methods is shown in Figure 13-4.

FIGURE 13-4:
A street and neighborhood represented as vector polygons and as a raster surface.

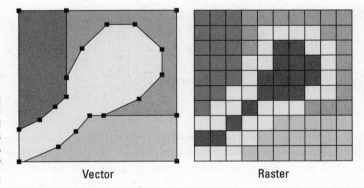

Vector   Raster

If you use GIS to create maps that show municipal boundaries, land cover, roads, attractions, or any other distinct spatial features, as shown in Figure 13-5, this type of spatial data is best stored in the vector file format. If you need to perform complex spatial analysis of multiple attributes for each feature in your dataset, keep your data in vector format. Vector data covers only the spatial areas where each discrete feature from your dataset is located on Earth. But with vector data, you get a lot of options on what attributes of that feature you want to analyze or display on a map.

The easiest way to analyze several attributes (that could be derived from one or several features) that spatially overlap one another over a particular piece of land is to put your data into raster format. Because a raster file can represent only one attribute at a time, you'd layer several rasters on top of each other to see how the overlapping attributes compare in a fixed geographic region. While you can do a similar type of spatial overlap comparison using vector files, raster files will give you a full and comprehensive coverage for each set of attribute values across an entire study area.

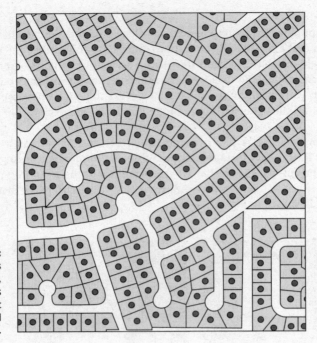

FIGURE 13-5:
An address
location map,
represented as
vector format
points and
polygons.

For example, to quantify volume data across a fixed area of land, raster files are definitely the way to go. Consider the snow example again. Your attribute in this example is snow height. Given that your raster data provides all height data for the snow (on a pixel-by-pixel basis) in a particular fixed region, you can use that to calculate the volume of snow on the ground in that area: Simply multiply the area of each pixel by the difference between the average snow surface height and the average ground elevation at that location. To find the area of snow that has accumulated in a fixed area, sum up the volume of snow that has fallen in each pixel of that area, as shown in Figure 13-6.

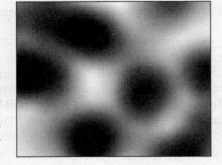

FIGURE 13-6:
Interpolated
surface of snow
depth repre-
sented in a raster
with low
resolution.

When you work with spatial data that's in vector format, you're focusing on *features*. You're doing things like drawing separate line features, cutting existing features, or performing a buffering analysis to get some determination about features that are within a certain proximity of the feature you're studying. When you work with spatial data that's in raster format, you're focusing on *surfaces*. You're working with a raster surface that covers the entire spatial area you're studying and describes the quantities, intensities, and changes in value of one attribute across an entire study area.

It's possible to convert a vector feature to a raster surface — but, you can convert only one attribute at a time. Imagine that you have a vector file that represents gas stations with "Leaking Underground Storage Tanks," represented as points on a map. The attribute table for this layer has data on the following four attributes: "Year Tank Was Installed," "Year Leak Was Detected," "Tank Depth," and "Contaminant Concentrations." When you convert all this data from vector to raster, you get four separate raster files, one for each attribute. The vector point format is converted to a raster surface that covers the entire study area and displays the attribute values, or lack thereof, on a pixel-by-pixel basis.

Map projections and coordinate systems

Map projections and coordinate systems give GIS a way to accurately represent a round Earth on a flat surface, translating Earth's arced 3-dimensional geometry into flat 2-dimensional geometry.

Projections and coordinate systems *project* spatial data. That is to say, they forecast and predict accurate spatial positions and geographic scale, depending on where those features are located on Earth. Although projection and coordinate systems are able to project most features rather accurately, they don't offer a one-size-fits-all solution. If features in one region are projected perfectly at scale, features in another region are inevitably projected with at least a slight amount of distortion. This distortion is sort of like looking at things through a magnifying glass — you can see the object in the center of the lens accurately and clearly, but the objects on the outer edge of the lens always appear distorted. No matter where you move the magnifying glass, this fact remains unchanged. Similarly, you can't represent *all* features of a rounded world accurately and to-scale on a flat map.

In GIS, the trick to getting around this distortion problem is to narrow your study area, focus on only a small geographic region, and use the map projection or coordinate system that's most accurate for this region.

A coordinate system is a referencing system that is used to *define* a feature's location on Earth. There are two types of coordinate systems:

» **Projected:** Also called *map projection*, a projected coordinate system is a mathematical algorithm you can use to transform the location of features on a round Earth to equivalent positions represented on a flat surface instead. The three common projection types are cylindrical, conical, and planar.

» **Geographic:** A coordinate system that uses sets of numbers and/or letters to define every location on Earth. In geographic coordinate systems, location is often represented by latitude/longitude, decimal degrees, or degrees-minutes-seconds (if you're familiar with old-fashioned surveying nomenclature).

Figure 13-7 shows these three types, in all their glory.

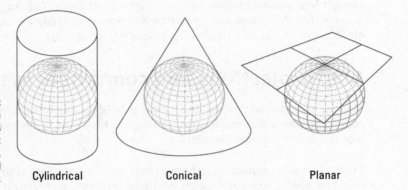

FIGURE 13-7: Three common projection types (left to right): cylindrical, conical, and planar.

Cylindrical   Conical   Planar

Now that you know what types of coordinate systems are out there, it's time to take a look at how you'd make practical use of them. This is the easy part! In almost all cases, when you import a spatial dataset into GIS, it comes in with its own predefined coordinate system. The GIS software then adopts that coordinate system and assigns it to the entire project. When you add additional datasets to that project in the future, they may be using that same coordinate system or an alternative one. In cases where the new data is coming in with a coordinate system that's different from that of the project, the GIS software transforms the incoming data so that it is represented correctly on the map.

As an example of how all of this works in practice, to determine how much agricultural land has been contaminated during a tanker spill at the Mississippi Delta, you import a spatial dataset named Contaminated Land. The Contaminated Land file already has a predefined coordinate system — State Plane Coordinate System Mississippi, West MS_W 4376 2302. When you import the dataset, GIS automatically detects its coordinate system, assigns that coordinate system to the project you've started, and transforms any subsequently added spatial datasets so that they come in with correct scale and positioning. It's that easy!

TIP

Information about a dataset's default map projection and coordinate system is stored in its metadata description. The default map projection and coordinate system are the fundamental reference systems from which you can re-project the dataset for your specific needs.

Analyzing Spatial Data

After you've imported your data, it's time to get into spatial data analysis. In the following sections, you find out how to use various querying, buffering, overlay, and classifying methods to extract valuable information from your spatial dataset.

Querying spatial data

In GIS, you can query spatial data in two ways: attribute querying and spatial querying. *Attribute querying* is just what it sounds like: You use this querying method when you want to summarize, extract, manipulate, sort, or group database records according to relevant attribute values. If you want to make sense of your data by creating order from its attribute values, use attribute querying.

Spatial querying, on the other hand, is all about querying data records according to their physical location in space. Spatial querying is based solely on the location of the feature and has nothing to do with the feature's attribute values. If your goal is to make sense of your data based on its physical location, use spatial querying.

TIP

Learning to quickly and fluidly switch between attribute and spatial querying can help you to quickly make sense of complex problems in GIS. A situation where this is true would be if you have a spatial point dataset that represents disease risk. If you want to find the average disease risk of people over the age of 50 who live within a 2-mile distance of a major power center, you could use spatial and attribute querying to quickly generate some results. The first step would be to use spatial querying to isolate data points so that you're analyzing only those people who live within the 2-mile radius. From this reduced dataset, you'd next use attribute querying to isolate the records of people who are over the age of 50, and then perform a quick mathematical operation to get the average value for disease risk from that subset.

TIP

You can either query the spatial database directly using SQL statements or use the simple built-in interfaces to query your data for you. Sometimes the quickest way to query results is to write the SQL statement yourself, but if your query is simple, you might as well make your life easy and use the point-and-click interface instead.

Referring back to the snow example, if you want to generate a list of all cities where snow depth was greater than 100mm, you simply use attribute querying to select all records that have a snow value that's greater than 100mm. But if you decide that you want to generate a list of cities with more than 100mm of snow that are located within 100 miles of Grand Forks, you'd use both an attribute and a spatial query.

Buffering and proximity functions

Within a GIS project, you can select or extract spatial features based on their physical *proximity*, or nearness, to a point, line, or polygon by using buffering and proximity functions. Buffering and proximity functions are fundamental, basic spatial querying methods.

Proximity analysis is a spatial querying operation you can use to select and extract features that are within a user-defined distance from your target feature. You can use proximity analysis to calculate distances between features or to calculate the shortest route in a network. *Buffering* is a proximity operation you can use to select and extract spatial features that are within a user-defined distance of your target feature. Figure 13-8 shows a schematic of a Buffer Zone Y that encompasses all areas within distance d of a target Polygon X. You can use Buffer Zone Y to isolate, extract, and analyze all spatial features within the d distance of Polygon X.

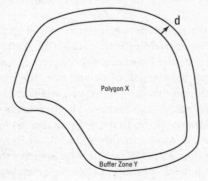

FIGURE 13-8: Buffered features at two different distances.

Using layer overlay analysis

One of the most powerful features of a GIS platform is its capability to overlay and derive meaning from multiple layers of data. By using *layer overlay analysis*, you can apply multiple operations to multiple layers of data that overlap the same spatial area.

Union, intersection, non-intersection, and *subtraction* are a few fundamental overlay operations. *Union* operations combine the total area of all features being overlain, whereas *intersection* operations retain only the areas of overlap between the features being overlain. *Non-intersection* operations are the reverse of intersection operations — they represent the areas of non-overlap between the features being overlain. Lastly, you can use a *subtraction* operation to subtract an area from one feature based on the area of other features that overlay it. I know this all sounds rather obscure, but it's not so bad. Take a look at Figure 13-9 to see how these operations work.

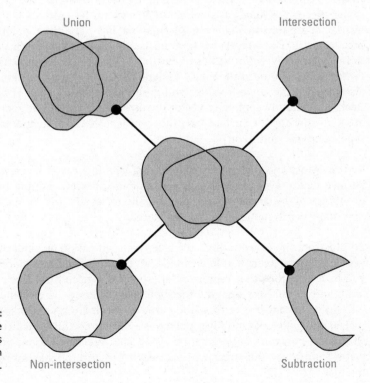

FIGURE 13-9: Simple operations applied on overlain features.

Overlay analysis is commonly used in suitability studies to determine which sites are best suited to support a particular function or type of business. For example, if you have to plan a new town settlement, you can use GIS to overlay spatial data layers and analyze the land's proximity to potable water sources, suitable terrain, suitable soil type, bodies of water, and so on. By overlaying these layers, you generate a map that shows which regions are more or less suitable to support the planned settlement.

REMEMBER

Vector format data is often a bit too big and clunky for complex overlay analyses. To reduce computing requirements, consider converting your vector data to raster data and then using overlay operations to make sense of the layers. This type of overlay analysis is called *raster algebra.*

Reclassifying spatial data

In GIS, *reclassification* is the act of changing or reclassifying the values of cells in a raster file, or the values of an attribute in a vector file. Although you can use layer overlay operations to analyze more than one layer at a time, you have to perform reclassification on a layer-by-layer basis. You can use reclassification if you want to reassign a new set of values to existing cells (in rasters) or attribute values (in vectors), but you need the newly assigned values to be proportional to, and consistent with, the current values and groupings of those cells or attribute values. Reclassification is applied to vector or raster data layers that generally represent attributes of Earth's surface (in other words, elevation, temperature, land cover type, soil type, and so on).

To fully grasp the concept of reclassifying data in a raster layer, imagine a raster surface where every cell is assigned a depth of snow. Simply by creating new groupings of depth ranges, you could easily reclassify this source data to uncover new snow depth patterns in the study area.

To illustrate the concept of vector layer reclassification, consider that you have a vector polygon layer that depicts land cover across your study area. In this layer, you have polygons that represent lakes, rivers, agricultural land, forests, grassland, and so on. Now imagine that you want to know where only the water and vegetation are located in this study area. You can simply repackage your map by reclassifying all Lake and River polygons as Water and all Agricultural, Forest, and Grassland polygons as Vegetation. With this reclassification, you can identify water from vegetation areas without needing to give the map more than a sweeping glance.

Getting Started with Open-Source QGIS

Earlier sections in this chapter focus on the basic concepts involved in GIS and spatial data analysis. The following sections let you finally get your hands dirty. I show you how to set up your interface, add data, and specify display settings in QGIS. To follow along, you must first start by downloading and installing QGIS (from `http://qgis.org/en/site/forusers/index.html`) and then download the QGIS Tutorial Data from the GitHub repository for this course (at `https://github.com/BigDataGal/Data-Science-for-Dummies/`).

Getting to know the QGIS interface

The main window of QGIS contains a lot of toolbars and menus, as shown in Figure 13-10. The toolbar on the far left is used to add data. You can add vector layers, raster layers, comma-delimited tables, and several other data types. The toolbar at the top contains many tools that allow you to navigate through the map you're creating. You can use the two toolbars below the topmost toolbar to manipulate and analyze data.

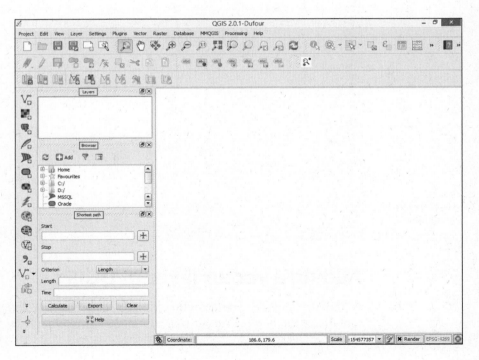

FIGURE 13-10:
The default QGIS setup.

These three embedded windows run down the left side of the main window:

>> **Browser:** Allows you to browse through your files and add data

>> **Layers:** Shows you what layers are active in your map

>> **Shortest Path:** Calculates the shortest path between two points on a map

You won't use the Browser or Shortest Path window in this chapter, so you can close those windows by clicking the X that appears in the top-right corner of each window.

Your screen should now look something like Figure 13-11.

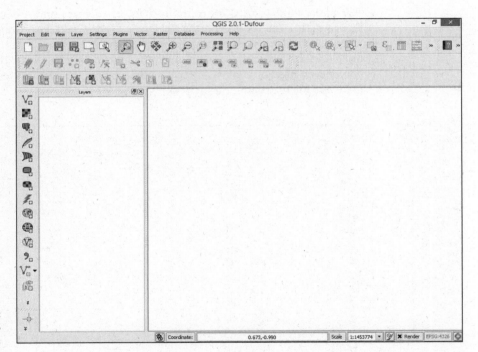

FIGURE 13-11: Your new QGIS setup.

Adding a vector layer in QGIS

To continue your exploration of the QGIS interface, add to your map a vector layer containing the borders for all counties in the United States by following these steps:

1. **Click the Add Vector Layer icon on the toolbar on the left of your screen.**

   The Add Vector Layer dialog box appears onscreen, as shown in Figure 13-12.

2. **Click the Add Vector Layer dialog box's Browse button.**

3. **In the Open an OGR Supported Vector Layer dialog box that appears, navigate to the folder where you choose to store the GIS data that you downloaded for this tutorial.**

4. **Choose the** county.shp **file, click OK, and then click Open.**

   A layer named County appears on the Layers menu, as shown in Figure 13-13.

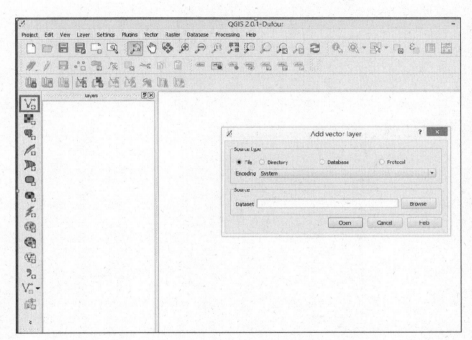

FIGURE 13-12:
Adding a vector
layer to QGIS.

Displaying data in QGIS

This county.shp file (a vector file) displays all counties in the United States. All these polygons have Attribute data connected to and stored in the dataset's Attribute table. To see what I mean, take a look at the kind of information this table contains. Follow these steps:

1. **Right-click the County layer in the Layers window and choose Open Attribute Table from the pop-up menu that appears.**

   The Attribute Table window containing all the data appears, as shown in Figure 13-14.

FIGURE 13-13:
A layer added
into QGIS.

	STATEFP	COUNTYFP	COUNTYNS	AFFGEOID	GEOID	NAME	LSAD	ALAND	AWATER
0	01	001	00161526	0500000US01001	01001	Autauga	06	1539584443	25773561
1	01	009	00161530	0500000US01009	01009	Blount	06	1670041814	15077461
2	01	023	00161537	0500000US01023	01023	Choctaw	06	2365954803	19059247
3	01	033	00161542	0500000US01033	01033	Colbert	06	1534878355	80029923
4	01	049	00161550	0500000US01049	01049	DeKalb	06	2012664422	4121499
5	01	089	00161570	0500000US01089	01089	Madison	06	2076115375	28770709
6	01	109	00161581	0500000US01109	01109	Pike	06	1740741440	2336918
7	01	133	00161592	0500000US01133	01133	Winston	06	1587615096	48922725
8	02	016	01419965	0500000US02016	02016	Aleutians West	05	11370496382	25190642141
9	02	090	01419969	0500000US02090	02090	Fairbanks North...	04	19006935117	272298859
10	02	270	01419985	0500000US02270	02270	Wade Hampton	05	44240303572	6712008910
11	04	007	00040471	0500000US04007	04007	Gila	06	12323010025	97111871
12	04	021	00025447	0500000US04021	04021	Pinal	06	13897002061	22331517
13	05	013	00063758	0500000US05013	05013	Calhoun	06	1627959476	9926129
14	05	017	00069160	0500000US05017	05017	Chicot	06	1668739972	120391647
15	05	073	00066864	0500000US05073	05073	Lafayette	06	1368208572	43539042
16	05	099	00069169	0500000US05099	05099	Nevada	06	1600189832	7257493
17	05	145	00069906	0500000US05145	05145	White	06	2680817964	18326633
18	06	003	01675840	0500000US06003	06003	Alpine	06	1912243146	12557256
19	06	005	01675841	0500000US06005	06005	Amador	06	1539947370	29470575
20	06	011	01675902	0500000US06011	06011	Colusa	06	2980373007	14581043
21	06	015	01682074	0500000US06015	06015	Del Norte	06	2606517997	578525673
22	06	025	00277277	0500000US06025	06025	Imperial	06	10817387352	790204642
23	06	027	01804637	0500000US06027	06027	Inyo	06	26358506526	119060126
24	06	033	00277281	0500000US06033	06033	Lake	06	3254241507	188959508
25	06	043	00277286	0500000US06043	06043	Mariposa	06	3752425637	36268140
26	06	079	00277304	0500000US06079	06079	San Luis Obispo	06	8543653416	820437991
27	06	089	01682610	0500000US06089	06089	Shasta	06	9778188422	186530228
28	06	099	00277314	0500000US06099	06099	Stanislaus	06	3870792977	51176485
29	06	105	00277317	0500000US06105	06105	Trinity	06	8234308383	73407638
30	08	001	00198116	0500000US08001	08001	Adams	06	3023994956	41935475
31	08	005	00198118	0500000US08005	08005	Arapahoe	06	2066561712	19528620

Attribute table - county :: Features total: 3234, filtered: 3234, selected: 0

Show All Features

FIGURE 13-14:
An Attribute
table in QGIS.

REMEMBER

Each record in this table represents a single polygon. Every record has its own row, and each attribute has its own column. Within the QGIS Layer Properties settings, you can set up your record attributes so that they display different colors, are grouped in certain ways, and do a lot of other nifty things.

The attribute STATEFP contains a unique number for each state. You can use this number to do things like represent all counties in the same state with the same color. The attribute ALAND represents the size of each county. You can use the data that belongs to this attribute category to do things like assign darker colors to larger counties.

Say that you're interested in only the counties that fall within the state of Colorado. Therefore, you need to tell QGIS what polygons should be shown.

2. **Close the Attribute Table window by clicking the red X in the top-right corner, and then double-click the County layer in the Layers window on the left.**

The Layer Properties window appears, as shown in Figure 13-15.

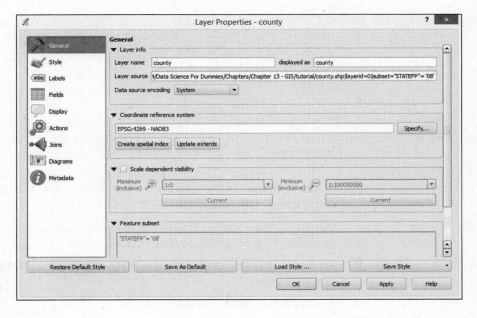

FIGURE 13-15:
Layer properties
in QGIS.

3. **Click the window's General tab (active by default) and scroll down until you find the Feature Subset section.**

4. In the Feature Subset section, click the Query Builder button.

The Query Builder dialog box appears, as shown in Figure 13-16.

The Fields box displays only those fields that are available in the Attribute table of the county . shp file.

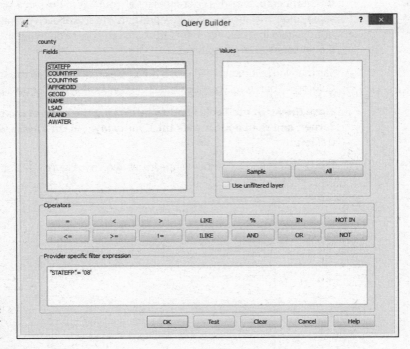

FIGURE 13-16: Query Builder in QGIS.

5. Double-click the STATEFP entry in the Fields box of the Query Builder dialog box.

The STATEFP field appears in the Provider Specific Filter Expression box, located near the bottom of the Query Builder dialog box.

6. Type = '08' after the "STATEFP" entry in the Provider Specific Filter Expression box.

The final expression should look like

"STATEFP" = '08'

TIP

STATEFP contains codes that represent the states in America, and in that code, 08 stands for Colorado.

7. **Click OK, and then click OK again.**

The main Layer Properties window reappears.

8. **Right-click the County layer in the Layers window and choose Zoom to Layer from the pop-up menu that appears.**

You can make these kinds of queries as complicated as you need. You can choose to display only polygons for which the value in a specific column is larger or smaller than a given value, or you can combine different arguments for different fields. QGIS relies on SQL queries.

The map shown in Figure 13-17 displays only the counties that are in Colorado.

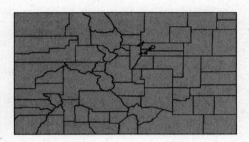

FIGURE 13-17:
A basic vector
layer mapped
in QGIS.

4
Computing for Data Science

Chapter **14**

Using Python for Data Science

lthough popular programming languages like Java and C++ are good for developing stand-alone desktop applications, Python's versatility makes it an ideal programming language for processing, analyzing, and visualizing data. For this reason, Python has earned a reputation of excellence in the data science field, where it has been widely adopted over the past decade. In fact, Python has become so popular that it seems to have stolen ground from R — the other free, widely adopted programming language for data science applications. Python's status as one of the more popular programming languages out there can be linked to the fact that it's relatively easy to master and it allows users to accomplish several tasks using just a few lines of code.

In this chapter, I first introduce you to the fundamental concepts of programming with Python (such as data types, function, and classes), and then I present the information you need to know to set up a standard Python working environment in Jupyter. I also introduce some of the best Python libraries for manipulating data, performing statistical computations, creating data visualizations, and completing other related tasks. Lastly, I walk you through some scenarios designed to illustrate how Python can best help you analyze data.

You can use Python to do anything, from simple mathematical operations to data visualization and even machine learning and predictive analytics. Here's an example of a basic math operation in Python (Figure 14-1 shows an example — taken from Python's MatPlotLib library — of a more advanced output):

```
>>> 2.5+3
5.5
```

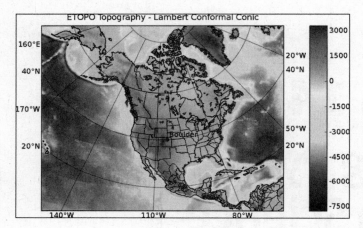

FIGURE 14-1:
Sample output
from Python's
MatPlotLib
library.

Regardless of the task at hand, you should always study the most basics concepts of a language before attempting to delve into its more specialized libraries.

Because Python is an object-oriented programming language, everything in Python is considered an object. In Python, an *object* is anything that can be assigned to a variable or passed as an argument to a function. The following items are all considered objects in the Python programming language:

- » Numbers
- » Strings
- » Lists
- » Tuples
- » Sets
- » Dictionaries
- » Functions
- » Classes

Additionally, all these items except for the last two in the list function as basic data types in plain ol' Python, which is Python with no external extensions added to it. (I introduce you to the external Python libraries NumPy, SciPy, Pandas, MatPlotLib, and Scikit-learn in the section "Checking Out Some Useful Python Libraries," later in this chapter; when you add these libraries, additional data types become available to you.)

In Python, functions do basically the same thing as they do in plain math — they accept data inputs, process them, and output the result. Output results depend wholly on the task the function was programmed to do. Classes, on the other hand, are prototypes of objects that are designed to output additional objects.

REMEMBER

If your goal is to write fast, reusable, easy-to-modify code in Python, you must use functions and classes. Doing so helps to keep your code efficient and organized.

Sorting Out the Python Data Types

If you do much work with Python, you need to know how to work with different data types. The main data types in Python and the general forms they take are described in this list:

>> **Numbers:** Plain old numbers, obviously

>> **Strings:** '. . .' or ". . ."

>> **Lists:** [. . .] or [. . ., . . ., . . .]

>> **Tuples:** (. . .)

>> **Sets:** Rarely used

>> **Dictionaries:** {'Key': 'Value', . . .}.

Numbers and strings are the most basic data types. You can incorporate them inside other, more complicated data types. All Python data types can be assigned to variables.

REMEMBER

In Python, numbers, strings, lists, tuples, sets, and dictionaries are classified as both object types and data types.

Numbers in Python

The numbers data type represents numeric values that you can use to handle all types of mathematical operations. Numbers come in the following types:

>> **Integers:** A whole-number format

>> **Long:** A whole-number format with an unlimited digit size

>> **Float:** A real-number format, written with a decimal point

>> **Complex:** An imaginary-number format, represented by the square root of –1

Strings in Python

Strings are the most often used data type in Python — and in every other programming language, for that matter. Simply put, a *string* consists of one or more characters written inside single or double quotes. The following code represents a string:

```
>>> variable1='This is a sample string'
>>> print(variable1)
This is a sample string
```

In this code snippet, the string is assigned to a variable, and the variable subsequently acts like a storage container for the string value.

To print the characters contained inside the variable, simply use the predefined function, `print`.

Python coders often refer to lists, tuples, sets, and dictionaries as data *structures* rather than data *types*. *Data structures* are basic functional units that organize data so that it can be used efficiently by the program or application you're working with.

Lists, tuples, sets, and dictionaries are data structures, but keep in mind that they're still composed of one or more basic data types (numbers and/or strings, for example).

Lists in Python

A *list* is a sequence of numbers and/or strings. To create a list, you simply enclose the elements of the list (separated by commas) within square brackets. Here's an example of a basic list:

```
>>> variable2=["ID","Name","Depth","Latitude","Longitude"]
>>> depth=[0,120,140,0,150,80,0,10]
>>> variable2[3]
'Latitude'
```

Every element of the list is automatically assigned an index number, starting from 0. You can access each element using this index, and the corresponding value of the list will be returned. If you need to store and analyze long arrays of data, use lists — storing your data inside a list makes it fairly easy to extract statistical information. The following code snippet is an example of a simple computation to pull the mean value from the elements of the depth list created in the preceding code example:

```
>>> sum(depth)/len(depth)
62.5
```

In this example, the average of the list elements is computed by first summing up the elements, via the sum function, and then dividing them by the number of the elements contained in the list. See, it's as simple as 1-2-3!

Tuples in Python

Tuples are just like lists, except that you can't modify their content after you create them. Also, to create tuples, you need to use normal brackets instead of squared ones. Here's an example of a tuple:

```
>>> depth=(0,120,140,0,150,80,0,10)
```

In this case, you can't modify any of the elements, like you would with a list. If you want to ensure that your data stays in a read-only format, use tuples.

Sets in Python

A *set* is another data structure that's similar to a list. In contrast to lists, however, elements of a *set* are unordered. This disordered characteristic of a set makes it impossible to index, so it's not a commonly used data type.

Dictionaries in Python

Dictionaries are data structures that consist of pairs of keys and values. In a dictionary, every value corresponds to a certain key, and consequently, each value can be accessed using that key. The following code snippet shows a typical key/ value pairing:

```
>>> variable4={"ID":1,"Name":"Valley City","Depth":0,
        "Latitude":49.6, "Longitude":-98.01}
>>> variable4["Longitude"]
-98.01
```

Putting Loops to Good Use in Python

When working with lists in Python, you typically access a list element by using the element index number. In a similar manner, you can access other elements of the list by using their corresponding index numbers. The following code snippet illustrates this concept:

```
>>>variable2=["ID","Name","Depth","Latitude","Longitude"]
>>> print(variable2[3])
Latitude
>>> print(variable2[4])
Longitude
```

WARNING

Don't let the index numbering system confuse you. Every element of the list is automatically assigned an index number starting from 0 — *not* starting from 1. That means the fourth element in an index actually bears the index number 3.

When you're analyzing considerable amounts of data and you need to access each element of a list, this technique becomes quite inefficient. In these cases, you should use a looping technique instead.

You can use *looping* to execute the same block of code multiple times for a sequence of items. Consequently, rather than manually access all elements one by one, you simply create a loop to automatically *iterate* (or pass through in successive cycles) each element of the list.

You can use two types of loops in Python: the for loop and the while loop. The most often used looping technique is the for loop — designed especially to iterate through sequences, strings, tuples, sets, and dictionaries. The following code snippet illustrates a for loop iterating through the variable2 list created in the preceding code:

```
>>> for element in variable2:print(element)
ID
```

```
Name
Depth
Latitude
Longitude
```

The other available looping technique in Python is the `while` loop. Use a `while` loop to perform actions while a given condition is true.

Looping is crucial when you work with long arrays of data, such as is the case when working with raster images. Looping allows you to apply certain actions to all data or to apply those actions to only predefined groups of data.

Having Fun with Functions

Functions (and classes, which I describe in the following section) are the crucial building blocks of almost every programming language. They provide a way to build organized, reusable code. Functions are blocks of code that take an input, process it, and return an output. Function inputs can be numbers, strings, lists, objects, or functions. Python has two types of functions: built-in and custom. *Built-in* functions are predefined inside Python. You can use them by just typing their names.

The following code snippet is an example of the built-in function `print`:

```
>>> print("Hello")
Hello
```

The highly used built-in function `print` prints out a given input. The code behind `print` has already been written by the people who created Python. Now that this code stands in the background, you don't need to know how to code it yourself — you simply call the `print` function. The people who created the Python library couldn't guess every possible function to satisfy everyone's needs, but they managed to provide users with a way to create and reuse their own functions when necessary.

In the section "Sorting Out the Python Data Types," earlier in this chapter, the code snippet from that section (listed again here) was used to calculate the average of elements in a list:

```
>>> depth=[0,120,140,0,150,80,0,10]
>>> sum(depth)/len(depth)
62.5
```

The preceding data actually represents snowfall and snow depth records from multiple point locations. As you can see, the points where snow depth measurements were collected have an average depth of 62.5 units. These are depth measurements taken at only one time, though. In other words, all the data bears the same time-stamp. When modeling data using Python, you often see scenarios in which sets of measurements were taken at different times — known as *time-series* data.

Here's an example of time-series data:

```
>>> december_depth=[0,120,140,0,150,80,0,10]
>>> january_depth=[20,180,140,0,170,170,30,30]
>>> february_depth=[0,100,100,40,100,160,40,40]
```

You could calculate December, January, and February average snow depth in the same way you averaged values in the previous list, but that would be cumbersome. This is where custom functions come in handy:

```
>>> def
        average(any_list):return(sum(any_list)/len(any_list))
```

This code snippet defines a function named average, which takes any list as input and calculates the average of its elements. The function is not executed yet, but the code defines what the function does when it later receives some input values. In this snippet, any_list is just a variable that's later assigned the given value when the function is executed. To execute the function, all you need to do is pass it a value. In this case, the value is a real list with numerical elements:

```
>>> average(february_depth)
72
```

Executing a function is straightforward. You can use functions to do the same thing repeatedly, as many times as you need, for different input values. The beauty here is that, once the functions are constructed, you can reuse them without having to rewrite the calculating algorithm.

Keeping Cool with Classes

Although *classes* are blocks of code that put together functions and variables to produce other objects, they're slightly different from functions. The set of functions and classes tied together inside a class describes the blueprint of a certain object. In other words, classes spell out what has to happen in order for an object to be created. After you come up with a class, you can generate the actual object instance by calling a class instance. In Python, this is referred to as *instantiating* an object — creating an instance of that class, in other words.

REMEMBER

Functions that are created inside of a class are called *methods,* and variables within a class are called *attributes.* Methods describe the actions that generate the object, and attributes describe the actual object properties.

To better understand how to use classes for more efficient data analysis, consider the following scenario: Imagine that you have snow depth data from different locations and times and you're storing it online on an FTP server. The dataset contains different ranges of snow depth data, depending on the month of the year. Now imagine that every monthly range is stored in a different location on the FTP server.

Your task is to use Python to fetch all the monthly data and then analyze the entire dataset, so you need to use different operations on the data ranges. First, download the data from within Python by using an FTP handling library, such as `ftplib`. Then, to be able to analyze the data in Python, you need to store it in proper Python data types (in lists, tuples, or dictionaries, for example). After you fetch the data and store it as recognizable data types in a Python script, you can then apply more advanced operations that are available through specialized libraries such as NumPy, SciPy, Pandas, MatPlotLib, and Scikit-learn.

In this scenario, you want to create a class that creates a list containing the snow depth data for each month. Every monthly list would be an object instance generated by the class. The class itself would tie together the FTP downloading functions and the functions that store the downloaded records inside the lists. You can then instantiate the class for as many months as you need in order to carry out a thorough analysis. The code to do something like this is shown in Listing 14-1.

LISTING 14-1: **Defining a Class in Python**

```
class Download:
    def __init__(self,ftp=None,site,dir,fileList=[]):
        self.ftp =ftp
        self.site=site
        self.dir=dir
        self.fileList=fileList
        self.Login_ftp()
            self.store_in_list()
    def Login_ftp(self):
        self.ftp=ftplib.FTP(self.site)
        self.ftp.login()
    def store_in_list(self):
        fileList=[]
        self.ftp.cwd("/")
        self.ftp.cwd(self.dir)
        self.ftp.retrlines('NLST',fileList.append)
        return fileList
```

Defining a class probably looks intimidating right now, but I simply want to give you a feeling for the basic structure and point out the class methods involved.

Delving into Listing 14-1, the keyword class defines the class, and the keyword def defines the class methods. The __init__ function is a default function that you should always define when creating classes, because you use it to declare class variables. The Login_ftp method is a custom function that you define to log in to the FTP server. After you log in through the Login_ftp method and set the required directory where the data tables are located, you then store the data in a Python list using the custom function store_in_list.

After you finish defining the class, you can use it to produce objects. You just need to instantiate the class:

```
>>> Download("ftpexample.com","ftpdirectory")
```

And that's it! With this brief snippet, you've just declared the particular FTP domain and the internal FTP directory where the data is located. After you execute this last line, a list appears, giving you data that you can manipulate and analyze as needed.

Checking Out Some Useful Python Libraries

In Python, a *library* is a specialized collection of scripts that were written by someone else to perform specialized sets of tasks. To use specialized libraries in Python, you must first complete the installation process. (For more on installing Python and its various libraries, check out the "Analyzing Data with Python — an Exercise" section, later in this chapter.) After you install your libraries on your local hard drive, you can import any library's function into a project by simply using the import statement. For example, if you want to import the ftplib library, you write

```
>>> import ftplib
```

REMEMBER

Be sure to import the library into your Python project before attempting to call its functions in your code.

After you import the library, you can use its functionality inside any of your scripts. Simply use *dot notation* (a shorthand way of accessing modules, functions, and classes in one line of code) to access the library. Here's an example of dot notation:

```
>>> ftplib.any_ftp_lib_function
```

REMEMBER

Though you can choose from countless libraries to accomplish different tasks in Python, the Python libraries most commonly used in data science are NumPy, SciPy, Pandas, MatPlotLib, and Scikit-learn. The NumPy and SciPy libraries were specially designed for scientific uses, Pandas was designed for optimal data analysis performance, and MatPlotLib library was designed for data visualization. Scikit-learn is Python's premiere machine learning library.

Saying hello to the NumPy library

NumPy is the Python package that primarily focuses on working with n-dimensional array objects, and SciPy, described next, extends the capabilities of the NumPy library. When working with plain Python (Python with no external extensions, such as libraries, added to it), you're confined to storing your data in 1-dimensional lists. But if you extend Python by using the NumPy library, you're provided a basis from which you can work with n-dimensional arrays. (Just in case you were wondering, *n-dimensional* arrays are arrays of one dimension or of multiple dimensions.)

REMEMBER

To enable NumPy in Python, you must first install and import the library. After that, you can generate multidimensional arrays.

To see how generating n-dimensional arrays works in practice, start by checking out the following code snippet, which shows how you'd create a 1-dimensional NumPy array:

```
import numpy
>>> array_1d=numpy.arange(8)
>>> print(array_1d)
[0 1 2 3 4 5 6 7]
```

After importing numpy, you can use it to generate n-dimensional arrays, such as the 1-dimensional array just shown. One-dimensional arrays are referred to as *vectors.* You can also create multidimensional arrays using the reshape method, like this:

```
>>> array_2d=numpy.arange(8).reshape(2,4)
>>> print(array_2d)
[[0 1 2 3]
 [4 5 6 7]]
```

The preceding example is a 2-dimensional array, otherwise known as a 2 × 4 *matrix*. Using the `arange` and `reshape` method is just one way to create NumPy arrays. You can also generate arrays from lists and tuples.

In the snow dataset that I introduce in the earlier section "Having Fun with Functions," I store my snow depth data for different locations inside three separate Python lists — one list per month:

```
>>> december_depth=[0,120,140,0,150,80,0,10]
>>> january_depth=[20,180,140,0,170,170,30,30]
>>> february_depth=[0,100,100,40,100,160,40,40]
```

It would be more efficient to have the measurements stored in a better-consolidated structure. For example, you could easily put all those lists in a single NumPy array by using the following code snippet:

```
>>>depth=numpy.array([december_depth,january_depth,february_
        depth])
>>> print(depth)
[[  0 120 140   0 150  80   0  10]
 [ 20 180 140   0 170 170  30  30]
 [  0 100 100  40 100 160  40  40]]
```

Using this structure allows you to pull out certain measurements more efficiently. For example, if you want to calculate the average of the snow depth for the first location in each of the three months, you'd extract the first elements of each horizontal row (values 0, 20, and 0, to be more precise). You can complete the extraction in one line of code by applying slicing and then calculating the mean through the NumPy `mean` function. Here's an example:

```
>>> numpy.mean(depth[:,0])
6.666666666666667
```

Beyond using NumPy to extract information from single matrices, you can use it to interact with different matrices as well. You can use NumPy to apply standard mathematical operations between matrices, or even to apply nonstandard operators, such as matrix inversion, summarize, and minimum/maximum operators.

REMEMBER

Array objects have the same rights as any other objects in Python. You can pass them as parameters to functions, set them as class attributes, or iterate through array elements to generate random numbers.

Getting up close and personal with the SciPy library

SciPy is a collection of mathematical algorithms and sophisticated functions that extends the capabilities of the NumPy library. The SciPy library adds some specialized scientific functions to Python for more specific tasks in data science. To use SciPy's functions within Python, you must first install and import the SciPy library.

Some sticklers out there consider SciPy to be an extension of the NumPy library. That's because SciPy was *built on top of* NumPy — it uses NumPy functions, but adds to them.

SciPy offers functionalities and algorithms for a variety of tasks, including vector quantization, statistical functions, discrete Fourier transform–algorithms, orthogonal distance regression, airy functions, sparse eigenvalue solvers, maximum entropy fitting routines, n-dimensional image operations, integration routines, interpolation tools, sparse linear algebra, linear solvers, optimization tools, signal-processing tools, sparse matrices, and other utilities that are not served by other Python libraries. Impressive, right? Yet that's not even a complete listing of the available SciPy utilities. If you're dying to get hold of a complete list, running the following code snippet in Python will open an extensive help module that explains the SciPy library:

```
>>> import scipy
>>> help(scipy)
```

You need to first download and install the SciPy library before you can use this code.

The `help` function used in the preceding code snippet returns a script that lists all utilities that comprise SciPy and documents all of SciPy's functions and classes. This information helps you understand what's behind the prewritten functions and algorithms that make up the SciPy library.

Because SciPy is still under development, and therefore changing and growing, regularly check the `help` function to see what's changed.

Peeking into the Pandas offering

The Pandas library makes data analysis much faster and easier with its accessible and robust data structures. Its precise purpose is to improve Python's performance with respect to data analysis and modeling. It even offers some data visualization functionality by integrating small portions of the MatPlotLib library. The two main Pandas data structures are described in this list:

>> **Series:** A Series object is an array-like structure that can assume either a horizontal or vertical dimension. You can think of a Pandas Series object as being similar to one row or one column from an Excel spreadsheet.

>> **DataFrame:** A DataFrame object acts like a tabular data table in Python. Each row or column in a DataFrame can be accessed and treated as its own Pandas Series object.

Indexing is integrated into both data structure types, making it easy to access and manipulate your data. Pandas offers functionality for reading in and writing out your data, which makes it easy to use for loading, transferring, and saving datasets in whatever formats you want. Lastly, Pandas offers excellent functionality for reshaping data, treating missing values, and removing outliers, among other tasks. This makes Pandas an excellent choice for data preparation and basic data analysis tasks. If you want to carry out more advanced statistical and machine learning methods, you'll need to use the Scikit-learn library. The good news is that Scikit-learn and Pandas play well together.

Bonding with MatPlotLib for data visualization

Generally speaking, data science projects usually culminate in visual representations of objects or phenomena. In Python, things are no different. After taking baby steps (or some not-so-baby steps) with NumPy and SciPy, you can use Python's MatPlotLib library to create complex visual representations of your dataset or data analysis findings. MatPlotLib, when combined with NumPy and SciPy, creates an excellent environment in which to work when solving problems using data science.

Looking more closely at MatPlotLib, I can tell you that it is a 2-dimensional plotting library you can use in Python to produce figures from data. You can use MatPlotLib to produce plots, histograms, scatter plots, and a variety of other data graphics. What's more, because the library gives you full control of your visualization's symbology, line styles, fonts, and colors, you can even use MatPlotLib to produce publication-quality data graphics.

REMEMBER

As is the case with all other libraries in Python, to work with MatPlotLib you first need to install and import the library into your script. After you complete those tasks, it's easy to get started producing graphs and charts.

To illustrate how to use MatPlotLib, consider the following NumPy array (which I came up with in the "Saying hello to the NumPy library" section, earlier in this chapter):

```
>>> print(depth)
[[   0 120 140    0 150  80    0  10]
 [  20 180 140    0 170 170   30  30]
 [   0 100 100   40 100 160   40  40]]
```

With the following few lines of code, using just a for loop and a MatPlotLib function — pyplot — you can easily plot all measurements in a single graph within Python:

```
>>> import matplotlib.pyplot as plt
>>> for month in depth:
        plt.plot(month)
>>> plt.show()
```

This code snippet instantly generates the line chart you see in Figure 14-2.

Each line in the graph represents the depth of snow at different locations in the same month. The preceding code you use to build this graph is simple; if you want to make a better representation, you could add color or text font attributes to the plot function. Of course, you can also use other types of data graphics, depending on which types best show the data trends you want to display. What's important here is that you know when to use each of these important libraries and that you understand how you can use the Python programming language to make data analysis both easy and efficient.

Learning from data with Scikit-learn

Scikit-learn is far and away Python's best machine learning library. With it, you can execute all sorts of machine learning methods, including classification, regression, clustering, dimensionality reduction, and more. The library also offers a preprocessing module that is wonderfully supportive whenever you need to prepare your data for predictive modeling. Lastly, Scikit-learn offers a model selection module that's readily available with all sorts of metrics to help you build your models and choose the best performing model among a selection.

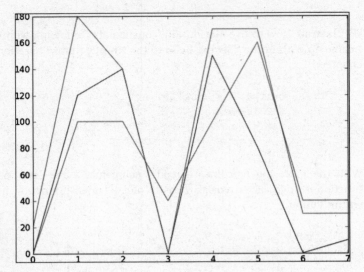

FIGURE 14-2:
Time-series plot of monthly snow depth data.

Analyzing Data with Python — an Exercise

Most of Python's recent growth has been among users from the science community, which means that most users probably didn't study computer science in school yet find programming to be a skill they must have in order to work in their respective fields. Python's uncomplicated, human-readable syntax and its welcoming user community have created a large and dedicated user base. The remainder of this chapter can help get you started in analyzing data using Python.

In the exercise I spell out in this section, I refer to a hypothetical classroom dataset, but I want to start out by showing you where to go to do an easy install-and-setup of a good Python programming environment. From there, I show you how to import the classroom-data CSV file into Python, how to use Python to calculate a weighted grade average for students in the class, and how to use Python to generate an average trendline of student grades.

Installing Python on the Mac and Windows OS

The Mac comes with a basic version of Python preinstalled; Windows doesn't ship with Python. Whether you're on the Mac or a Windows PC, I recommend downloading a free Python distribution that gives you easy access to as many useful modules as possible. I've tried several distributions — the one I recommend is Anaconda, by Continuum Analytics (available from `https://store.continuum.io/cshop/anaconda`). It comes with more than 150 Python packages, including NumPy, SciPy, Pandas, MatPlotLib, and Scikit-learn.

To do something of any magnitude in Python, you also need a programming environment. Anaconda comes with the IPython programming environment, which I recommend. IPython, which runs in Jupyter Notebooks (from directly within your web browser), allows you to write code in separate cells and then see the results for each step. To open Jupyter in your web browser after installing Anaconda, just navigate to, and open, the Jupyter Notebook program. That program automatically launches the web browser application, shown in Figure 14-3.

REMEMBER

When you're using data science to solve problems, you aren't writing the programs yourself. Rather, you're using prebuilt programming tools and languages to interact with your data.

TECHNICAL STUFF

When you download your free Python distribution, you have a choice between version 2 or version 3. In 2010, the Python language was completely overhauled to make it more powerful in ways that only computer scientists would understand. The problem is that the new version is not *backward-compatible* — in other words, Python 2 scripts aren't compatible with a Python 3 environment. Python 2 scripts need syntax changes to run in Python 3. This sounds like a terrible situation, and though it's not without controversy, most *pythonistas* (Python users) are fine with it.

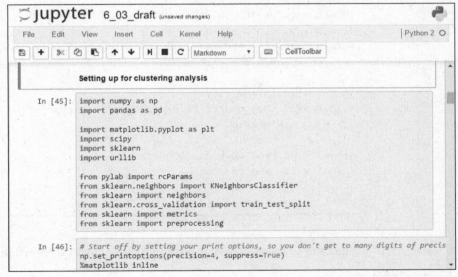

FIGURE 14-3:
The Jupyter Notebook / IPython programming environment.

Source: Lynda.com, Python for DS

TIP

I highly recommend that you use the final Python 2 release, version Python 2.7. As of late 2016, that version is still being used by the majority of Python users (caveat: except perhaps those whom hold a degree in Computer Science). It performs great for data science, it's easier to learn than Python 3, and sites such as GitHub have millions of snippets and scripts that you can copy to make your life easier.

Loading CSV files

To load data from a comma-separated values (CSV) file, use the Pandas library. I walk you through the process in the code shown in Listing 14-2. For this exercise, you'll need to download the class_grades.csv file from the GitHub repository for this course (at https://github.com/BigDataGal/Data-Science-for-Dummies). Before getting started, make sure to place your data file — the class_grades.csv file, to be precise — in the Jupyter Notebooks folder. By default, IPython always looks at the Jupyter Notebooks folder to find any external files that are called by your code.

REMEMBER

Just in case you don't know about commenting yet, in Python a coder can insert comments on the code by prefixing every comment line with the *hash symbol* (#). All comments are invisible to the application — they aren't acted on — but they are visible to the programmers and their buddies (and to their enemies, for that matter).

LISTING 14-2: Sample Code for Loading a CSV File into Python

```
import pandas as pd
import numpy as np
import matplotlib.pyplot as plt
from scipy import stats
# This loads the modules I'll use throughout this notebook, giving
        each a short alias.


%matplotlib inline
# This will show charts below each cell instead of in a separate
        viewer.


grades = pd.read_csv('class_grades.csv')
# That's it, you're done!

print grades.head()
```

Figure 14-4 shows you what IPython comes up with when fed this code.

TIP

If you want to limit the code output to the first five rows only, you can use the head() function.

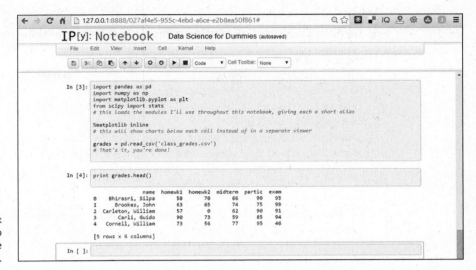

FIGURE 14-4:
Using Pandas to
import a CSV file
into Jupyter.

Calculating a weighted average

Okay, so you've fed IPython (if you've read the preceding section) a lot of student grades that were stored in a CSV file. The question is, how do you want these grades calculated? In other words, how do you want to weigh each separate component of the grade?

I'm just going to make a command decision and say that final grades are to be calculated this way:

» Homework assignment 1 = 10 percent

» Homework assignment 2 = 10 percent

» Midterm = 25 percent

» Class participation = 10 percent

» Final exam = 45 percent

With Pandas, you can easily calculate each student's weighted final grade. Listing 14-3 shows you how it's done.

LISTING 14-3: **Sample Code for Calculating a Weighted Average in Python**

```
import pandas as pd
import numpy as np
import matplotlib.pyplot as plt
from scipy import stats
%matplotlib inline
grades = pd.read_csv('class_grades.csv')
grades['grade'] = np.round((0.1 * grades.homewk1 + 0.1 * grades.
        homewk2 + 0.25 * grades.midterm + 0.1 * grades.partic +
        0.45 * grades.exam), 0)

# This creates a new column called 'grade' and populates it based on
        the values of other columns, rounded to an integer.

print grades.tail()
```

Figure 14-5 shows the results of your new round of coding.

REMEMBER

If you want to limit your code output to the last five rows only, you can use the `tail()` function.

Just for fun, you can calculate letter grades with a `letter_grade` function and `if` commands. The code is shown in Listing 14-4, and the results are shown in Figure 14-6.

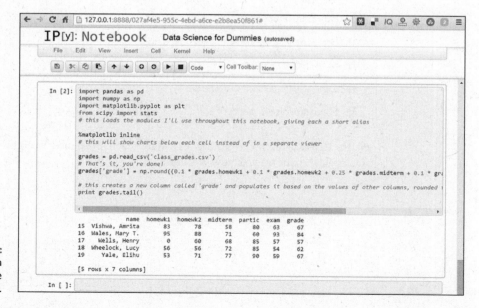

FIGURE 14-5:
Calculating a
weighted average
in IPython.

LISTING 14-4: **Using a `letter_grade` Function and an `if` Command in Python**

```python
def calc_letter(row):
    if row.grade >= 90:
        letter_grade = 'A'
    elif row['grade'] > 75:
        letter_grade = 'B'
    elif row['grade'] > 60:
        letter_grade = 'C'
    else:
        letter_grade = 'F'
    return letter_grade

# See how in Python there are no "then" statements, no braces, and
    few brackets or parentheses. Flow is determined by colons and
    indents.

grades['ltr'] = grades.apply(calc_letter, axis=1)

# "apply" with axis=1 applies a function to an entire column using
    values from the same row.

print grades
```

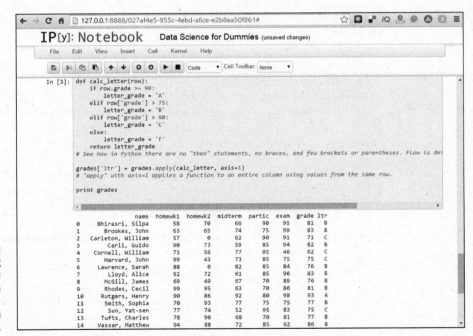

FIGURE 14-6:
Calculating
a weighted
average using a
letter_grade
function and an
if command.

Drawing trendlines

Using SciPy, you can easily draw a *trendline* — a line on a chart that indicates the overall trend of a dataset. Popular kinds of trendlines include best-fit lines, regression lines, and ordinary least squares lines. In this section, I show you how to track the progress of any student in our hypothetical class, from the beginning of the semester to the end. For this example, I've created a trendline for the first student, Silpa Bhirasri. You can generate a trendline for any student, however, simply by plugging that person's name into the student variable.

To use SciPy, you first need to make a basic Python ordered list (denoted by numbers or strings in square brackets) and then turn those numbers or strings into a NumPy array. This new array allows you to run calculations on all values at one time, rather than have to write code to run over each of the values separately. Lastly, you calculate the best-fit line for *y*-values (the *x*-values are always the same as the original series) and draw the chart in the Jupyter Notebook using four lines of code from the MatPlotLib library. Listing 14-5 puts it all together for you.

LISTING 14-5: **Sample Code for Creating a Trendline in Python**

```
student = 'Bhirasri, Silpa'

y_values = [] # create an empty list
for column in ['homewk1', 'homewk2', 'midterm', 'partic', 'exam']:
    y_values.append(grades[grades.name == student][column].iloc[0])
# Append each grade in the order it appears in the dataframe.
print y_values

x = np.array([1, 2, 3, 4, 5])
y = np.array(y_values)
slope, intercept, r, p, slope_std_err = stats.linregress(x, y)
# This automatically calculates the slope, intercept, Pearson
            correlation, coefficient (r), and two other statistics I
            won't use here.

bestfit_y = intercept + slope * x
# This calculates the best-fit line to show on the chart.

plt.plot(x, y, 'ko')
# This plots x and y values; 'k' is the standard printer's
            abbreviation for the color 'blacK', and 'o' signifies
            markers to be circular.
```

```
plt.plot(x, bestfit_y, 'r-')
# This plots the best fit regression line as a 'r'ed line('-').

plt.ylim(0, 100)
# This sets the upper and lower limits of the y axis.
# If it were not specified, the minimum and maximum values would
        be used.

plt.show() # since the plot is ready, it will be shown below the
        cell
print 'Pearson coefficient (R) = ' + str(r)
```

Figure 14-7 shows the trendline for the student named Silpa Bhirasri.

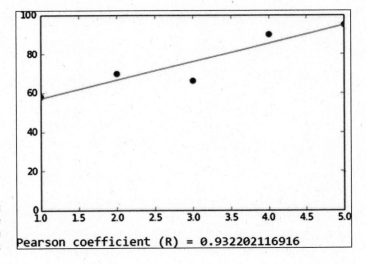

FIGURE 14-7:
A trendline
generated in
IPython.

Pearson coefficient (R) = 0.932202116916

From the trendline shown in the figure, you can see that Silpa's grades steadily improved all semester, except for a little dip at the midterm. At about 0.93, the Pearson correlation coefficient is high, indicating that Silpa's grades improved, and it's close to a linear progression. For more on the Pearson coefficient, check out Chapter 5.

Chapter **15**

Using Open Source R for Data Science

R is an open-source, free statistical software system that, like Python, has been widely adopted across the data science sector over the past decade. In fact, a somewhat never-ending squabble takes place among data science types about which programming language is best suited for data science. Practitioners who favor R generally do so because of its advanced statistical programming and data visualization capabilities — capabilities that simply can't be replicated in Python. When it comes to data science practitioners, specifically, R's user base is broader than Python's. (For more on Python, see Chapter 14.)

You can download the R programming language and the packages that support it from `http://cran.r-project.org`.

R is not as easy to learn as Python, but R can be more powerful for certain types of advanced statistical analyses. Although R's learning curve is somewhat steeper than Python's, the programming language is nonetheless relatively straightforward. All you really need to do is master the basic vocabulary used to describe the language and then it shouldn't be too hard to get a grasp on how the software works.

R's Basic Vocabulary

Although the vocabulary associated with R may sound exotic at first, you can quickly master it through practice. For starters, you can run R in one of these two modes:

» **Non-interactive:** You run your R code by executing it as a .r file (the .r file extension is the one that's assigned to script files created for execution by the R program) directly from the command line.

» **Interactive:** You generally work in a software application that interacts with you by prompting you to enter your data and R code. In an R session within interactive mode, you can import datasets or enter the raw data directly; assign names to variables and data objects; and use functions, operators, and built-in iterators to help you gain some insight into your source data.

REMEMBER

R is an *object-oriented* language, which simply means that the different parts that comprise the language belong to classes — each class has its own specific definition and role. A specific example of a class is known as an *instance* of that class, and so it inherits the class's characteristics. Classes are *polymorphic:* The subclasses of a class can have their own set of unique behaviors yet share some of the same functionality of the parent class. To illustrate this concept, consider R's print function: print( ). Because this function is polymorphic, it works slightly differently depending on the class of the object it's told to print. Thus, this function and many others perform the same general job in many classes but differ slightly according to class. In the section "Observing How Objects Work," later in this chapter, I elaborate on object-oriented programming and its advantages, but for now I want to introduce objects and their names and definitions.

R works with the following main object types:

» **Vector:** A *vector* is an ordered list of the same mode — character (alphanumeric), numeric, or Boolean. Vectors can have any number of dimensions. For instance, the vector A = ["a", "cat", "def"] is a 3-dimensional vector of mode character. B = [2, 3.1, –5, 33] is a 4-dimensional vector of mode numerical. To identify specific elements of these vectors, you could enter the following codes at the prompt in interactive mode to get R to generate the following returns: A[[1]] = "a" or A[[2]] = "cat" or A[[3]] = "def" or B[[1]] = 2 or B[[2]] = 3.1 or B[[3]] = –5 or B[[4]] = 33. R views a single number as a vector of dimension one. Because they can't be broken down further in R, vectors are also known as *atomic vectors* (which are not the same as *generic vectors* that are actually list objects, as I discuss under "Lists").

R's treatment of atomic vectors gives the language tremendous advantages with respect to speed and efficiency (as I describe in the section "Iterating in R," later in this chapter).

>> **Matrix:** Think of a *matrix* as a collection of vectors. A matrix can be of any mode (numerical, character, or Boolean), but all elements in the matrix must be of the same mode. A matrix is also characterized by its number of dimensions. Unlike a vector, a matrix has only two dimensions: number of rows and number of columns.

>> **List:** A *list* is a list of items of arbitrary modes, including other lists or vectors.

Lists are sometimes also called *generic vectors* because some of the same operations performed on vectors can be performed on lists as well.

TECHNICAL STUFF

>> **Data frame:** A *data frame* is a type of list that's analogous to a table in a database. Technically speaking, a data frame is a list of vectors, each of which is the same length. A row in a table contains the information for an individual record, but elements in the row most likely will not be of the same mode. All elements in a specific column, however, are all of the same mode. Data frames are structured in this same way — each vector in a data frame corresponds to a column in a data table, and each possible index for these vectors is a row.

There are two ways to access members of vectors, matrices, and lists in R:

>> **Single brackets** [ ] give a vector, matrix, or list (respectively) of the element(s) that are indexed.

>> **Double brackets** [[ ]] give a single element.

R users sometimes disagree about the proper use of the brackets for indexing. Generally speaking, the double bracket has several advantages over the single bracket. For example, the double bracket returns an error message if you enter an index that's out of bounds. If, however, you want to indicate more than one element of a vector, matrix, or list, you should use a single bracket.

Now that you have a grasp of R's basic vocabulary, you're probably eager to see how it works with some actual programming. Imagine that you're using a simple EmployeeRoll dataset and entering the dataset into R by hand. You'd come up with something that looks like Listing 15-1.

LISTING 15-1: **Assigning an Object and Concatenating in R**

```
> EmployeeRoll <- data.frame(list(EmployeeName=c("Smith,
      John","O'Bannon, Tom","Simmons, Sarah"),Grade=c(10,8,12),
      Salary=c(100000,75000,125000), Union=c(TRUE, FALSE,
      TRUE)))
> EmployeeRoll
    EmployeeName Grade Salary Union
1      Smith,John    10 100000   TRUE
2  O'Bannon, Tom     8  75000 FALSE
3 Simmons, Sarah    12 125000   TRUE
```

The combined symbol <– in the first line of Listing 15-1 is pronounced "gets." It assigns the contents on its right to the name on its left. You can think of this relationship in even simpler terms by considering the following statement, which assigns the number 3 to the variable c:

```
> c <- 3
```

Line 1 of Listing 15-1 also exhibits the use of R's concatenate function — c( ) — which is used to create a vector. The concatenate function is being used to form the atomic vectors that comprise the vector list that makes up the EmployeeRoll data frame. Line 2 of Listing 15-1, EmployeeRoll, instructs R to display the object's contents on the screen. (Figure 15-1 breaks out the data in more diagrammatic form.)

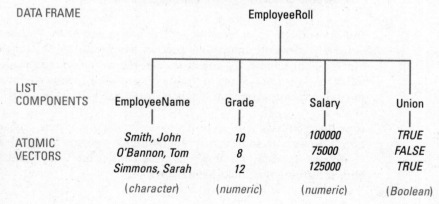

FIGURE 15-1: The relationship between atomic vectors, lists, and data-frame objects.

One other object within R is vitally important: the function. *Functions* use atomic vectors, matrices, lists, and data frames to accomplish whatever analysis or computation you want done. (In the following section, I discuss functions more thoroughly. For now, you should simply understand their general role.) Each analysis you perform in R may be done in one or more sessions, which consists of entering a set of instructions that tells R what you want it to do with the data you've entered or imported. In each session, you specify the functions of your script. Then the blocks of code process any input that's received and return an output. A function's input (also known as a function's *arguments*) can be any R object or combination of objects — vectors, matrices, arrays, data frames, tables, or even other functions.

Invoking a function in R is known as *calling* a function.

TECHNICAL STUFF

Commenting in R works the same as in Python. (Python is covered in Chapter 14.) As an R coder, you'd insert any comments you may have on the code by prefixing them with a *hash symbol* — the # symbol, in other words.

Delving into Functions and Operators

You can choose one of two methods when writing your functions: a quick, simple method and a more complex, but ultimately more useful, method. Of course, you achieve the same result from choosing either approach, but each method is advantageous in its own ways. If you want to call a function and generate a result as simply and as quickly as possible, and if you don't think you'll want to reuse the function later, use Method 1. If you want to write a function that you can call for different purposes and use with different datasets in the future, then use Method 2 instead.

To illustrate the difference between these two methods, consider again the EmployeeRoll dataset defined in Listing 15-1. Say you want to come up with a function you can use to derive a mean value for employee salary. Using the first, simpler method, you call a single function to handle that task: You simply define an operation by writing the name of the function you want to use, and then include whatever argument(s) the function requires in the set of parentheses following the function name. More specifically, you call the built-in statistical function mean( ) to calculate the mean value of employee salaries, as shown here:

```
> #Method 1 of Calculating the Mean Salary
> MeanSalary1 <- mean(EmployeeRoll$Salary)
> MeanSalary1
[1] 1e+05
```

In this method, the mean( ) function calculates and saves the average salary, 100,000 (or 1e+05, in scientific notation) as an object (a vector, of course!) named MeanSalary1.

The $ symbol refers R to a particular field in the dataset. In this example, it's referring R to the `Salary` field of the `EmployeeRoll` dataset.

Method 2 illustrates a more complicated but possibly more useful approach. Rather than define only a single operation, as in Method 1, Method 2's function can define a series of separate operations if they're needed; therefore, the method can oftentimes get quite complex. In the following chunk of code, the statement `MeanSalary2 <- function(x)` creates a function named `MeanSalary2`, which takes one argument, x. The statements between the curly braces ({ }) make up this function. The job of {`return(mean(x))`} is to calculate the mean of some entity x and then return that value as a result to the computer screen:

```
> #Method 2 of Calculating the Mean Salary
> #This method allows the user to create a custom set of
        instructions for R that can be used again and again.
> MeanSalary2 <- function(x) {return(mean(x))}
>
> MeanSalary2(EmployeeRoll$Salary)
[1] 1e+05
```

The argument of the function definition isn't the `Salary` field from the `EmployeeRoll` dataset, because this type of function can be called and used for different purposes on different datasets and different fields of said datasets. Also, nothing happens when you finish typing the function and press Return after entering the ending curly brace; in the next line, you just get another prompt (>). That's because you set up the function correctly. (You know it's correct because you didn't get an error message.) You now can call this function when you actually need it — that's what the last instruction entered at the prompt in the preceding code does. Typing `MeanSalary2(EmployeeRoll$Salary)` is a *function call,* and it replaces the function's placeholder argument x with `EmployeeRoll$Salary` — a real object that allows the function to generate a solution.

Of course, the function that's written in Method 2 yields the same mean salary as did the function in Method 1, but the Method 2 function can now be reused for different applications. To illustrate how you'd use this same function on a different dataset, imagine that you have another business with its own payroll. It has five employees with the following salaries: $500,000; $1,000,000; $75,000; $112,000; and $400,000. If you want to call and use the `MeanSalary2` function to find the mean salary of these employees, you could simply write the following:

```
> MeanSalary2(c(500000,1000000,75000,112000,400000))
[1] 417400
```

As instructed in Method 2, the MeanSalary2 function quickly generates a mean value for this new dataset — in this case, $417,400.

The primary benefit of using functions in R is that they make it easier to write cleaner, more concise code that's easy to read and more readily reusable. But at the most fundamental level, R is simply using functions to apply operators. Although applying operators and calling functions both serve the same purpose, you can distinguish the two techniques by their differing syntaxes. R uses many of the same operators that are used in other programming languages. Table 15-1 lists the more commonly used operators.

Operators act as functions in R. (I *warned* you that learning the vocabulary of R can be tricky!)

REMEMBER

TABLE 15-1

Popular Operators

Operation	Operator
plus	+
minus	–
times	*
divide	/
modulo	%%
power	^
greater than	>
greater than or equal to	>=
less than	<
less than or equal to	<=
equals	==
not equals	!=
not (logical)	!
and (logical)	&
or (logical)		
is assigned; gets	<-
is assigned to	->

This code snippet shows several examples of where operators are used as functions:

```
> "<"(2,3)
[1] TRUE
> "<"(100,10)
[1] FALSE
> "+"(100,1)
[1] 101
> "/"(4,2)
[1] 2
> "+"(2,5,6,3,10)
Error in `+`(2, 5, 6, 3, 10) : operator needs one or two
          arguments
```

In the preceding code, the Boolean operators less than (<) and greater than (>) return a value of either TRUE or FALSE. Also, do you see the error message that's generated by the last line of code? That error happened because the operator + can take only one or two arguments, and in that example, I provided three arguments more than it could handle.

TIP

You can use the + operator to add two numbers or two vectors. In fact, all arithmetic operators in R can accept both numbers and vectors as arguments. For more on arithmetic operators, check out the following section.

Iterating in R

Because of the way R handles vectors, programming in R offers you an efficient way to handle loops and iterations. Essentially, R has built-in iterators that automatically loop over elements without the added hassle of you having to write out the loops yourself.

To better conceptualize this process, called *vectorization*, imagine that you want to add a constant c = 3 to a series of three numbers that you've stored as a vector, m = [10, 6, 9]. You can use the following code:

```
> c <- 3
> m <- c(10, 6, 9)
> m <- m + c
> m
[1] 13  9 12
```

The preceding method works because of an R property known as *recyclability:* If you're performing operations on two vectors that aren't the same length, R repeats and reuses the smaller vector to make the operation work. In this example, c was a 1-dimensional vector, but R reused it to convert it to a 3-dimensional vector so that the operation could be performed on m.

Here's the logic behind this process:

```
10          3          13
6     +     3     =     9
9           3          12
```

This method works also because of the vectorization of the + operator, which performs the + operation on the vectors m and c — in effect, looping through each of the vectors to add their corresponding elements.

Here's another way of writing this process that makes the vectorization of the + operator obvious:

```
> m <- "+"(m,c)
```

TIP

R vectorizes all arithmetic operators, including +, −, /, *, and ^.

When you're using conditional statements within iterative loops, R uses vectorization to make this process more efficient. If you've used other programming languages, you've probably seen a structure that looks something like this:

```
for (y = 1 through 5) {     if (3*y <= 4) then z = 1     else
    z = 0}
```

This loop iterates the code within the brackets ({ }) sequentially for each y equal to 1, 2, 3, 4, and 5. Within this loop, for each y-value, the conditional statement 3*y <= 4 generates either a TRUE or a FALSE statement. For y-values that yield TRUE values, z is set to 1; otherwise, it's set to 0. This loop thus generates the following:

```
| y | 3*y | 3*y <= 4 | z |
| 1 | 3 | TRUE | 1 |
| 2 | 6 | FALSE | 0 |
| 3 | 9 | FALSE | 0 |
| 4 | 12 | FALSE | 0 |
| 5 | 15 | FALSE | 0 |
```

Now check out how you can do this same thing using R:

```
> y <- 1:5
> z <- ifelse(3*y <= 4, 1, 0)
> z
[1] 1 0 0 0 0
```

It's much more compact, right? In the preceding R code, the y term represents the numerical vector [1, 2, 3, 4, 5]. As was the case earlier, in the R code the operator <= is vectorized, and recyclability is again applied so that the apparent scalar 4 is treated as a 5-dimensional vector [4, 4, 4, 4, 4] to make the vector operation work. As before, only where y = 1 is the condition met and, consequently, z[[1]] = 1 and z[2:5] = 0.

TIP

In R, you often see something that looks like 1:10. This *colon operator* notates a sequence of numbers — the first number, the last number, and the sequence that lies between them. Thus, the vector 1:10 is equivalent to 1, 2, 3, 4, 5, 6, 7, 8, 9, 10 and 2:5 is equal to 2, 3, 4, 5.

Observing How Objects Work

R's object-oriented approach makes deploying and maintaining code relatively quick and easy. As part of this object-oriented functionality, objects in R are distinguished by characteristics known as *attributes*. Each object is defined by its attributes; more specifically, each object is defined by its class attribute.

As an example, the USDA provides data on the percentages of insect-resistant and herbicide-tolerant corn planted per year, for years ranging from 2000 through 2014. You could take this information and use a linear regression function to predict the percentage of herbicide-tolerant corn planted in Illinois during 2000 to 2014, from the percentage of insect-resistant corn planted in Illinois during these same years. The dataset and function are shown in Listing 15-2.

LISTING 15-2: **Exploring Objects in R**

```
> GeneticallyEngineeredCorn <- data.frame(list(year=c(2000, 2001,
        2002, 2003, 2004, 2005, 2006, 2007, 2008, 2009, 2010,
        2011, 2012, 2013, 2014),Insect =c(13,
        12,18,23,26,25,24,19,13,  10,  15,  14,  14,  4,  3),
        herbicide=c(3,3,3,4,5,6,12,15,15,15,15,17,18,7,5)))
> GeneticallyEngineeredCorn
```

```
     year Insect herbicide
1    2000     13        3
2    2001     12        3
3    2002     18        3
4    2003     23        4
5    2004     26        5
6    2005     25        6
7    2006     24       12
8    2007     19       15
9    2008     13       15
10   2009     10       15
11   2010     15       15
12   2011     14       17
13   2012     14       18
14   2013      4        7
15   2014      3        5
> PredictHerbicide <-
         lm(GeneticallyEngineeredCorn$herbicide ~
         GeneticallyEngineeredCorn$Insect)
> attributes(PredictHerbicide)$names
 [1] "coefficients"  "residuals"    "effects"     "rank"
 [5] "fitted.values" "assign"       "qr"          "df.residual"
 [9] "xlevels"       "call"         "terms"       "model"
> attributes(PredictHerbicide)$class
 [1] "lm"
> PredictHerbicide$coef
              (Intercept) GeneticallyEngineeredCorn$Insect
         10.52165581                      -0.06362591
```

In Listing 15-2, the expression PredictHerbicide <- lm(GeneticallyEngineered Corn$herbicide ~ GeneticallyEngineeredCorn$Insect) instructs R to perform a linear regression and assign the results to the PredictHerbicide object. In the linear regression, GeneticallyEngineeredCorn is defined as the source dataset, the Insect column acts as the independent variable, and the herbicide column acts as the dependent variable.

R's attribute function allows you to get information about an object's attributes. In this example, typing in the function attribute(PredictHerbicide)$names instructs R to name all attributes of the PredictHerbicide object, and the function attribute(PredictHerbicide)$class instructs R to identify the object's classes. You can see from Listing 15-2 that the PredictHerbicide object has 12 attributes and has class lm (which stands for linear model).

R allows you to request specifics on each of these attributes; but to keep this example brief, simply ask R to specify the coefficients of the linear regression equation. Looking back, you can see that this is the first attribute that's provided for the `PredictHerbicide` object. To ask R to show the coefficients obtained by fitting the linear model to the data, enter `PredictHerbicide$coef`, as shown in Listing 15-2, and R returns the following information:

```
(Intercept) GeneticallyEngineeredCorn$Insect
10.52165581                           -0.06362591
```

In plain math, the preceding result translates into the equation shown in Figure 15-2.

FIGURE 15-2:
Linear regression coefficients from R, translated into a plain math equation.

$$\left(\%_{\text{herbicide-resistant corn}}\right)_{\text{Illinois, 2000-2014}} = 10.52165581 - 0.06362591\left(\%_{\text{insect-resistance corn}}\right)_{\text{Illinois, 2000-2014}}$$

Translated into mathematical terms, this is equivalent to the following:

Percentage of Genetically Engineered Herbicide-Tolerant Corn = 10.5 – 0.06*Percentage of Genetically Engineered Insect-Resistant Corn

Thus the relationship between the two variables appears rather weak, so the percentage of genetically engineered, insect-resistant corn planted wouldn't provide a good predictor of percentage of herbicide-resistant corn planted.

This example also illustrates the polymorphic nature of generic functions in R — that is, where the same function can be adapted to the class it's used with, so that function is applicable to many different classes. The polymorphic function of this example is R's `attributes( )` function. This function is applicable to the `lm` (linear model) class, the `mean` class, the `histogram` class, and many others.

REMEMBER

If you want to get a quick orientation when working with instances of an unfamiliar class, R's polymorphic generic functions can come in handy. These functions generally tend to make R a more efficiently mastered programming language.

Sorting Out Popular Statistical Analysis Packages

R has a plethora of easy-to-install packages and functions, many of which are quite useful in data science. In an R context, *packages* are bundles composed of specific functions, data, and code suited for performing specific types of analyses or sets of analyses. The CRAN site lists the current packages available for download at http://cran.r-project.org/web/packages, along with directions on how to download and install them. In this section, I discuss some popular packages and then delve deeper into the capabilities of a few of the more advanced packages that are available.

The robust R packages can help you do things like forecasting, multivariate analysis, and factor analysis. In this section, I quickly present an overview of a few of the more popular packages that are useful for this type of work.

R's forecast package contains various forecasting functions that you can adapt to use for ARIMA (*AutoRegressive Integrated Moving Average* time series forecasting), or for other types of univariate time series forecasts. Or perhaps you want to use R for quality management. You can use R's Quality Control Charts package (qcc) for quality and statistical process control.

In the practice of data science, you're likely to benefit from almost any package that specializes in multivariate analysis. If you want to carry out logistic regression, you can use R's *multinomial logit model* (mlogit), in which observations of a known class are used to "train" the software so that it can identify classes of other observations whose classes are unknown. (For example, you could use logistic regression to train software so that it can successfully predict customer churn, which you can read about in Chapter 3.)

If you want to use R to take undifferentiated data and identify which of its factors are significant for some specific purpose, you can use factor analysis. To better illustrate the fundamental concept of factor analysis, imagine that you own a restaurant. You want to do everything you can to make sure your customer satisfaction rating is as high as possible, right? Well, factor analysis can help you determine which exact factors have the largest impact on customer satisfaction ratings — those could coalesce into the general factors of ambience, restaurant layout, and employee appearance/attitude/knowledge. With this knowledge, you can work on improving these factors to increase customer satisfaction and, with that, brand loyalty.

REMEMBER

Few people enter data manually into R. Data is more often imported from either Microsoft Excel or a relational database. You can find driver packages available to import data from various types of relational databases, including RSQLite, RPostgreSQL, RMySQL, and RODBC, as well as packages for many other RDBMSs. One of R's strengths is how it equips users with the ability to produce publication-quality graphical illustrations or even just data visualizations that can help you understand your data. The ggplot2 package offers a ton of different data visualization options; I tell you more about this package later in this chapter.

For information on additional R packages, look through the R Project website at www.r-project.org. You can find a lot of existing online documentation to help you identify what packages best suit your needs. Also, coders in R's active community are making new packages and functions available all the time.

Examining Packages for Visualizing, Mapping, and Graphing in R

If you've read earlier sections in this chapter, you should have (I hope!) a basic understanding of how functions, objects, and R's built-in iterators work. You also should be able to think of a few data science tasks that R can help you accomplish. In the remainder of this chapter, I introduce you to some powerful R packages for data visualization, network graph analysis, and spatial point pattern analysis.

Visualizing R statistics with ggplot2

If you're looking for a fast and efficient way to produce good-looking data visualizations that you can use to derive and communicate insights from your datasets, look no further than R's ggplot2 package. It was designed to help you create all different types of data graphics in R, including histograms, scatter plots, bar charts, boxplots, and density plots. It offers a wide variety of design options as well, including choices in colors, layout, transparency, and line density. ggplot2 is useful if you want to do data showcasing, but it's probably not the best option if you're looking to do data storytelling or data art. (You can read about these data visualization design options in Chapter 9.)

To better understand how the ggplot2 package works, consider the following example. Figure 15-3 shows a simple scatter plot that was generated using ggplot2. This scatter plot depicts the concentrations (in parts per million, or ppm) of four types of pesticides that were detected in a stream between the years 2000 to 2013. The scatter plot could have been designed to show only the pesticide concentrations for each year, but ggplot2 provides an option for fitting a regression line to each of the pesticide types. The regression lines are the solid lines shown on the plot. ggplot2 can also present these pesticide types in different colors. The colored areas enclosing the regression lines represent 95 percent confidence intervals for the regression models.

The scatter plot chart makes it clear that all pesticides except for ryanoids are showing decreasing stream concentrations. Organochlorides had the highest concentration in 2000, but then exhibited the greatest decrease in concentration over the 13-year period.

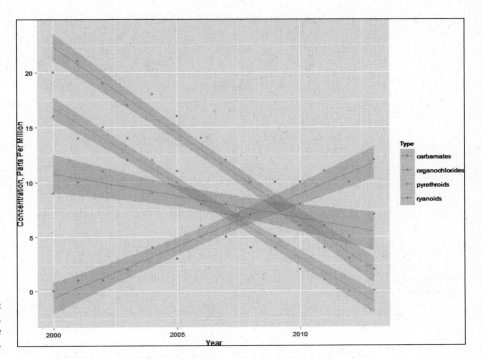

FIGURE 15-3:
A scatter plot,
generated in the
ggplot2 package.

Analyzing networks with statnet and igraph

Social networks and social network data volumes have absolutely exploded over the past decade. Therefore, knowing how to make sense of network data has become increasingly important for analysts. Social network analysis skills enable you to analyze social networks to uncover how accounts are connected and the ways in which information is shared across those connections. You can use network analysis methods to determine how fast information spreads across the Internet. You can even use network analysis methods in genetic mapping to better understand how one gene affects and influences the activity of other genes, or use them in hydraulic modeling to figure out how to best design a water-distribution or sewer-collection system.

Two R packages were explicitly written for network analysis purposes: statnet and igraph. You can use either statnet or igraph to collect network statistics or statistics on network components. Figure 15-4 shows sample output from network analysis in R, generated using the statnet package. This output is just a simple network in which the direction of the arrows shows the direction of flow within the network, from one vertex to another. The network has five vertices and nine *faces* — connections between the vertices.

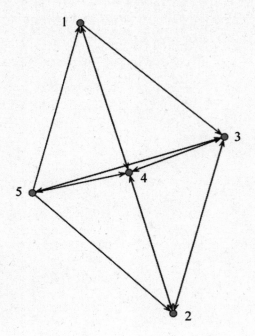

Mapping and analyzing spatial point patterns with spatstat

If you want to analyze spatial data in R, you can use the spatstat package. This package is most commonly used in analyzing point pattern data, but you can also use it to analyze line patterns, pixels, and linear network data. By default, the package installs with geographical, ecological, and environmental datasets that you can use to support your analyses, if appropriate. With its space-time point pattern analysis capabilities, spatstat can help you visualize a spatiotemporal change in one or several variables over time. The package even comes with 3-dimensional graphing capabilities. Because spatstat is a geographic data analysis package, it's commonly used in ecology, geosciences, and botany, or for environmental studies, although the package could easily be used for location-based studies that relate to business, logistics, sales, marketing, and more.

» **Designing great relational databases**

» **Doing data science tasks with SQL functions**

Chapter **16**

Using SQL in Data Science

S QL, or *Structured Query Language,* is a standard for creating, maintaining, and securing relational databases. It's a set of rules that you can use to quickly and efficiently query, update, modify, add, or remove data from large and complex databases. You use SQL, rather than Python or Excel, to do these tasks because SQL is the simplest, fastest way to get the job done. It offers a plain and standardized set of core commands and methods that are easy to use when performing these tasks. In this chapter, I introduce you to basic SQL concepts and explain how you can use SQL to do cool things, like query, join, group, sort, and even text-mine structured datasets.

Although you can use SQL to work with structured data that resides in relational database management systems, you can't use standard SQL as a solution for handling big data, because you can't handle big data using relational database technologies. I give you more solutions for handling big data in Chapter 2, where I discuss data engineering and its components. For now, suffice it to say that SQL is simply a tool you can use to manipulate and edit structured data tables. It's nothing exceedingly innovative, but it can be helpful to use SQL for the data querying and manipulation tasks that often arise in the practice of data science. In this chapter, I introduce the basics of relational databases, SQL, and database design.

Getting a Handle on Relational Databases and SQL

Although the name Structured Query Language suggests that SQL is a programming language, don't be misled. SQL is not a programming language like R or Python. Rather, it's a language of commands and syntax that you can use only to create, maintain, and search relational database systems. SQL supports a few common programming forms, like conditionals and loops, but to do anything more complex, you'd have to import your SQL query results into another programming platform and then do the more complex work there.

TECHNICAL STUFF

SQL has become so ubiquitous in the data field that its passionate users commonly debate whether SQL should be pronounced "ess-cue-el" or "sequel." Most users I've met lean toward the latter.

One fundamental characteristic of SQL is that you can use it on only structured data that sits in a relational database. SQL database management systems (DBMSs) optimize their own structure with minimal user input, which enables blazing-fast operational performance.

REMEMBER

An *index* is the lookup table you create in order to index (and point to) data in tables of a database. Although SQL DBMSs are known for their fast structured database querying capabilities, this speed and effectiveness are heavily dependent on good indexing. Good indexing is vital for fast data retrieval in SQL.

Similar to how different web browsers comply with, add to, and ignore different parts of the HTML standard in different ways, SQL rules are interpreted a bit differently, depending on whether you're working open-source or commercial vendor software applications. Because not every SQL solution is the same, it's a good idea to know something about the benefits and drawbacks of some of the more popular SQL solutions on the market. Here are the three most popular open-source SQL implementations among data scientists:

>> **SQLite:** This software is more limited than other SQL implementations, especially when it comes to user management and performance-enhancing customizations, but it's a fantastic place to get started when you're first learning to use SQL.

>> **MySQL:** MySQL is by far the most popular open-source version of SQL. It offers a complete and powerful version of SQL, and it's used on the back end of millions of websites.

>> **PostgreSQL:** This software adds object-oriented elements to SQL's relational language, making it popular with programmers who want to integrate SQL objects into their own platforms' object model.

REMEMBER

Other powerful commercial SQL implementations, such as Oracle and Microsoft SQL Server, are great solutions as well, but they're designed for use in business rather than as a data science tool.

As you might guess from the name, the most salient aspect of *relational* databases is that they're relational: They're composed of related tables. To illustrate the idea of a relational database, first imagine an Excel spreadsheet with rows, columns, and predefined relationships between shared columns. Then imagine having an Excel workbook with many worksheets (tables), in which every worksheet has a column with the same name as a column in one or more *other* worksheets. Because these worksheets have a shared relationship, if you use SQL you can use that shared relationship to look up data in all related worksheets. This type of relationship is illustrated in Figure 16-1.

REMEMBER

The *primary key* of a table is a column of values that uniquely identifies every row in that table. A good example of primary keys is the use of ISBN numbers for a table of books or employee ID numbers for a table of employees. A *foreign key* is a column in one table that matches the primary key of another and is used to link tables.

Foreign Key

Lake Name	Max Water Depth (ft)	Average Annual Depth Change (in)
Lake Monroe	...	...
Lake Lilly	...	...
Lake Conway	...	...

Primary Key

Lake Name	Alkalinity (mEq/L)	Total Dissolved Solids (ppm)	Phosphates (u g/L)
Lake Monroe	...	...	...
Lake Lilly	...	...	...
Lake Conway	...	...	...

Foreign Key

Lake Name	Subdivision Name	Taxing District
Lake Monroe	...	...
Lake Lilly	...	...
Lake Conway	...	...

FIGURE 16-1:
A relationship between data tables that share a column.

Keeping the focus on terminology, remember that proper database science often associates particular meanings to particular words, as you can see in this list:

» **Columns,** called fields, keys, and attributes

» **Rows,** called records

» **Cells,** called values

REMEMBER

Database science uses a *lot* of synonyms. For simplicity's sake, I try to stick to using the words *column, row,* and *cell.* And because *primary key* and *foreign key* are standard terms, I use them to describe these two special column types.

The main benefits of using relational database management systems (RDBMSs, for short) is that they're fast, they have large storage and handling capacity (compared to spreadsheet applications such as Excel), and they're ideal tools to help you maintain *data integrity* — the consistency and accuracy of data in your database. If you need to make quick and accurate changes and updates to your datasets, you can use SQL and a RDBMS.

Let the following scenario serve as an illustration. This table describes films and lists ratings from viewers:

id	title	genre	rating timestamp	rating
1	The Even Couple	NULL	2011-08-03 16:04:23	4
2	The Fourth Man	Drama	2014-02-19 19:17:16	5
2	The Fourth Man	Drama	2010-04-27 10:05:36	4
3	All About Adam	Drama	2011-04-05 21:21:05	4
3	All About Adam	Drama	2014-02-21 00:11:07	3
4	Dr. Yes	Thriller	NULL	

What happens if you find out that *All About Adam* is a comedy rather than a drama? If the table were in a simple spreadsheet, you'd have to open the data table, find all instances of the film, and then manually change the genre value for that record. That's not so difficult in this sample table because only two records are related to that film. But even here, if you forget to change one of these records, this inconsistency would cause a loss of data integrity, which can cause all sorts of unpredictable problems for you down the road.

In contrast, the relational database solution is simple and elegant. Instead of one table for this example, you'd have three:

Film	id	title
	1	The Even Couple
	2	The Fourth Man

```
        3    All About Adam
        4    Dr. Yes


Genre   id    genre
        2     Drama
        3     Drama
        4     Thriller


Rating  timestamp             id   rating
        2011-08-03 16:04:23   1    4
        2014-02-19 19:17:16   2    5
        2010-04-27 10:05:36   2    4
        2011-04-05 21:21:05   3    4
        2014-02-21 00:11:07   3    3
```

The primary key for the Film and Genre tables is id. The primary key for the Rating table is timestamp — because a film can have more than one rating, id is not a unique field and, consequently, it can't be used as a primary key. In this example, if you want to look up and change the genre for *All About Adam*, you'd use Film.id as the primary key and Genre.id as the foreign key. You'd simply use these keys to query the records you need to change and then apply the changes systematically. This systematic approach eliminates the risk of stray errors.

Investing Some Effort into Database Design

If you want to ensure that your database will be useful to you for the foreseeable future, you need to invest time and resources into excellent database design. If you want to create databases that offer fast performance and error-free results, your database design needs to be flawless, or as flawless as you can manage. Before you enter any data into a data table, first carefully consider the tables and columns you want to include, the kinds of data those tables will hold, and the relationships you want to create between those tables.

REMEMBER

Every hour you spend planning your database and anticipating future needs can save you countless hours down the road, when your database might hold a million records. Poorly planned databases can easily turn into slow, error-ridden monstrosities — avoid them at all costs.

Keep just a few principles in mind when you design databases:

>> Data types

>> Constraints

>> Normalization

In the next few sections, I help you take a closer look at each topic.

Defining data types

When creating a data table, one of the first things you have to do is define the data type of each column. The data type can be designated from any of the following options:

>> **Text:** If your column is to contain text values, you can classify it as a Character data type with a fixed length or a Text data type of indeterminate length.

>> **Numerical:** If your column is to hold number values, you can classify it as a Numerical data type. These can be stored as integers or floats.

>> **Date:** If your column is to hold date- or time-based values, you can designate this as a Date data type or Date-Time data type.

Text data types are handy, but they're terrible for searches. If you plan to query a column, assign that column a fixed length.

REMEMBER

Designing constraints properly

Properly designed constraints are an important consideration in database design. You can think of them, in the context of SQL, as rules that are used to control the type of data that can be placed in a table. When you're considering adding constraints, first decide whether each column is allowed to hold a NULL value. (NULL is not the same as blank or zero data; it indicates a total absence of data in a cell.)

For example, if you have a table of products you're selling, you probably don't want to allow a NULL in the Price column. In the Product Description column, however, some products may have *long* descriptions, so you might allow some of the cells in this column to contain NULL values.

Within any data type, you can also constrain exactly what type of input values the column accepts. Imagine that you have a text field for Employee ID, which must contain values that are exactly two letters followed by seven numbers, like this:

SD0154919. Because you don't want your database to accept a typo, you'd define a constraint that requires all values entered into the cells of the Employee ID column to have exactly two letters followed by seven numbers.

Normalizing your database

After you've defined the data types and designed constraints, you need to deal with *normalization* — structuring your database so that any changes, additions, or deletions to the data have to be done only once and won't result in anomalous, inconsistent data. There are many different degrees and types of normalization (at least seven), but a good, robust, normalized SQL database should have at least the following properties:

>> **Primary keys:** Each table has a *primary key,* which is a unique value for every row in that column.

>> **Non-redundancy of columns:** No two tables have the same column, unless it's the primary key of one and the foreign key of the other.

>> **No multiple dependencies:** Every column's value must depend on only one other column, whose value does not in turn depend on any other column. *Calculated values* — values such as the total for an invoice, for example — must therefore be done on the fly for each query and should not be hard-coded into the database. This means that Zip codes should be stored in a separate table because a Zip code depends on three columns — address, city, and state.

>> **Column indexes:** As you may recall, in SQL an index is a lookup table that points to data in tables of a database. When you make a *column index* — an index of a particular column — each record in that column is assigned a unique key value that's indexed in a lookup table. Column indexing enables faster data retrieval from that column.

It's an excellent idea to create a column index for frequent searches or to be used as a search criterion. The column index takes up memory, but it increases your search speeds tremendously. It's easy to set up, too. Just tell your SQL DBMS to index a certain column, and then the system sets it up for you.

TIP

If you're concerned that your queries are slow, first make sure that you have all the indexes you need before trying other, perhaps more involved, trouble-shooting efforts.

>> **Subject-matter segregation:** Another feature of good database design is that each table contains data for only one kind of subject matter. This is not exactly a normalization principle *per se,* but it helps to achieve a similar end.

Consider again the film rating example, from an earlier section:

```
Film    id   title
        1    The Even Couple
        2    The Fourth Man
        3    All About Adam
        4    Dr. Yes


Genre   id   genre
        2    Drama
        3    Drama
        4    Thriller


Rating  timestamp             id   rating
        2011-08-03 16:04:23   1    4
        2014-02-19 19:17:16   2    5
        2010-04-27 10:05:36   2    4
        2011-04-05 21:21:05   3    4
        2014-02-21 00:11:07   3    3
```

I could have designated Genre to be a separate column in the Film table, but it's better off in its own table because that allows for the possibility of missing data values (NULLs). Look at the Film table shown above. Film 1 has no genre assigned to it. If the Genre column were included in this table, then Film 1 would have a NULL value there. Rather than have a column that contains a NULL value, it's much easier to make a separate Genre data table. The primary keys of the Genre table don't align exactly with those of the Film table, but they don't need to when you go to join them.

TIP

NULL values can be quite problematic when you're running a SELECT query. When you're querying based on the value of particular attribute, any records that have a null value for that attribute will not be returned in the query results. Of course, these records would still exist, and they may even fall within the specified range of values you've defined for your query, but if the record has a null value, it will be omitted from the query results. In this case, you're likely to miss them in your analysis.

Any data scientist worth her salt must address many challenges, when dealing with either the data or the science. SQL takes some of the pressure off when you're dealing with the time-consuming tasks of storing and querying data, saving precious time and effort.

Integrating SQL, R, Python, and Excel into Your Data Science Strategy

Some data scientists are resistant to learning SQL because of the cognitive overhead. They think, "I've already memorized a bunch of commands for dealing with data in R or Python. Won't it be confusing to switch over to a whole new language?" In the case of SQL, no, it's not that confusing, and it's worth the small degree of hassle. Although the SQL standard is lengthy, a user commonly needs fewer than 20 commands, and the syntax is human-readable. Making things even easier, SQL commands are written in ALL CAPS, which helps to keep the language distinct and separate in your mind from other programming languages.

If you want to integrate SQL capabilities into your R or Python workflow, every DBMS has a library or module that you can use. Generally, it's a good idea to take advantage of SQL's speed by doing as much work in SQL as possible, and then accessing the SQL database from within your scripting language only when necessary. In this type of procedure, you'd translate query results into native R or Python data forms only when you finish with SQL and have all the data you need.

You can also integrate Microsoft Excel with your work in SQL. You can use MySQL to import your databases into Excel using the Data Ribbon (the Ribbon's Other Sources button, to be precise), or you can save your Excel tables as text files and import them into the DBMS. If you're not working in MySQL, look around online and you'll be sure to find plug-ins for integrating other DBMSs into Excel. Some plug-ins are even free.

Narrowing the Focus with SQL Functions

When working with SQL commands, you use *functions* to perform tasks, and *arguments* to more narrowly specify those tasks. To query a particular set from within your data tables, for example, use the SELECT function. To combine separate tables into one, use the JOIN function. To place limits on the data that your query returns, use a WHERE argument. As I say in the preceding section, fewer than 20 commands are commonly used in SQL. This section introduces SELECT, FROM, JOIN, WHERE, GROUP, MAX(), MIN(), COUNT(), AVG(), and HAVING.

The most common SQL command is SELECT. You can use this function to generate a list of search results based on designated criteria. To illustrate, imagine the film-rating scenario mentioned earlier in this chapter with a tiny database of movie ratings that contains the three tables Film, Genre, and Rating.

To generate a printout of all data FROM the Rating table, use the SELECT function. Any function with SELECT is called a *query,* and SELECT functions accept different arguments to narrow down or expand the data that is returned. Since an asterisk (∗) represents a wildcard, the asterisk in SELECT ∗ tells the *interpreter* — the SQL component that carries out all SQL statements — to show every column in the table. You can then use the WHERE argument to limit the output to only certain values. For example, here is the complete Rating table:

```
Rating  timestamp              id   rating
        2011-08-03 16:04:23    1    4
        2014-02-19 19:17:16    2    5
        2010-04-27 10:05:36    2    4
        2011-04-05 21:21:05    3    4
        2014-02-21 00:11:07    3    3
```

If you want to limit your ratings to those made after a certain time, you'd use code like that shown in Listing 16-1.

LISTING 16-1: **Using SELECT, WHERE, and DATE() to Query Data**

```
SELECT ∗ FROM Rating
WHERE Rating.timestamp >= date('2014-01-01')
timestamp              id   rating
2014-02-19 19:17:16    2    5
2014-02-21 00:11:07    3    3
```

In Listing 16-1, the DATE() function turns a string into a date that can then be compared with the timestamp column.

You can also use SQL to join columns into a new data table. Joins are made on the basis of shared (or compared) data in a particular column (or columns). There are several ways you can execute a join in SQL, but the ones listed here are probably the most popular:

>> **Inner join:** The default JOIN type; returns all records that lie in the intersecting regions between the tables being queried

>> **Outer join:** Returns all records that lie outside the overlapping regions between queried data tables

>> **Full outer join:** Returns all records that lie both inside and outside the overlapping regions between queried data tables — in other words, returns all records for both tables

» **Left join:** Returns all records that reside in the leftmost table

» **Right join:** Returns all records that reside in the rightmost table

REMEMBER

Be sure to differentiate between an inner join and an outer join because these functions handle missing data in different ways. As an example of a join in SQL, if you want a list of films that includes genres, you use an inner join between the Film and Genre tables to return only the results that intersect (overlap) between the two tables.

To refresh your memory, here are the two tables you're interested in:

```
Film    id    title
        1     The Even Couple
        2     The Fourth Man
        3     All About Adam
        4     Dr. Yes


Genre   id    genre
        2     Drama
        3     Drama
        4     Thriller
```

Listing 16-2 shows how you'd use an inner join to get the information you want.

LISTING 16-2: **An Inner JOIN Function**

```
SELECT Film.id, Film.title, Genre.genre
FROM Film
JOIN Genre On Genre.id=Film.id
id    title              genre
2     The Fourth Man     Drama
3     All About Adam     Drama
4     Dr. Yes            Thriller
```

In Listing 16-2, I name specific columns (Film.title and Genre.genre) after the SELECT command. I do this to avoid creating a duplicate id column in the table that results from the JOIN — one id from the Film table and one id from the Genre table. Since the default for JOIN is inner, and inner joins return only records that are overlapping or shared between tables, Film 1 is omitted from the results (due to its missing genre value).

If you want to return all rows, even ones with NULL values, simply do a full outer join, like the one shown in Listing 16-3.

A Full Outer JOIN

```
SELECT Film.id, Film.title, Genre.genre
FROM Film
FULL JOIN Genre On Genre.id=Film.id
id    title              genre
1     The Even Couple    NULL
2     The Fourth Man     Drama
3     All About Adam     Drama
4     Dr. Yes            Thriller
```

To aggregate values so that you can figure out the average rating for a film, use the GROUP statement. (GROUP statement commands include MAX(), MIN(), COUNT(), or AVG().) Listing 16-4 shows one way you could aggregate values.

In Listing 16-4, the average rating of films was returned; the AS statement was used in SELECT to rename the column, to make sure it was properly labeled. The Film and Ratings tables had to be joined, and because *Dr. Yes* had no ratings and an inner join was used, that film was left out.

Using a GROUP Statement to Aggregate Data

```
SELECT Film.title, AVG(rating) AS avg_rating
FROM Film
JOIN Rating On Film.id=Rating.id
GROUP BY Film.title

title              avg_rating
All About Adam     3.5
The Even Couple    4.0
The Fourth Man     4.5
```

To narrow the results even further, add a HAVING clause at the end, as shown in Listing 16-5.

LISTING 16-5: **A HAVING Clause to Narrow Results**

```
SELECT Film.title, AVG(rating) AS avg_rating
FROM Film
JOIN Rating On Film.id=Rating.id
GROUP BY Film.title
HAVING avg_rating >= 4
title            avg_rating
The Even Couple  4.0
The Fourth Man   4.5
```

The code in Listing 16-5 limits the data your query returns so that you get only records of titles that have an average rating greater than or equal to 4.

TECHNICAL STUFF

Though SQL can do some basic text mining, packages such as Natural Language Toolkit in Python (NLTK, at www.nltk.org) and General Architecture for Text Engineering (GATE, at https://gate.ac.uk) are needed in order to do anything more complex than counting words and combinations of words. These more advanced packages can be used for preprocessing of data to extract linguistic items such as parts of speech or syntactic relations, which can then be stored in a relational database for later querying.

MINING TEXT WITH SQL

In this era of big data, more and more analysis is being done on larger and larger amounts of raw text — from books to government procedures and even Twitter feeds. You can use the tm and nltk packages in R and Python, respectively, to process such data, but as scripting languages, they can be rather slow. That's why users commonly do some text mining in SQL. If you want to generate quick statistics on word counts and frequencies, you can use SQL to your advantage.

When the first SQL standard was published, its originators likely had no idea it would be used for these purposes, but the boundaries of SQL are being pushed and expanded all the time. This flexibility is yet another reason that SQL maintains its place as an indispensable tool among data science practitioners.

Chapter **17**

Doing Data Science with Excel and Knime

In this day and age, when it seems like every organization is reliant upon cloud-based applications, standard installable desktop applications are fewer and farther between. Nonetheless, there are still a few programs out there that you can install on your computer and use for data science tasks. In this chapter, I explain how you can use Microsoft Excel to perform some basic tasks to help simplify your project work in data science. I also introduce a free, open-source analytics platform called KNIME and discuss how you can use it to perform advanced data science tasks without having to learn how to code.

Making Life Easier with Excel

Microsoft Excel holds a special place among data science tools. It was originally designed to act as a simple spreadsheet. Over time, however, it has become the people's choice in data analysis software. In response to user demands, Microsoft has added more and more analysis and visualization tools with every release. As Excel advances, so do its data munging and data science capabilities. Excel 2013 includes easy-to-use tools for charting, pivot tables, and macros. It also supports scripting in Visual Basic so that you can design scripts to automate repeatable tasks.

The benefit of using Excel in a data science capacity is that it offers a fast and easy way to get up close and personal with your data. If you want to browse every data point in your dataset, you can quickly and easily do this using Excel. Most data scientists start in Excel and eventually add other tools and platforms when they find themselves pushing against the boundaries of the tasks Excel is designed to do. Still, even the best data scientists out there keep Excel as an important tool in their tool belt. When working in data science, you might not use Excel every day, but knowing how to use it can make your job easier.

REMEMBER

Although you have many different tools available to you when you want to see your data as one big forest, Excel is a great first choice when you need to look at the trees. Excel attempts to be many different things to many different kinds of users. Its functionality is well-compartmentalized, to avoid overwhelming new users, while still providing power users with the more advanced functionality they crave. In the following sections, I show you how you can use Excel to quickly get to know your data. I also introduce Excel pivot tables and macros, and tell you how you can use those to greatly simplify your data cleanup and analysis tasks.

Using Excel to quickly get to know your data

If you're just starting off with an unfamiliar dataset and you need to spot patterns or trends as quickly as possible, use Excel. Excel offers effective features for exactly these purposes. Its main features for a quick-and-dirty data analysis are

>> **Filters:** Filters are useful for sorting out all records that are irrelevant to the analysis at hand.

>> **Conditional formatting:** Specify a condition, and Excel flags records that meet that condition. By using conditional formatting, you can easily detect outliers and trends in your tabular datasets.

>> **Charts:** Charts have long been used to visually detect outliers and trends in data, so charting is an integral part of almost all data science analyses.

To see how these features work in action, consider the sample dataset shown in Figure 17-1, which tracks sales figures for three employees over six months.

Filtering in Excel

To narrow your view of your dataset to only the data that matters for your analysis, use Excel filters to filter irrelevant data out of the data view. Simply select the data and click the Home tab's Sort & Filter button, and then choose Filter from the

Salesperson	Month	Total Sales
Abbie	Jan	$ 10,144.75
Abbie	Feb	$ 29,008.52
Abbie	Mar	$ 208,187.70
Abbie	Apr	$ 21,502.13
Abbie	May	$ 23,975.73
Abbie	Jun	$ 20,172.20
Brian	Jan	$ 9,925.44
Brian	Feb	$ 9,183.93
Brian	Mar	$ 12,691.39
Brian	Apr	$ 19,521.37
Brian	May	$ 16,579.38
Brian	Jun	$ 14,161.52
Chris	Jan	$ 2,792.18
Chris	Feb	$ 5,669.46
Chris	Mar	$ 4,909.24
Chris	Apr	$ 8,731.14
Chris	May	$ 11,747.29
Chris	Jun	$ 13,856.17

FIGURE 17-1: The full dataset that tracks employee sales performance.

options that appear. A little drop-down option then appears in the header row of the selected data so that you can select the classes of records you want to have filtered from the selection. Using the Excel Filter functionality allows you to quickly and easily sort or restrict your view to only the subsets of the data that interest you the most.

Take another look at the full dataset shown in Figure 17-1. Say you want to view only data related to Abbie's sales figures. If you select all records in the Salesperson column and then activate the filter functionality (as just described), from the drop-down menu that appears you can specify that the filter should isolate only all records named Abbie, as shown in Figure 17-2. When filtered, the table is reduced from 18 rows to only 6 rows. With this particular example, that change doesn't seem so dramatic, but when you have hundreds, thousands, or even a million rows, this feature comes in very, very handy.

Excel lets you store only up to 1,048,576 rows per worksheet.

WARNING

Salesperson	Month	Total Sales
Abbie	Jan	$10,144.75
Abbie	Feb	$29,008.52
Abbie	Mar	$208,187.70
Abbie	Apr	$21,502.13
Abbie	May	$23,975.73
Abbie	Jun	$20,172.20

FIGURE 17-2: The sales performance dataset, filtered to show only Abbie's records.

Conditional formatting to spot outliers and trends in tabular data

To quickly spot outliers in your tabular data, use Excel's Conditional Formatting feature. Imagine after a data entry error that Abbie's March total sales showed $208,187.70 but was supposed to be only $20,818.77. You're not quite sure where the error is located, but you know that it must be significant because the figures seem off by about $180,000.

To quickly show such an outlier, select all records in the Total Sales column and then click the Conditional Formatting button on the Ribbon's Home tab. When the button's menu appears, choose the Data Bars option. Doing so displays the red data bar scales shown in Figure 17-3. With data bars turned on, the bar in the $208,187.70 cell is so much larger than any of the others that you can easily see the error.

If you want to quickly discover patterns in your tabular data, you can choose the Color Scales option (rather than the Data Bars option) from the Conditional Formatting menu. After correcting Abbie's March Total Sales figure to $20,818.77, select all cells in the Total Sales column and then activate the Color Scales version of conditional formatting. Doing so displays the result shown in Figure 17-4. From the red-white-blue heat map, you can see that Abbie has the highest sales total and that Brian has been selling more than Chris. (Okay, you can't see the red-white-blue in my black-and-white figures, but you can see the light-versus-dark contrast.)

Excel charting to visually identify outliers and trends

Excel's Charting tool gives you an incredibly easy way to visually identify both outliers and trends in your data. An XY (scatter) chart of the original dataset (refer to Figure 17-1) yields the scatter plot shown in Figure 17-5. As you can see, the outlier is overwhelmingly obvious when the data is plotted on a scatter chart.

Salesperson	Month	Total Sales
Abbie	Jan	$ 10,144.75
Abbie	Feb	$ 29,008.52
Abbie	Mar	$ 208,187.70
Abbie	Apr	$ 21,502.13
Abbie	May	$ 23,975.73
Abbie	Jun	$ 20,172.20
Brian	Jan	$ 9,925.44
Brian	Feb	$ 9,183.93
Brian	Mar	$ 12,691.39
Brian	Apr	$ 19,521.37
Brian	May	$ 16,579.38
Brian	Jun	$ 14,161.52
Chris	Jan	$ 2,792.18
Chris	Feb	$ 5,669.46
Chris	Mar	$ 4,909.24
Chris	Apr	$ 8,731.14
Chris	May	$ 11,747.29
Chris	Jun	$ 13,856.17

FIGURE 17-3: Spotting outliers in a tabular dataset with conditional formatting data bars.

Salesperson	Month	Total Sales
Abbie	Jan	$ 10,144.75
Abbie	Feb	$ 29,008.52
Abbie	Mar	$ 20,818.77
Abbie	Apr	$ 21,502.13
Abbie	May	$ 23,975.73
Abbie	Jun	$ 20,172.20
Brian	Jan	$ 9,925.44
Brian	Feb	$ 9,183.93
Brian	Mar	$ 12,691.39
Brian	Apr	$ 19,521.37
Brian	May	$ 16,579.38
Brian	Jun	$ 14,161.52
Chris	Jan	$ 2,792.18
Chris	Feb	$ 5,669.46
Chris	Mar	$ 4,909.24
Chris	Apr	$ 8,731.14
Chris	May	$ 11,747.29
Chris	Jun	$ 13,856.17

FIGURE 17-4: Spotting outliers in a tabular dataset with color scales.

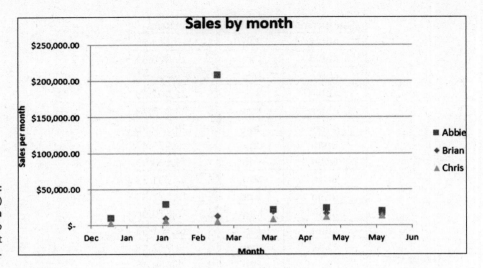

Alternatively, if you want to visually detect trends in a dataset, you can use Excel's Line Chart feature. The data from Figure 17-4 is shown as a line chart in Figure 17-6.

As you can clearly see from the figure, Chris's sales performance is low. He's in last place among the three salespeople, but he's gaining momentum. Because he seems to be improving, maybe management would want to wait a few months before making any firing decisions based on sales performance data.

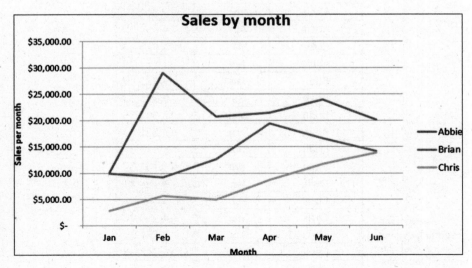

Reformatting and summarizing with pivot tables

Excel developed the pivot table to make it easier for users to extract valuable insights from large sets of spreadsheet data. If you want to generate insights by quickly restructuring or reclassifying your data, use a pivot chart. One of the main differences between a traditional spreadsheet and a dataset is that spreadsheets tend to be wide (with a lot of columns) and datasets tend to be long (with a lot of rows). Figure 17-7 clearly shows the difference between a long dataset and a wide spreadsheet.

Long format:

Salesperson	Month	Total Sales
Abbie	Jan	$ 10,144.75
Abbie	Feb	$ 29,008.52
Abbie	Mar	$ 208,187.70
Abbie	Apr	$ 21,502.13
Abbie	May	$ 23,975.73
Abbie	Jun	$ 20,172.20
Brian	Jan	$ 9,925.44
Brian	Feb	$ 9,183.93
Brian	Mar	$ 12,691.39
Brian	Apr	$ 19,521.37
Brian	May	$ 16,579.38
Brian	Jun	$ 14,161.52
Chris	Jan	$ 2,792.18
Chris	Feb	$ 5,669.46
Chris	Mar	$ 4,909.24
Chris	Apr	$ 8,731.14
Chris	May	$ 11,747.29
Chris	Jun	$ 13,856.17

Wide format:

Salesperson	Jan	Feb	Mar	Apr	May	Jun
Abbie	$10,144.75	$29,008.52	$208,187.70	$21,502.13	$23,975.73	$20,172.20
Brian	$ 9,925.44	$ 9,183.93	$ 12,691.39	$19,521.37	$16,579.38	$14,161.52
Chris	$ 2,792.18	$ 5,669.46	$ 4,909.24	$ 8,731.14	$11,747.29	$13,856.17

FIGURE 17-7: A long dataset and a wide spreadsheet.

The way that Excel is designed leads many users to intuitively prefer the wide format — which makes sense because it's a spreadsheet application. To counter this preference, however, Excel offers the table feature so that you can quickly convert between long and wide formats. You can also use pivot tables to quickly calculate subtotals and summary calculations on your newly formatted and rearranged data tables.

TIP

Creating pivot tables is easy: Just select all cells that comprise the table that you seek to analyze. Then click the Pivot Table button on the Insert tab. This opens the Create PivotTable dialog box, where you can define where you want Excel to construct the pivot table. Select OK, and Excel automatically generates a PivotTables Fields interface on the page you've specified. From this interface, you can specify the fields you want to include in the pivot table and how you want them to be laid out.

The table shown in Figure 17-8 was constructed using the long-format sales performance data shown in Figure 17-7. It's an example of the simplest possible pivot table that can be constructed, but even at that, it automatically calculates subtotals for each column, and those subtotals automatically update when you make changes to the data. What's more, pivot tables come with *pivot charts* — data plots that automatically change when you make changes to the pivot table filters based on the criteria you're evaluating.

FIGURE 17-8:
Creating a wide data table from the long dataset via a pivot table.

Total_Sales	Month						
Salesperson	Jan	Feb	Mar	Apr	May	Jun	Grand Total
Abbie	$10,144.75	$29,008.52	$20,818.77	$21,502.13	$23,975.73	$20,172.20	$125,622.10
Brian	$9,925.44	$9,183.93	$12,691.39	$19,521.37	$16,579.38	$14,161.52	$82,063.03
Chris	$2,792.18	$5,669.46	$4,909.24	$8,731.14	$11,747.29	$13,856.17	$47,705.48
Grand Total	$22,862.37	$43,861.91	$38,419.40	$49,754.64	$52,302.40	$48,189.89	$255,390.61

Automating Excel tasks with macros

Within Excel, macros act as a set of functions and commands that you can use to automate tasks. If you want to save time (and hassle) by automating Excel tasks that you routinely repeat, use macros.

Macros are pre-scripted routines written in Visual Basic for Applications (VBA). You can use macros to decrease the amount of manual processing you need to do when working with data in Excel.

To access macros, first activate Excel's Developer tab from within the Options menu on the File tab. (When the Options menu opens, choose Customize Ribbon from your choices on the left, and then click to select the Developer check box in the column on the right.) Using the Developer tab, you can record a macro, import one that was created by someone else, or code your own in VBA.

To illustrate macros in action, imagine that you have a column of values and you want to insert an empty cell between each one of the values, as shown in Figure 17-9. Excel has no easy, out-of-the-box way to make this insertion. Using Excel macros, however, you can ask Excel to record you while you step through the process one time, and then assign a key command to this recording to create the macro. After you create the macro, every time you need to repeat the same task in the future, just run the macro by pressing the key command, and the script then performs all the required steps for you.

Before macro:	After macro:
one	one
two	
three	two
four	
five	three
six	
seven	four
eight	
nine	five
ten	
	six
	seven
	eight
	nine
	ten

FIGURE 17-9:
Using a macro to insert empty cells between values.

TIP

When you record a macro, it will record in Absolute mode by default. If you want it to record the macro in Relative mode instead, you'll need to select the Use Relative References option before recording the macro:

» **Relative:** Every action and movement you make is recorded as relative to the cell that was selected when you began the recording. When you run the macro in the future, it will run in reference to the cell that's selected, acting as though that cell were the same cell you had initially selected when you recorded the macro.

» **Absolute:** After you start recording the macro, every action and movement you make is repeated when you run the macro in the future, and those actions or movements are not made in any relative reference to whatever cell was active when you started recording. The macro routine is repeated exactly as you recorded it.

In the preceding example, the macro was recorded in Relative mode. This enables the macro to be run continuously, anywhere, and on top of results from any preceding macros run. Since, in this scenario, the macro recorded only one iteration of the process, if it had been recorded in Absolute mode, every time it was run, the macro would have kept adding a space between only the one and two values. It would not operate on any cells other than the ones it was recorded upon.

Macro commands are not entered into Excel's Undo stack. If you use a macro to change or delete data, you're stuck with that change.

Test your macros first and save your worksheets before using them so that you can revert to the saved file if something goes wrong.

Excel power users often graduate to programming their own macros using VBA. Because VBA is a full-fledged programming language, the possibilities from pairing Excel with VBA are almost endless. Still, ask yourself this question: If you're going to invest time in learning a programming language, do you need to work within the confines of Excel's spreadsheet structure? If not, you might consider learning a scientific computing language, like R or Python. These open-source languages have a more user-friendly syntax and are much more flexible and powerful.

Using KNIME for Advanced Data Analytics

If you don't know how to code but still want the benefits that custom predictive analytics has to offer, you can download and install KNIME and use its visual environment to access these features. KNIME offers services, solutions, and open-source software to fulfill the advanced analytics requirements of today's data-driven business enterprise. The company's purpose is to provide an open platform that meets the data-mining and analytics needs of the masses.

If you want data-mining software that you can install on your PC and use for predictive analytics, look no further than KNIME Analytics Platform. KNIME is easy to use, so even beginners who don't know how to code can use the program. For more advanced users, however, KNIME offers plug-ins that can be used to integrate Weka's preconstructed analysis modules or to run R and Python scripts from within the application. Beginners and advanced users alike can use KNIME predictive analytics to

>> **Upsell and cross-sell:** Build cross-selling and upselling models that enable you to increase sales by making optimal recommendations of other products that customers are likely to be interested in purchasing as well.

>> **Churn reduction:** Mine customer data and identify which customers you're most likely to lose and why.

>> **Sentiment and network analysis:** Analyze the sentiment of people and organizations in your social networks, to help identify which areas of your business are performing well and which ones may need some work.

>> **Energy usage prediction and auditing:** Perform time series analyses and build regression models from energy usage data.

If you're curious about KNIME and how you can use it to increase revenues and streamline business workflows, the good news is that KNIME's Analytics Platform is available for free. In the following sections, I discuss how KNIME can be used to reduce churn, perform sentiment analysis, and predict energy usage.

Reducing customer churn via KNIME

I talk a bit about customer churn in Chapter 20, where I spell out how you can use clustering techniques to maintain customer loyalty. Within KNIME, you use the k-means algorithm to perform this type of churn analysis. (For more on the k-means algorithm, see Chapter 6.) If you want to use KNIME to help reduce customer churn, it offers a cool churn analysis workflow (see `www.knime.org/knime-applications/churn-analysis`) that shows exactly how to use the platform to perform this type of analysis.

Using KNIME to make the most of your social data

You can use sentiment analysis (as I discuss in Chapter 20) to monitor and detect, early on, your customer satisfaction rates. KNIME offers a social media clustering workflow (see `www.knime.org/knime-applications/social-media-sentiment-analysis`) and a text processing plug-in (see `https://tech.knime.org/knime-text-processing`) that you can use against your social media data to keep a close eye on how customers and potential customers are feeling about your brand and its offerings.

In Chapter 20, I also discuss the benefits that strategic social networking can bring to your business. If you want to identify and forge alliances with thought leaders and online social influencers who operate in your target niche, use KNIME's Social Media Leader/Follower Analysis workflow and network analysis plug-in at `www.knime.org/knime-applications/social-media-leaderfollower-analysis`.

Using KNIME for environmental good stewardship

Everyone knows that energy usage predictions and audits are essential to responsible energy planning. Within KNIME, you use time series analysis and autoregressive modeling to generate a predictive model from historical data and data trends. (For more on time series analysis and regression models, see Chapter 5.) If you want to use KNIME to build predictive models for energy usage, you can use the Energy Usage Prediction (Time Series Prediction) workflow (see www.knime.org/knime-applications/energy-usage-prediction) that the platform provides at its public workflow server (see www.knime.org/example-workflows).

5

Applying Domain Expertise to Solve Real-World Problems Using Data Science

Chapter **18**

Data Science in Journalism: Nailing Down the Five Ws (and an H)

For as long as newsrooms have been around, reporters have been on a mission to cover answers to questions about the "Five Ws and an H" (or 5W1H) — the who, what, when, where, why, and how of a given topic. The tools have changed over the years and the data sources — such as data generated on social media networks — have grown, but this only provides journalists with deeper and more insightful answers to their questions. In this era of digital media, traditional journalists can't survive if they cannot quickly find sufficient answers to these questions — they simply won't be fast enough or relevant enough to compete with other, more data-savvy journalists. Indeed, any journalist who wants to stay competitive in her field has to develop at least basic data science skills and hone those skills to help her develop, design, and publish content that consistently demonstrates competitive readership and engagement rates (metrics that indicate the content's popularity).

In a quest to stay relevant, many traditional media venues have turned to the same technological advances that previously threatened to annihilate them. This adoption of more advanced digital technologies resulted in the birth of data journalism as an independent field. Data journalism — also known as *data-driven journalism* — is proving to be a potent marriage between traditional journalism and the power of data.

Modern data journalists — the experts who craft all the cool data-driven stories you see out there — must be masters at collecting, analyzing, and presenting data. In its simplest form, data journalism can be described as a process involving these three distinct steps:

1. *Data collection:* This step may involve *web-scraping* (setting up automated programs to scour and extract the data you need straight from the Internet) and configuring automated data feeds.

2. *Data analysis:* Spot trends, analyze outliers, and evaluate context.

3. *Data presentation:* Design the data visualization and draft concise, well-written story narratives.

REMEMBER

Let me emphasize here, at the beginning of the chapter, that data journalists have an ethical responsibility to always represent data accurately. Data journalists should never distort the message of the data to fit a story they want to tell. Readers rely on data journalists to provide honest and accurate representations, thus amplifying the level of ethical responsibility that the journalist must assume. Data journalists must first find out what the data really says and then either tell that story (even if it wasn't the journalist's first idea for the story) or, in the alternative, drop the story altogether.

Who Is the Audience?

When most people think of data, questions about *who* (as it relates to the data) don't readily come to mind. In data journalism, however, answers to questions about *who* are profoundly important to the success of any data-driven story. You must consider who created and maintains the sources of your datasets to determine whether those datasets are a credible basis for a story. If you want to write a story that appeals to your target readership, you must consider who comprises that readership and the most pressing needs and concerns of those people.

Who made the data

The answer to the question "Who made your data?" is the most fundamental and important answer to any of the five W questions. No story can pass the litmus test unless it's been built upon highly credible sources. If your sources aren't valid and accurate, you could spend countless hours producing what, in the end, amounts to a worthless story.

You must be scrupulous about knowing who made your data because you need to be able to validate those sources' accuracy and credibility. You definitely don't want to go public with a story you generated from noncredible sources, because if anyone questions the story's validity, you have no ground on which to stand.

REMEMBER

News is only as good as its source, so protect your own credibility by reporting on data from only credible sources. Also, it's important to use as many relevant data sources as can be acquired, to avoid bias or accusations of cherry-picking.

If you want to create a meaningful, credible data-driven story that attracts a maximum amount of attention from your audience, you can use the power and clout of reputable data sources to make your stories and headlines that much more compelling. In any type of data journalism piece you publish, it's critical that you disclose your data sources. You don't have to provide a live web link back to those sources, but you should at least make a statement about where you found your information, in case people want to investigate further on their own.

Who comprises the audience

Research your target audience and get to know their interests, reading preferences, and even their aesthetics preferences (for choosing the best images to include in your story) before planning your story so that you can craft something that's of maximum interest and usefulness to them. You can present the same interesting, high-quality story in countless different lights — with some lights beaming in a *much* more compelling way than others.

To present your story in a way that most attracts readers' attention, spend some serious time researching your target audience and evaluating what presentation styles work well with readers of that group. One way to begin getting to know your readers is to gather data on stories that have performed well with that audience in the recent past.

TIP

If you search social bookmarking sites — StumbleUpon, for example, (http://stumbleupon.com), or Digg (http://digg.com) or Delicious (http://delicious.com) — or if you just mine some Twitter data, you can quickly generate a list of headlines that perform well with your target audience. Just get in there and start searching for content that's based on the same topic as that of your own. Identify what headlines seem to have the best performance — the highest engagement counts, in other words — among them.

After you have a list of related headlines that perform well with your target audience, note any similarities between them. Identify any specific keywords or hashtags that are getting the most user engagement. Leverage those as main draws to generate interest in your article. Lastly, examine the *emotional value* of the headlines — the emotional pull that draws people in to read the piece, in other words.

Speaking of emotions, news articles generally satisfy at least one of the following core human desires:

>> **Knowledge:** Often, but not always, closely tied to a desire for profit.

>> **Safety:** The desire to protect one's property, income, and well-being, or that of friends and family.

>> **Personal property:** A person's innate desire to have things that bring him comfort, safety, security, and status.

>> **Self-esteem:** People are sometimes interested in knowing about topics that help them feel good about themselves. These topics often include ideas about philanthropy, charity, service, or grassroots causes for social change.

Ask yourself what primary desires your headlines promise to satisfy. Then craft your headlines in a way designed to appeal most strongly to that desire. Try to determine what type of articles perform the best with your target audience or what your target audience most strongly seeks when looking for new content to consume. With that info in hand, make sure to exact-target your writing and headlines in a way that clearly meets a core desire among your target audience.

What: Getting Directly to the Point

The *what*, in data journalism, refers to the gist of the story. In all forms of journalism, a journalist absolutely must be able to get straight to the point. Keep it clear, concise, and easy to understand.

When crafting data visualizations to accompany your data journalism piece, make sure that the visual story is easy to discern at a moment's glance. If it takes longer than that, the data visualization is not focused enough. The same principle applies to your writing. No one wants to drag through loads of words trying to figure out *what* you're trying to say. Readers appreciate it when you make their lives easier by keeping your narrative clear, direct, and to the point.

The more people have to work to understand your content, the less they tend to like it. If you want to provide readers with information they enjoy consuming, make your writing and data visualizations clear and to the point.

Bringing Data Journalism to Life: The Black Budget

Any chapter on data science in journalism would be utterly incomplete without a solid case study to demonstrate the power of data journalism in action. The *Washington Post* story "The Black Budget" is one incredible example of such a piece. (Check it out for yourself at `www.washingtonpost.com/wp-srv/special/national/black-budget`.)

When former NSA contractor Edward Snowden leaked a trove of classified documents, he unleashed a storm of controversy not only among the public but also among the data journalists who were tasked with analyzing the documents for stories. The challenge for data journalists in this case was to discover and disclose data insights that were relevant to the public without compromising the safety of ordinary citizens.

Among the documents leaked by Snowden was the so-called *Black Budget* for fiscal year 2013, a 178-page line-by-line breakdown of the funds that were earmarked for 16 various U.S. federal intelligence agencies. Through the *Washington Post's* "The Black Budget," the American public was informed that $52.6 billion taxpayer dollars had been spent on mostly covert federal intelligence services in 2013 alone.

The *Washington Post* did a phenomenal job in its visual presentation of the data. The opening title is a somber visual pun: The words *The Black Budget* are written in a huge black box contrasted only with gray and white. This layout visually implies the serious and murky nature of the subject matter. The only touch of color is a navy blue, which conjures a vaguely military image and barely contrasts with the black. This limited palette is continued throughout the visual presentation of the data.

Washington Post data journalists used unusual blocky data graphics — an unsettling, strangely horizontal hybrid of a pie chart, a bar graph, and a tree map — to hint at the surreptitious and dangerous nature of the topic, as well as the shady manner in which the information was obtained.

The data graphics used in the piece exhibited a low *data-to-ink ratio* — in other words, only a little information is conveyed with a lot of screen space. Although normally a low data-to-ink ratio indicates bad design, the data-to-ink ratio here effectively hints that mountains of data lie underneath the layers being shown, and that these layers remain undisclosed so as not to endanger intelligence sources and national security.

Traditional infographic elements used in this piece include stark, light gray seals of the top five intelligence agencies, only three of which the average person would have ever seen. Simple bar charts outlined funding trends, and people-shaped icons represented the army of personnel involved in intelligence gathering.

A lot of thought went into the collection, analysis, and presentation of this story. Its ensemble is an unsettling, yet overwhelmingly informative, piece of data journalism. Although this sort of journalism was in its infancy even just a decade ago, now the data and tools required for this type of work are widely available for journalists to use to quickly develop high-quality data journalism articles.

When Did It Happen?

As the old adage goes, timing is everything. It's a valuable skill to know how to refurbish old data so that it's interesting to a modern readership. Likewise, in data journalism, it's imperative to keep an eye on contextual relevancy and know when is the optimal time to craft and publish a particular story.

When as the context to your story

If you want to craft a data journalism piece that really garners a lot of respect and attention from your target audience, consider *when* — over what time period — your data is relevant. Stale, outdated data usually doesn't help the story make breaking news, and unfortunately you can find tons of old data out there. But if you're skillful with data, you can create data mashups (described a little later in this chapter) that take trends in old datasets and present them in ways that are interesting to your present-day readership.

For example, take gender-based trends in 1940s employment data and do a *mashup* — integration, comparison, or contrast — of that data and employment data trends from the five years just previous to the current one. You could then use this combined dataset to support a truly dramatic story about how much things have changed or how little things have changed, depending on the angle you're after with your piece.

REMEMBER

Returning once again to the issue of ethical responsibilities in journalism, as a data journalist you walk a fine line between finding datasets that most persuasively support your storyline and finding facts that support a factually challenged story you're trying to push. Journalists have an ethical responsibility to convey an honest message to their readers. When building a case to support your story, don't take things too far — in other words, don't take the information into the realm of fiction. There are a million facts that could be presented in countless ways to support any story you're looking to tell. Your story should be based in reality, and not be some divisive or fabricated story that you're trying to promote because you think your readers will like it.

TIP

You may sometimes have trouble finding interesting or compelling datasets to support your story. In these situations, look for ways to create data mashups that tie your less-interesting data into some data that's extremely interesting to your target audience. Use the combined dataset as a basis for your data-driven story.

When does the audience care the most?

If your goal is to publish a data journalism piece that goes viral, then you certainly want to consider the story's *timeliness*: When would be the prime time to publish an article on this particular topic?

For obvious reasons, you're not going to do well by publishing a story in 2017 about who won the 1984 election for U.S. president; everyone knows, and no one cares. Likewise, if a huge, present-day media scandal has already piqued the interest of your readership, it's not a bad idea to ride the tailwinds of that media hype and publish a related story. The story would likely perform pretty well, if it's interesting.

As a recent example, you could have created a data journalism piece on Internet user privacy assumptions and breaches thereof and then published it in the days just after news of the Edward Snowden/NSA controversy broke. Keeping relevant and timely publishing schedules is one way to ensure that your stories garner the attention they need to keep you employed.

Where Does the Story Matter?

Data and stories are always more relevant to some places than others. From where is a story derived, and where is it going? If you keep these important facts in mind, the publications you develop are more relevant to their intended audience.

The *where* aspect in data journalism is a bit ambiguous because it can refer to a geographical location or a digital location, or both.

Where is the story relevant?

You need to focus on where your story is most relevant so that you can craft the most compelling story by reporting on the most relevant trends.

If your story is *location independent* — you're reporting on a trend that's irrelevant to location — of course you want to use data sources that most clearly demonstrate the trend on which you're reporting. Likewise, if you're reporting a story that's tied to a specific geographic location, you probably want to report statistics that are generated from regional areas demonstrating the greatest degree of extremes — either as greatest value fluxes or as greatest value differences for the parameters on which you're reporting.

Sometimes you find multiple geographic or digital locations that exemplify extreme trends and unusual outliers. In other words, you find more than one excellent information source. In these cases, consider using all of them by creating and presenting a *data mashup* — a combination of two or more data sources that are analyzed together in order to provide readers with a more complete view of the situation at hand.

Where should the story be published?

Another important question to consider in data journalism is, "Where do you intend to publish your story?" This *where* can be a geographical place, a particular social media platform, or certain series of digital platforms that are associated with a particular brand — Facebook, Twitter, Pinterest, and Instagram accounts, as well as blogs, that are all tied together to stream data from one branded source.

Just as you need to have a firm grasp on who your audience is, you should clearly understand the implications of where your publication is distributed. Spelling out where you'll be publishing helps you conceptualize to whom you're publishing, what you should publish, and how you should present that publication. If your goal is to craft high-performing data journalism articles, your headlines and storylines should cater to the interests of the people that are subscribed to the channels in which you're distributing. Since the collective interest of the people at each channel may slightly differ, make sure to adapt to those differences before posting your work.

Why the Story Matters

The human capacity to question and understand why things are the way they are is a clear delineation point between the human species and other highly cognitive mammals. Answers to questions about *why* help you to make better-informed decisions. These answers help you to better structure the world around you and help you develop reasoning beyond what you need for mere survival.

In data journalism, as in all other types of business, answers to the question *why* help you predict how people and markets respond. These answers help you know how to proceed to achieve an outcome of most probable success. Knowing why your story matters helps you write and present it in a way that achieves the most favorable outcomes — presumably, that your readers enjoy and take tremendous value from consuming your content.

Asking why in order to generate and augment a storyline

No matter what topic you're crafting a story around, it's incredibly important to generate a storyline around the wants and needs of your target audience. After you know who your audience is and what needs they most often try to satisfy by consuming content (which I talk about in the section "Who comprises the audience," earlier in this chapter), use that knowledge to help you craft your storyline. If you want to write a story and design a visualization that precisely targets the needs and wants of your readership, take the time to pinpoint why people would be interested in your story, and create a story that directly meets that desire in as many ways as possible.

Why your audience should care

People care about things that matter to them and that affect their lives. Generally, people want to feel happy and safe. They want to have fulfilling relationships. They want to have good status among their peers. People like to learn things, particularly things that help them earn more money. People like possessions and things that bring them comfort, status, and security. People like to feel good about themselves and what they do. This is all part of human nature.

The desires I just described summarize *why* people care about anything — from the readers of your story to the person down the street. People care because it does something for them, it fills one of their core desires. Consequently, if your goal is to publish a high-performing, well-received data journalism piece, make sure to craft it in a way that fulfills one or two core desires of your target readership.

To better understand your audience and what they most desire in the content they consume, flip back to the section "Who Is the Audience," earlier in this chapter.

How to Develop, Tell, and Present the Story

By thinking through the *how* of a story, you are putting yourself in position to craft better data-driven stories. Looking at your data objectively and considering factors like how it was created helps you to discover interesting insights that you can include in your story. Also, knowing how to quickly find stories in potential data sources helps you to quickly sift through the staggering array of options.

And, how you present your data-driven story determines much about how well that story is received by your target audience. You could have done everything right — really taken the time to get to know who your audience is, boiled your story down so that it says exactly what you intend, published it at just the right time, crafted your story around what you know about why people care, and even published it to just the right venue — but if your data visualization looks bad, or if your story layout makes it difficult for readers to quickly gather useful information, then your positive response rates are likely to be low.

Integrating how as a source of data and story context

You need to think about how your data was generated because that line of thinking often leads you into more interesting and compelling storylines. Before drawing up a final outline for your story, brainstorm about how your source data was generated. If you find startling or attention-grabbing answers that are relevant to your story, consider introducing those in your writing or data visualization.

Finding stories in your data

If you know how to quickly and skillfully find stories in datasets, you can use this set of skills to save time when you're exploring the array of stories that your datasets offer. If you want to quickly analyze, understand, and evaluate the stories in datasets, then you need to have solid data analysis and visualization skills. With these skills, you can quickly discover which datasets to keep and which to discard. Getting up to speed in relevant data science skills also helps you quickly find the most interesting, relevant stories in the datasets you select to support your story.

Presenting a data-driven story

How you present your data-driven story determines much about whether it succeeds or fails with your target audience. Should you use an infographic? A chart? A map? Should your visualization be static or interactive? You have to consider countless aspects when deciding how to best present your story. (For much more on data visualization design, check out Chapter 9.)

Collecting Data for Your Story

A data-journalism piece is only as good as the data that supports it. To publish a compelling story, you must find compelling data on which to build. That isn't always easy, but it's easier if you know how to use *scraping* and *autofeeds* to your advantage.

Scraping data

Web-scraping involves setting up automated programs to scour and extract the exact and custom datasets that you need straight from the Internet so you don't have to do it yourself. The data you generate from this process is commonly called *scraped* data. Most data journalists scrape source data for their stories because it's the most efficient way to get datasets for unique stories. Datasets that are easily accessible have usually already been exploited and mined by teams of data journalists who were looking for stories. To generate unique data sources for your data-driven story, scrape the data yourself.

WARNING

If you find easy-to-access data, beware that most of the stories in that dataset have probably been told by a journalist who discovered that data before you.

To illustrate how you'd use data scraping in data journalism, imagine the following example: You're a data journalist living in a U.S. state that directly borders Mexico. You've heard rumors that the local library's selection of Spanish-language children's books is woefully inadequate. You call the library, but its staff fear negative publicity and won't share any statistics with you about the topic.

Because the library won't budge on its data-sharing, you're forced to scrape the library's online catalog to get the source data you need to support this story. Your scraping tool is customized to iterate over all possible searches and keep track of the results. After scraping the site, you discover that 25 percent of children's books at the library are Spanish-language books. Spanish-speakers make up 45 percent of the primary-school population; is this difference significant enough to form the basis of a story? Maybe, maybe not.

To dig a little deeper and possibly discover a reason behind this difference, you decide to scrape the catalog once a week for several weeks, and then compare patterns of borrowing. When you find that a larger proportion of Spanish books are being checked out, this indicates that there is, indeed, a high demand for children's books in Spanish. This finding, coupled with the results from your previous site scrape, give you all the support you need to craft a compelling article around the issue.

Setting up data alerts

To generate hot stories, data journalists must have access to the freshest, newest data releases that are coming from the most credible organizations. To stay on top of what datasets are being released where, data journalists subscribe to alert systems that send them notifications every time potentially important data is released. These alert systems often issue notifications via RSS feeds or via email. It's also possible to set up a custom application like DataStringer (https://github.com/pudo/datastringer) to send push notifications when significant modifications or updates are made to source databases.

After you subscribe to data alerts and form a solid idea about the data-release schedule, you can begin planning for data releases in advance. For example, if you're doing data journalism in the business analytics niche and know that a particularly interesting quarterly report is to be released in one week, you can use the time you have before its release to formulate a plan on how you'll analyze the data when it does become available.

TECHNICAL STUFF

Many times, after you're alerted to important new data releases, you still need to scrape the source site in order to get that data. In particular, if you're pulling data from a government department, you're likely to need to scrape the source site. Although most government organizations in western countries are legally obligated to release data, they aren't required to release it in a format that's readily consumable. Don't expect them to make it easy for you to get the data you need to tell a story about their operations.

Finding and Telling Your Data's Story

Every dataset tells a story, but not every story is newsworthy. To get to the bottom of a data-driven story, you need an analytical mind, plus basic skills in data science and a solid understanding of journalistic procedure for developing a story.

Spotting strange trends and outliers

One quick way to identify interesting stories in a dataset is to do a quick spot-check for unusual trends or extreme outliers. These anomalies usually indicate that an external force is affecting a change that you see reflected in the data.

If you want to do a quick-and-dirty spot-check for easy-to-identify stories, you can simply throw your data into an *x-y* scatter plot and visually inspect the result for obvious trends and outliers. After you spot these anomalies, look into reasons behind why the data behaves oddly. In doing so, you can usually uncover some juicy stories.

Illustrating this fact, consider the World Bank Global Development Indicator (GDI) open dataset, available for review at `http://data.worldbank.org`. Looking at this data, you can easily see a clear correlation between a country's gross domestic product and the life expectancy of its citizens. The reason for this correlation is obvious: More affluent people can afford better healthcare.

But say you're searching through the hundreds of GDI indicators for the year 2013 and you come across something less obvious — the survival rate of newborns is reasonably well-correlated with the percentage of employed females who receive wages or salaries instead of only performance-based remuneration, as illustrated in Figure 18-1.

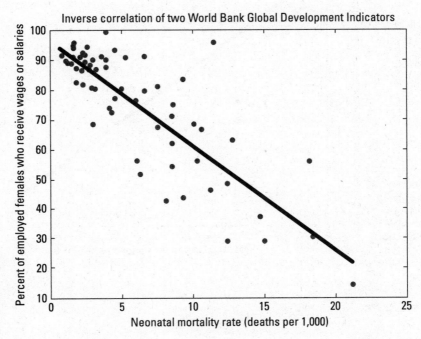

FIGURE 18-1:
A scatter plot of the inverse correlation between two GDI indicators.

The relationship in this data is a little murky. Although you naturally expect two metrics based on health and economic well-being to be related, after analyzing your data a bit, you find a Pearson correlation coefficient of 0.86. That's quite high. Is there a story here? Does this qualify as a newsworthy trend? An effective and time-efficient way to explore answers to this question is to try to find the exception that proves the rule. In Figure 18-2, the simple least-squares best-fit line is in black, and the two data points that most differ (horizontally and vertically) from this line are indicated with light gray lines.

TECHNICAL STUFF

A *Pearson coefficient* is a statistical correlation coefficient that measures the linear correlation between two variables. A high (nearer to 1) or low (nearer to −1) Pearson correlation coefficient indicates a high degree of correlation between the variables. The closer the coefficient is to 0, the smaller the correlation between the variables. The maximum value for a Pearson coefficient is 1, and the minimum is −1.

TIP

You could also look for exceptions at the largest perpendicular distance from the line, but it's a little more difficult to calculate. The topmost point in Figure 18-2 would fulfill that criterion.

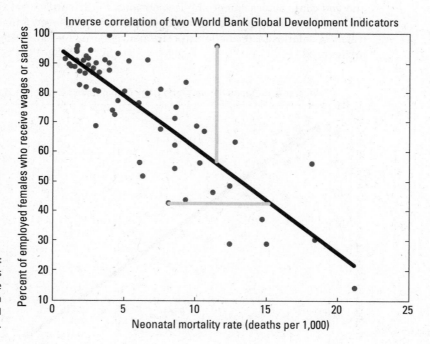

FIGURE 18-2:
A least-squares line of the inverse correlation between two GDI indicators.

Examining context to understand the significance of data

By pinpointing strange trends or outliers in your dataset, you can subsequently focus in on those patterns and look for the interesting stories about the external factors that cause them. If you want to cultivate the most thought-provoking story about what's happening in your source dataset, you need to further investigate, compare, and contrast these factors you've identified. By examining the context in which competing causative factors are creating extreme trends and outliers, you can then begin to get a solid understanding of your data's significance.

For example, think about the World Bank Global Development Indicator (GDI) in the preceding section. The topmost point in Figure 18-2 represents the country of Jordan. For a given level of child mortality, Jordan has an unusual number of women with predictable income. If you dig a little deeper into factors that might account for this outlier, you see that the overall employment rate for women in Jordan is among the lowest in the world. In a country where few women work, the women who do work in Jordan are earning relatively stable wages or salaries. This might indicate that the precariously paid work is being given mostly to men. Maybe the underlying story here is about gender roles in Jordan? If so, what conclusions could you draw by looking at another outlier country in the dataset — Peru, for example?

Well, because only 41 percent of Peruvian women are employed with a stable income, Peru is near the bottom ranks in terms of employed women with stable incomes. Perhaps this is to be expected in a country with so much agriculture by hand. And, in all honesty, Peruvian men aren't much better off either, indicated by the fact that only 51 percent of them are reporting stable employment. But the Peruvian neonatal mortality rate is unusually low. Does Peru have an exceptionally well-funded healthcare system? Not really — it spends less, per capita, on healthcare than most of its neighbors. So what could be the cause for the low neonatal mortality rate?

Introducing contextually relevant datasets, the Social Institutions and Gender Index (SIGI) data ranks Peru low on the scale for economic gender equality, but quite high — at 17th — on an overall scale for gender equality that includes legal, societal, and educational metrics (http://genderindex.org/country/peru). Perhaps there's a story there!

Although the possible stories identified in this exercise are not exceptionally dramatic or earth-shaking, that's okay — not all stories have to be.

You shouldn't expect to find a groundbreaking story in a dataset as accessible as World Bank's open data. Again, the more accessible a dataset is, the more likely it is that the dataset has been thoroughly picked over and exploited by other data journalists.

Emphasizing the story through visualization

When it comes to data-visualization design, you always want to pick the colors, styles, and data graphic types that most dramatically convey the visual story you're trying to tell. You want to make your visual stories as clear, concise, and easy to understand as possible. In making selections among visual elements for your data visualization, find the best way to visually convey your story without requiring your audience to have to strain and work to understand it.

Looking back to the World Bank Global Development Indicator (GDI) example from the preceding sections, imagine that you decide to go with the Peru story. Because the SIGI dataset is so relevant to the Peru story, you need to make a thorough study of that dataset, as well as any other datasets you've identified to be relevant. Time-series data on different statistics is likely to be quite informative because it should indicate several relevant metrics — the proportion of total income earned by women, survival rates of pregnant mothers, legal-based gender equality metrics, and so on.

After you gather and appraise the most relevant metrics that are available to you, pick and choose the metrics whose datasets show the most extreme trends. Subtle changes in data don't lend themselves to dramatic and easy-to-understand visual stories. After you select the most dramatic metrics to use in telling your story, it's time to decide the best way to represent that story visually.

For the Peruvian example, imagine that its legal system's gender-based equality metric is the most striking statistic you've found in all the data that covers the topic of women's status in that country. The dramatic impact of that metric makes it an excellent choice for the fundamental basis of your visual story. With that impact in mind, you decide to use a static infographic to show how the Peruvian legal system is more equitable when it comes to gender than that of its neighboring countries. Whatever story you decide to cover, just be sure that the visualizations you create are well *branded* — be sure to pick a common color palette, font type, and symbol style to unify your visualizations.

Solid visual branding practices govern that you make subtle associations between each of your related visualizations by using color, font type, or symbol style. If you choose to brand with color choices, for instance, then independent of the data graphics you use to display data on a metric, make sure to always use the same color to represent that metric across every graphic you employ.

Creating compelling and highly focused narratives

As you well know, no one wants to wade through a bunch of needless, complicated words to try to figure out what your story says. It's frustrating, and it simply takes too much work. Presuming that your purpose for creating a data-driven story is to publish something that has impact and value in the lives of your readers, you must work hard to whittle your narrative down to its simplest, most-focused form. Failure to do so decreases the impact and performance of your data-driven story.

Narrow each of your stories down to its hook and lede before going any further into the process of writing a full narrative. In journalism, a *hook* is a dramatic angle that cultivates interest in potential readers and draws them into your piece. A *lede* is the first sentence of your story — it introduces the story and shows readers why the story is newsworthy. After you go through your story and flesh out a hook, a lede, and a full narrative, you always need to go back through the piece once or twice and cut unnecessary words or restructure sentences so that they most directly express the ideas you seek to convey.

Referring back to the Peru example from the preceding sections, gender equality is quite a broad subject. So, start by creating a *hook* — in this case, the hook could be a description of the most dramatic metrics indicating that Peruvian women are far better off than women in neighboring South American countries. Next, get to work on the *lede* — perhaps something like, "In Peru, economically disadvantaged women experience the highest chance of dying during childbirth, yet their children have among the highest chances of surviving." Lastly, go back through and clean things up so that the lede is as clear and easy to understand as possible. For this example, you might rewrite the lede so that it reads, "Poor Peruvian mothers have the greatest childbirth mortality rates of any South America women yet, oddly, Peruvian infants demonstrate the highest chances of surviving childbirth."

Chapter **19**

Delving into Environmental Data Science

B ecause data science can be used to successfully reverse-engineer business growth and increase revenues, many of its more noble applications often slide by, completely unnoticed. *Environmental* data science, one such application, is the use of data science techniques, methodologies, and technologies to address or solve problems that are related to the environment. This particular data science falls into three main categories — environmental intelligence, natural resource modeling, and spatial statistics — to predict environmental variation. In this chapter, I discuss each type of environmental data science and how it's being used to make a positive impact on human health, safety, and the environment.

Modeling Environmental-Human Interactions with Environmental Intelligence

The purpose of environmental intelligence (EI) is to convert raw data into insights that can be used for data-informed decision making about matters that pertain to environmental-human interactions. EI solutions are designed to support the decision making of community leaders, humanitarian response decision-makers, public health advisors, environmental engineers, policy makers, and more. If you want to collect and analyze environmentally relevant data in order to produce content that's crucial for your decision making process — like real-time maps, interactive data visualizations, and tabular data reports — look into an EI solution.

In the following four sections, I discuss the type of problems being solved by using EI technologies and specify which organizations are out there using EI to make a difference. I explain the ways in which EI is similar to business intelligence (BI) and the reasons it qualifies as applied data science despite those similarities. I wrap up this main section with a real-world example of how EI is being used to make a positive impact.

Examining the types of problems solved

EI technologies are used to monitor and report on interactions between humans and the natural environment. This information provides decision-makers and stakeholders with real-time intelligence about on-the-ground happenings, in the hope of avoiding preventable disasters and community hardships through proactive, data-informed decision making. EI technologies are being used to achieve the following types of results:

>> **Make responsible energy-consumption plans:** EI technology is just what you need in order to audit, track, monitor, and predict energy consumption rates. Here, energy is the natural resource, and people's consumption of energy is the human interaction. (Note that you can use KNIME to help you build this type of EI solution directly on your desktop computer; check out Chapter 17 for more on KNIME.)

>> **Expedite humanitarian relief efforts:** EI of this type involves *crisis mapping*, where EI technology is used to collect, map, visualize, analyze, and report environmental data that is relevant to the crisis at hand. Crisis mapping provides real-time humanitarian decision support. Here, water supply,

sanitation, natural disaster, and hygiene status are measures of natural resources, and the effects that these resources have on the health and safety of people is the human interaction.

>> **Improve water resource planning:** You can use EI technologies to generate predictive models for water consumption, based on simple inference from statistically derived population forecasts, historical water-consumption rates, and spatial data on existing infrastructure. Water supply is the natural resource here, and people's consumption of it is the human interaction.

>> **Combat deforestation:** EI technologies are being used in real-time, interactive, map-based data visualization platforms to monitor deforestation in remote regions of developing nations. This type of solution utilizes conditional autoregressive modeling, spatial analysis, web-based mapping, data analytics, data cubes, and time series analyses to map, visualize, analyze, and report deforestation in near–real-time. These uses of EI increase transparency and public awareness on this important environmental issue. In this application, forestry and land are the natural resources, and the act of cutting down trees is the human interaction.

Defining environmental intelligence

Although environmental intelligence (EI) and business intelligence (BI) technologies have a lot in common, EI is still considered applied data science. Before I delve into the reasons for this difference, first consider the following ways in which EI and BI are similar:

>> **Simple inference from mathematical models:** As discussed in Chapter 3, BI generates predictions based on simple mathematical inference, and not from complex statistical predictive modeling. Many of the simpler EI solutions derive their predictions from simple mathematical inference as well.

>> **Data structure and type:** Like BI, many of the simpler EI products are built solely from structured data that sits in a relational SQL database.

>> **Decision-support product outputs:** Both EI and BI produce data visualizations, maps, interactive data analytics, and tabular data reports as decision-support products.

Much of the EI approach was borrowed from the BI discipline. However, EI evolved away from BI technologies when its features were upgraded and expanded to solve real-world environmental problems. When you look into the data science features that are central to most solutions, the evolution of EI away from standard BI becomes increasingly obvious. Here are a few data science processes you won't find used in BI but will find in EI technology:

>> **Statistical programming:** The most basic EI solutions deploy time series analysis and autoregressive modeling. Many of the more advanced solutions make use of complex statistical models and algorithms as well.

>> **GIS technology:** Because environmental insights are location-dependent, it's almost impossible to avoid integrating geographic information systems (GIS) technologies into EI solutions. Not only that, but almost all web-based EI platforms require advanced spatial web programming. (For more on GIS technologies, check out Chapter 13.)

>> **Web-based data visualization:** Almost all web-based EI platforms offer interactive, near–real-time data visualizations that are built on the JavaScript programming language.

>> **Data sources:** Unlike BI, EI solutions are built almost solely from external data sources. These sources often include data autofeeds derived from image, social media, and SMS sources. Other external data comes in the form of satellite data, scraped website data, or .pdf documents that need to be converted via custom optical text-recognition scripts. In EI, the reported data is almost always updating in real-time.

REMEMBER

Web-scraping is a process that involves setting up automated programs to scour and extract the data you need straight from the Internet. The data you generate from this type of process is commonly called *scraped* data.

>> **Coding requirements:** EI solutions almost always require advanced custom coding. Whether in the form of web programming or statistical programming, extra coding work is required in order to deliver EI products.

Identifying major organizations that work in environmental intelligence

Because EI is a social–good application of data science, there aren't a ton of funding sources out there, which is probably the chief reason not many people are working in this line of data science. EI is small, but some folks in dedicated organizations have found a way to earn a living by creating EI solutions that serve the public good. In the following list, I name a few of those organizations, as well as the umbrella organizations that fund them. If your goal is to use EI technologies to build products that support decision making for the betterment of environmental health and safety, one of these organizations will likely be willing to help you with advice or even support services:

>> **DataKind** (www.datakind.org): A nonprofit organization of data science volunteers who donate their time and skills to work together in the service of humanity, DataKind was started by the data science legend Jake Porway. The organization has donated EI support to projects in developing nations and first-world countries alike. DataKind's sponsors include *National Geographic*, IBM, and Pop! Tech.

>> **Elva** (www.elva.org): A nongovernmental organization, Elva was built by a small, independent group of international *digital humanitarians* — knowledge workers who use data and disruptive technologies to build solutions for international humanitarian problems. Elva founders gave their time and skills to build a mobile-phone platform, which allows marginalized communities to map local needs and to work with decision-makers to develop effective joint-response plans. Elva offers EI support for environmental projects that are centered in underserved, developing nations. Elva is directed by Jonne Catshoek and is sponsored by UNDP, USAID, and Eurasia Partnership.

>> **Vizzuality** (www.vizzuality.com): Here's a business started by the founders of CartoDB — a technology that's discussed further in Chapter 11. Almost all of Vizzuality's projects involve using EI to serve the betterment of the environment. Vizzuality was founded by Javier de la Torre, and some of the organization's bigger clients have included Google, UNEP, NASA, the University of Oxford, and Yale University.

>> **QCRI** (www.qcri.com): The Qatar Computing Research Institute (QCRI) is a national organization that's owned and funded by a private, nonprofit, community development foundation in Qatar. The social-innovation section delivers some ongoing environmental projects, including Artificial Intelligence in Disaster Response (AIDR) and a crowdsourced verification-for-disaster-response platform (Verily).

Making positive impacts with environmental intelligence

Elva is a shining example of how environmental intelligence technologies can be used to make a positive impact. This free, open-source platform facilitates cause mapping and data visualization reporting for election monitoring, human rights violations, environmental degradation, and disaster risk in developing nations.

In one of its more recent projects, Elva has been working with Internews, an international nonprofit devoted to fostering independent media and access to information in an effort to map crisis-level environmental issues in one of the most impoverished, underdeveloped nations of the world, the Central African Republic. As part of these efforts, local human rights reporters and humanitarian organizations are using Elva to monitor, map, and report information derived from environmental data on natural disasters, infrastructure, water, sanitation, hygiene, and human health. The purpose of Elva's involvement on this project is to facilitate real-time humanitarian-data analysis and visualization to support the decision making of international humanitarian-relief experts and community leaders.

With respect to data science technologies and methodologies, Elva implements

>> **Autofeeds for data collection:** The data that's mapped, visualized, and reported through the Elva platform is actually created by citizen activists on the ground who use SMS and smartphones to report environmental conditions by way of reports or surveys. The reporting system is built so that all reports come in with the correct structure, are collected by service-provider servers, and then are pushed over to the Elva database.

>> **Non-relational database technologies:** Elva uses a non-relational NoSQL database infrastructure to store survey data submitted by smartphone and SMS, as well as other sources of structured, unstructured, and semistructured data.

>> **Open data:** OpenStreetMap powers the map data that the Elva platform uses. You can find out more about OpenStreetMap in Chapter 22, where I focus on *open data* resources — data resources that have been made publicly available for use, reuse, modification, and sharing with others.

>> **Inference from mathematical and statistical models:** Elva's data analysis methods aren't overly complex, but that's perfect for producing fast, real-time analytics for humanitarian decision support. Elva depends mostly on time series analysis, linear regression, and simple mathematical inference.

>> **Data visualization:** Elva produces data visualizations directly from reported data and also from inferential analyses. These are interactive JavaScript visualizations built from the Highcharts API.

>> **Location-based predictions:** Such predictions are based on simple inference and not on advanced spatial statistics, as discussed in the section "Using Spatial Statistics to Predict for Environmental Variation across Space," later in this chapter. Elva staff can infer locations of high risk based on historical time series reported in the region.

Modeling Natural Resources in the Raw

You can use data science to model natural resources in their raw form. This type of environmental data science generally involves some advanced statistical modeling to better understand natural resources. You model the resources *in the raw* — water, air, and land conditions as they occur in nature — to better understand the natural environment's organic effects on human life.

In the following sections, I explain a bit about the type of natural-resource issues that most readily lend themselves to exploration via environmental data science. Then I offer a brief overview about which data science methods are particularly relevant to environmental resource modeling. Lastly, I present a case in which environmental data science has been used to better understand the natural environment.

Exploring natural resource modeling

Environmental data science can model natural resources in the raw so that you can better understand environmental processes in order to comprehend how those processes affect life on Earth. After environmental processes are clearly understood, then and only then can environmental engineers step in to design systems to solve problems that these natural processes may be creating. The following list describes the types of natural-resource issues that environmental data science can model and predict:

>> **Water issues:** Rainfall rates, geohydrologic patterns, groundwater flows, and groundwater toxin concentrations

>> **Air issues:** The concentration and dispersion of particulate-matter levels and greenhouse gas concentrations

>> **Land issues:** Soil contaminant migration and geomorphology as well as geophysics, mineral exploration, and oil and gas exploration

If your goal is to build a predictive model that you can use to help you better understand natural environmental processes, you can use natural resource modeling to help you. Don't expect natural-resource modeling to be easy, though. The statistics that go into these types of models can be incredibly complex.

Dabbling in data science

Because environmental processes and systems involve many different interdependent variables, most natural-resource modeling requires the use of incredibly complex statistical algorithms. The following list shows a few elements of data science that are commonly deployed in natural-resource modeling:

>> **Statistics, math, and machine learning:** Bayesian inference, multilevel hierarchical Bayesian inference, multitaper spectral analysis, copulas, Wavelet Autoregressive Method (WARM), Autoregressive Moving Averages (ARMAs), Monte Carlo simulations, structured additive regression (STAR) models, regression on order statistics (ROS), maximum likelihood estimations (MLEs), expectation-maximization (EM), linear and nonlinear dimension reduction, wavelets analysis, frequency domain methods, Markov chains, k-nearest neighbor (kNN), kernel density, and logspline density estimation, among other methods

>> **Spatial statistics:** Generally, something like probabilistic mapping

>> **Data visualization:** As in other data science areas, needed for exploratory analysis and for communicating findings with others

>> **Web-scraping:** Many times, required when gathering data for environmental models

>> **GIS technology:** Spatial analysis and mapmaking

>> **Coding requirements:** Using Python, R, SPSS, SAS, MATLAB, Fortran, and SQL, among other programming languages

Modeling natural resources to solve environmental problems

The work of Columbia Water Center's director, Dr. Upmanu Lall, provides a world-class example of using environmental data science to solve incredibly complex water resource problems. (For an overview of the Columbia Water Center's work, see http://water.columbia.edu/.) Dr. Lall uses advanced statistics, math, coding, and a staggering subject-matter expertise in environmental engineering to uncover complex, interdependent relationships between global water-resource characteristics, national gross domestic products (GDPs), poverty, and national energy consumption rates.

In one of Dr. Lall's recent projects, he found that in countries with *high rainfall variability* — countries that experience extreme droughts followed by massive flooding — the instability results in a lack of stable water resources for agricultural development, more runoff and erosion, and overall decreases in that nation's GDP. The inverse is also true, where countries that have stable, moderate rainfall rates have a better water resource supply for agricultural development, better environmental conditions overall, and higher average GDPs. So, using environmental data science, Dr. Lall has been able to draw strong correlations between a nation's rainfall trends and its poverty rates.

With respect to data science technologies and methodologies, Dr. Lall implements these tools:

>> **Statistical programming:** Dr. Lall's arsenal includes multilevel hierarchical Bayesian models, multitaper spectral analysis, copulas, Wavelet Autoregressive Moving Averages (WARMs), Autoregressive Moving Averages (ARMAs), and Monte Carlo simulations.

>> **Mathematical programming:** Tools here include linear and nonlinear dimension reduction, wavelets analysis, frequency domain methods, and nonhomogeneous hidden Markov models.

>> **Clustering analysis:** In this case, Dr. Lall relies on the tried-and-true methods, including k-nearest neighbor, kernel density, and logspline density estimation.

>> **Machine learning:** Here, Dr. Lall focuses on minimum variance embedding.

Using Spatial Statistics to Predict for Environmental Variation across Space

By their very nature, environmental variables are location-dependent: They change with changes in geospatial location. The purpose of modeling environmental variables with spatial statistics is to enable accurate spatial predictions so that you can use those predictions to solve problems related to the environment.

Spatial statistics is distinguished from natural-resource modeling because it focuses on predicting how changes in space affect environmental phenomenon. Naturally, the time variable is considered as well, but spatial statistics is all about using statistics to model the inner workings of spatial phenomenon. The difference is in the manner of approach.

In the following three sections, I discuss the types of issues you can address with spatial statistical models and the data science that goes into this type of solution. You can read about a case in which spatial statistics has been used to correlate natural concentrations of arsenic in well water with incidence of cancer.

Addressing environmental issues with spatial predictive analytics

You can use spatial statistics to model environmental variables across space and time so that you can predict changes in environmental variables across space. The following list describes the types of environmental issues that you can model and predict using spatial statistical modeling:

» **Epidemiology and environmental human health:** Disease patterns and distributions

» **Meteorology:** Weather phenomenon

» **Fire science:** The spread of a fire (by channeling your inner Smokey the Bear!)

» **Hydraulics:** Aquifer conductivity

» **Ecology:** Microorganism distribution across a sedimentary lake bottom

If your goal is to build a model that you can use to predict how change in space will affect environmental variables, you can use spatial statistics to help you do this. In the next section, I quickly overview the basics that are involved in spatial statistics.

Describing the data science that's involved

Because spatial statistics involves modeling the x-, y-, z-parameters that comprise spatial datasets, the statistics involved can get rather interesting and unusual. Spatial statistics is, more or less, a marriage of GIS spatial analysis and advanced predictive analytics. The following list describes a few data science processes that are commonly deployed when using statistics to build predictive spatial models:

» **Spatial statistics:** Spatial statistics often involves krige and kriging, as well as variogram analysis. The terms "kriging" and "krige" denote different things. *Kriging* methods are a set of statistical estimation algorithms that curve-fit known point data and produce a predictive surface for an entire study area. *Krige* represents an automatic implementation of kriging algorithms, where you use simple default parameters to help you generate predictive surfaces. A *variogram* is a statistical tool that measures how different spatial data becomes as the distance between data points increases. The variogram is a measure of "spatial dissimilarity". When you krige, you use variogram models with internally defined parameters to generate interpolative, predictive surfaces.

- » **Statistical programming:** This one involves probability distributions, time series analyses, regression analyses, and Monte Carlo simulations, among other processes.

- » **Clustering analysis:** Processes can include nearest-neighbor algorithms, k-means clustering, or kernel density estimations.

- » **GIS technology:** GIS technology pops up a lot in this chapter, but that's to be expected because its spatial analysis and map-making offerings are incredibly flexible.

- » **Coding requirements:** Programming for a spatial statistics project could entail using R, SPSS, SAS, MATLAB, and SQL, among other programming languages.

Addressing environmental issues with spatial statistics

A great example of using spatial statistics to generate predictions for location-dependent environmental variables can be seen in the recent work of Dr. Pierre Goovaerts. Dr. Goovaerts uses advanced statistics, coding, and his authoritative subject-matter expertise in agricultural engineering, soil science, and epidemiology to uncover correlations between spatial disease patterns, mortality, environmental toxin exposure, and sociodemographics.

In one of Dr. Goovaerts recent projects, he used spatial statistics to model and analyze data on groundwater arsenic concentrations, location, geologic properties, weather patterns, topography, and land cover. Through his recent environmental data science studies, he discovered that the incidence of bladder, breast, and prostate cancers is spatially correlated to long-term arsenic exposure.

With respect to data science technologies and methodologies, Dr. Goovaerts commonly implements the following:

- » **Spatial statistical programming:** Once again, kriging and variogram analysis top the list.

- » **Statistical programming:** Least squares regression and Monte Carlo (a random simulation method) are central to Dr. Goovaerts's work.

- » **GIS technologies:** If you want map-making functionality and spatial data analysis methodologies, you're going to need GIS technologies.

To find out more about Dr. Goovaerts's work, check out his website at https://sites.google.com/site/goovaertspierre.

Chapter **20**

Data Science for Driving Growth in E-Commerce

Big data and analytics aren't really new topics to most people these days. However, the creative ways in which big data and analytics are being used to transform lives and businesses *are* new. Businesses are quickly catching on to the fact that in this fast-paced era, an organization's survival hinges on its ability to integrate data science and analytics into every major decision that's made — particularly in relation to strategic marketing decision making. In fact, the demand for marketing analytics practitioners has increased by 136 percent in the past three years alone. Marketing analytics professionals use data science and analytics to drive sales growth and user adoption rates for today's *e-commerce business* — a business that sells products or services on the Internet.

These days, even the most traditional, old-fashioned business enterprise has at least some sort of web presence that would qualify as an e-commerce operation. Other e-commerce businesses are 100 percent digital and have no real on-the-ground presence to speak of. Because many businesses use blogging to build a well-branded online space where visitors receive access to insightful or entertaining content in exchange for their website visits and brand loyalty, even an individual blogger who has a website and a strong social presence can be considered an e-commerce business.

In recent years, the practice of using marketing analytics and data science to develop tactical strategies for e-commerce business growth came to be known as *growth hacking* — growth hacking is also referred to as *growth engineering,* or simply *growth*. Growth hacking is particularly well suited for start-up growth because of the lower-cost, more-innovative methods that growth hackers generally employ. In marketing, the word *conversion* describes the scenario in which a marketing effort is successful in getting a user, or prospective user, to take a desired action. Examples of conversions include the act of getting someone to visit your website, subscribe to your newsletter, follow your social media channel, or purchase your product.

In the growth game, the only goals are to get visitors to convert and to move them along in a swift and steady flow through all layers of the sales funnel. This chapter provides you with some simple concepts and methods you can use to get started in growing your e-commerce business. This chapter gives you only the tip of the growth iceberg. For brevity, I've omitted many of the more advanced and complicated tactics.

True growth hacking is a hybridization of the following fields:

>> **Engineering:** In an e-commerce context, this includes systems design, process design, systems thinking, and iterative design.

>> **Marketing:** Subcategories of marketing include psychology, branding, and aesthetic design.

>> **Business intelligence:** Think *intelligence* as in Central Intelligence Agency, rather than smarts. Subcategories here include metric selection, descriptive analytics, diagnostic analytics, and prescriptive analytics based on simple inference.

>> **Data science:** Casting its web rather widely, data science requires math and statistics know-how, web programming chops, the ability to code in Python or R, SQL skills, and subject-matter expertise in e-commerce business and Internet marketing.

In this chapter, I discuss the data science that's involved in growth hacking, and how you can use it to supercharge your online business growth. Just keep in mind that marketing analytics professionals who engage in data science for e-commerce growth may have to wear many hats — for example, Digital Analytics Consultant,

Web Analytics Engagement Analyst, Digital Web Marketing Analytics, or Optimization Manager. For simplicity's sake, I refer to all of these roles as *e-commerce data science*.

Here's a look at the data science that's involved in this line of work:

» **Math and statistics requirements:** Practitioners should understand and know how to apply significance testing, time series analysis, trend and seasonal analysis, regression analysis, multivariate regression, segmentation analysis, A/B split testing, and multivariate testing.

» **Programming requirements:** Data scientists working in growth should be solid in SQL, as well as web-programming languages like JavaScript, HTML, DHTML, and AJAX. Python and R programming could come in handy for segmentation analysis, data visualization, or building a recommendation engine, although not many growth specialists are required to do this type of work, because of the high availability of applications designed specifically for these purposes.

» **Subject-matter expertise:** Data scientists working in this field must have a deep understanding of e-commerce business, its various structures, its systems, and its channels. They must also understand Internet marketing fundamentals.

Data scientists in e-commerce generally use applications for their analyses, although sometimes they need to use coding to carry out a customized analysis. E-commerce data scientists use data science to formulate highly focused, results-oriented business strategies. They do *not* focus on exploratory data analysis. In e-commerce data science, your job is to use data in order to better understand users so that you can devise ways to drive growth results. You use algorithms and data visualizations only to achieve these goals. It's all about how you as a data scientist can derive insights from a wide variety of software and web applications — many of which I discuss in the section "Appraising popular web analytics applications," later in this chapter, by the way.

Data scientists in this field are often asked to analyze click-stream data, site performance data, and channel performance data in order to provide decision support on the effectiveness of tactical optimization strategies. They often have to design, develop, and manage *tag deployments* — the placing of code snippets in the header of a web page used to collect data for use in third-party analytics applications. Data scientists in this field also work on A/B split testing, multivariate testing, and mouse-click heat map analytics (all explained later in the section "Checking out common types of testing in growth").

Advanced data scientists in this field may also be expected to build personalization and recommendation engines. Practitioners need to communicate data insights in a clear, direct, and meaningful manner, using written words, spoken words, and data visualizations. Lastly, any data scientist who works in growth has to have a solid understanding of e-commerce and Internet marketing.

Making Sense of Data for E-Commerce Growth

Data science in e-commerce serves the same purpose that it does in any other discipline — to derive valuable insights from raw data. In e-commerce, you're looking for data insights that you can use to optimize a brand's marketing return on investment (ROI) and to drive growth in every layer of the sales funnel. How you end up doing that is up to you, but the work of most data scientists in e-commerce involves the following:

» **Data analysis:** Simple statistical and mathematical inference. Segmentation analysis gets rather complicated when trying to make sense of e-commerce data. You also use a lot of trend analysis, outlier analysis, and regression analysis.

» **Data wrangling:** *Data wrangling* involves using processes and procedures to clean and convert data from one format and structure to another so that the data is accurate and in the format that analytics tools and scripts require for consumption. In growth work, source data is usually captured and generated by analytics applications. Most of the time, you can derive insight within the application, but sometimes you need to export the data so that you can create data mashups, perform custom analyses, and create custom visualizations that aren't available in your out-of-the-box solutions. These situations could demand that you use a fair bit of data wrangling to get what you need from the source datasets.

» **Data visualization design:** Data graphics in e-commerce are usually quite simple. Expect to use a lot of line charts, bar charts, scatter charts, and map-based data visualizations. Data visualizations should be simple and to the point, but the analyses required to derive meaningful insights may take some time.

» **Communication:** After you make sense of the data, you have to communicate its meaning in clear, direct, and concise ways that decision makers can easily understand. E-commerce data scientists need to be excellent at communicating data insights via data visualizations, a written narrative, and conversation.

>> **Custom development work:** In some cases, you may need to design custom scripts for automated custom data analysis and visualization. In other cases, you may have to go so far as to design a personalization and recommendation system, but because you can find a ton of prebuilt applications available for these purposes, the typical e-commerce data scientist position description doesn't include this requirement.

Optimizing E-Commerce Business Systems

Time for a (brief) primer on how you can begin using web analytics, testing tactics, and segmentation and targeting initiatives to ignite growth in all layers of your e-commerce sales funnel. Before getting into the nitty-gritty of these methods, though, you first need to understand the fundamental structure and function of each layer in a sales funnel. In keeping with a logical and systematic approach, I'm breaking down the e-commerce sales funnel into the following five stages: acquisition, activation, retention, referral, and revenue.

REMEMBER

Acquisition, activation, retention, referral, and revenue are also referred to as AARRR, the pirate metrics. (Say "AARRR" out loud a few times and you'll know why it's called the pirate metrics.) This growth framework (see Figure 20-1) was originally suggested by famed angel investor and entrepreneur, Dave McClure. The term is now widely used throughout the growth-hacking community.

Here are the functions of each stage of the sales funnel:

>> **Acquisition:** Your brand acquires new users in the form of website visitors. New users are often acquired via social media marketing, search engine marketing, search engine optimization, content marketing, or partnerships.

FIGURE 20-1:
The AARRR of the e-commerce sales funnel.

- » **Activation:** Acquired users activate, either through email subscription, RSS subscription, or social followings.
- » **Retention:** Activated users take some sort of action — such as accepting an offer or responding to a call to action within your email marketing campaign.
- » **Referral:** Retained users refer new users to your brand's acquisition layer.
- » **Revenue:** Users make revenue-generating purchases.

Angling in on analytics

Web analytics can be described as the practice of generating, collecting, and making sense of Internet data in order to optimize web design and strategy. Configure web analytics applications to monitor and track absolutely all your growth tactics and strategies, because without this information, you're operating in the dark — and nothing grows in the dark.

Web analytics provide fast and clear results that gauge e-commerce growth strategy effectiveness. You can use web analytics as a diagnostic tool, to get to know your audience, to understand their preferences, to start doing more of what works, and to stop doing the things that clearly don't work. If you want to devise growth strategies that actually grow your business, you need to make sure you've configured web analytics to track and monitor all stages of the funnel, as well as every touch point between your brand and its prospective customers.

Appraising popular web analytics applications

Data scientists working in growth hacking should be familiar with (and know how to derive insights from) the following web analytics applications:

- » **Google Analytics** (www.google.com/analytics)**:** A free, easy-to-use, powerful web analytics tool, Google Analytics is great for monitoring not only the volumes of traffic that come to your website over time but also the demographics and summary statistics on your visitors, your website referral sources, your visitor flow patterns, real-time visitor behavior analytics, and much more. Google Analytics can show you benchmarking analytics that provide insights about how your website's performance compares to the performance of other websites in your industry.
- » **Adobe Analytics** (www.adobe.com/solutions/digital-analytics/ marketing-reports-analytics.html)**:** You can use Adobe Analytics for marketing attribution, mobile app performance, social media marketing performance, return-on-investment (ROI) investigation, and real-time visitor monitoring.

- » **IBM Digital Analytics (**`www-03.ibm.com/software/products/en/digital-analytics`**):** The perfect platform for integrating performance data from all your business's web channels — from data generated by website guests visiting using personal computers to mobile visitor statistics, and even social media channel performance — IBM Digital Analytics offers powerful analytics capabilities to keep you informed of real-time and historical visitor behaviors, as well as relevant cross-channel interactions. The platform also offers marketing attribution and tag management capabilities.

- » **Webtrends (**`http://webtrends.com`**):** Offering advanced multichannel analytics, real-time visitor behavior monitoring, and the technology you need to reclaim lost sales from shopping cart abandonment via email remarketing tactics, Webtrends is a powerhouse web analytics application. It even goes the extra mile by offering a campaign optimization feature that you can use to track, monitor, and optimize your search engine marketing efforts, as well as your search and social advertisement campaigns.

- » **Google Tag Manager (**`www.google.com/tagmanager`**):** Website tags — code snippets that collect data for use in your third-party analytics applications — can help you measure and manage the effectiveness of your Internet marketing campaigns, but the process of deploying tags is error-prone and requires coding. Google Tag Manager is a free tag-management tool that offers a code-free interface and a rules-based system that allows you to easily manage and deploy your website marketing and tracking tags.

- » **Assorted social analytics tools:** In addition to the more heavyweight offerings described in this list, you can find many free, easy-to-use social analytics applications to monitor and measure the effectiveness of your social media growth initiatives. These include Sendible (`www.sendible.com`), which has ample options for tracking statistics from your Twitter, Facebook Page, Instagram, and Google Analytics metrics on one custom dashboard; Facebook Page Insights (`www.facebook.com/Your_Facebook_Page_ID/insights`); Pinterest Analytics (`https://analytics.pinterest.com`); Iconosquare Statistics for Instagram (`http://iconosquare.com`); and Google URL Shortener for link tracking (`https://goo.gl`).

While a cookie is not a web analytic application, per se, it is a text file that tracks the activities, interests, and browsing patterns of a website's visitors. Almost all large-scale e-commerce businesses use cookies to collect visitor information that helps the business improve the overall user experience and optimize advertising efforts.

Accessing analytics for acquisitions

Analytics for acquisitions provide a measure and gauge of the effectiveness of your user acquisition tactics. If you want to optimize your brand's channels, to glean a deeper understanding of your audiences, or to evaluate the performance of your growth tactics, look to user acquisition analytics. In this list, I describe some means by which you can use web analytics to begin boosting your user acquisitions:

>> **Audience discovery:** By taking a close look at your web analytics and the sources from which your new users are being acquired, you can infer an idea about the interests of users in each of your channels.

>> **Channel optimization:** After discovering insights about your channel audiences, you can use those insights to optimize your channels — designing your channels and the offerings you extend along them so that they better align with the preferences of each channel audience.

>> **Optimized social-growth strategies:** Social media networks are brand channels. Each network functions for its own purpose, and the preferences of audience members in different networks tend to differ, even if the niche is the same. For example, content about news events tends to perform well on Twitter, whereas Facebook audiences seek to be entertained and inspired. News content doesn't fare so well on the Facebook network and vice versa. What's more, your specific audiences have their own, particular interests and nuances per social network. Use social analytics to deduce the interests of your audiences per social channel, and then you can use that information to optimize your efforts there. You can also use social network analytics to identify the main influencers in your niche so that you can begin forging friendships and strategic alliances.

Applying analytics for activation

User activation analytics provide a measure and gauge of your user activations over time. You can use activation analytics to gauge how your user-activation tactics are performing, allowing you to optimize your user sign-ups, even on a per-channel basis. The following are a few ways in which you can use web analytics to optimize your user activation growth rates:

>> **Sign-up rate monitoring:** Analytics that reflect the number of new user sign-ups, in the form of either email subscriptions or RSS subscriptions. This metric gives you an idea of how well your website's content is meeting the wants and needs of newly acquired users. These analytics are also a good gauge of the overall effectiveness of your *calls to action* — your prompts that tell users to sign up in exchange for some promised benefit to them.

>> **Average session duration:** You can easily derive information on average session duration by taking a quick and basic look at your Google Analytics. Average session duration is a good gauge of how compelling your visitors find

your website. And the more compelling your site, the more likely it is that your acquired users will convert to active users — and active users to refer their friends and convert to paying customers.

If you're working on growth for a client or employer, you can access their Google Analytics account by having them add your Google account as an authorized user of their Google Analytics account. If you're working on growth for your own brand or website, you must sign up for a free Google Analytics account (at www.google.com/analytics) and then install the Google Analytics Tracking code into your site.

Whether you're working on behalf of a client or yourself, you must have your own Google account. You can get one of those by registering through Google (at https://accounts.google.com/SignUp).

>> **Website heat maps for website optimization:** A website *heat map* is a visual graphic that uses colors to depict the areas of a web page where visitors are clicking with greatest and least intensity. Applications such as SessionCam (www.sessioncam.com/website-heatmaps) and ClickTale (www.clicktale.com/products/heatmap-suite) offer mouse-click heat map data visualizations that show you how your customers and user segments are using your website — in other words, what website features and areas are most attractive to users. This information tells you about the effectiveness of your activation tactics and your overall web design. If you see that user attention flow isn't focused toward your call-to-action areas, you should perhaps redesign your page in a way that helps to redirect user focus.

Your main goal should always be to push users toward the next stage of the sales funnel.

Reviewing analytics for retentions

Retention analytics provide a measure of your user retention tactics. Retention analytics can help you boost customer loyalty or increase the amount of time your users spend interacting with your brand. Boosting user retentions is, in large part, a function of marketing strategy and psychology, but web analytics are also an integral part of maintaining and growing your brand's retention rates. Here's how you can use web analytics to optimize your user retentions growth:

>> **Email marketing open rates:** Tracking and monitoring *time series* — collections of data on attribute values over time — that capture email open rates can give you an idea of how well your email marketing tactics are performing, in general. For example, if you see a steady decline in open rates, either your subscribers aren't that interested in the topics described in email headlines or you're sending emails too frequently and spamming your users'

inboxes — in other words, wearing out your welcome. High email-open rates reflect a high level of subscriber loyalty, which is always a good thing.

>> **RSS view rates:** Tracking and monitoring time series that capture RSS view rates can give you an idea of how well your blog post titles are performing with your RSS subscribers — in other words, how well the blog content topic is matched to your subscribers' interests. This metric can also tell you whether your headline copy is intriguing enough to draw RSS subscribers in for a read. High RSS view rates reflect higher levels of loyalty among your RSS subscribers.

>> **Customer satisfaction monitoring:** Sentiment analysis is an analysis technique where you apply text mining and data categorization techniques to web data in order to identify the feelings and attitudes of people (and customers) in your networks. Some social analytics applications offer a built-in sentiment analysis feature. You can use one of these applications or code something up yourself. Whatever you choose, be sure to stay on top of what people are saying about your brand across your social media channels, because it's vital for the protection and proactive management of your brand's reputation. As they say, "The customer is always right."

Talking about testing your strategies

In growth, you use testing methods to optimize your web design and messaging so that it performs at its absolute best with the audiences to which it's targeted. Although testing and web analytics methods are both intended to optimize performance, testing goes one layer deeper than web analytics. You use web analytics to get a general idea about the interests of your channel audiences and how well your marketing efforts are paying off over time. After you have this information, you can then go in deeper to test variations on live visitors in order to gain empirical evidence about what designs and messaging your visitors actually prefer.

Testing tactics can help you optimize your website design or brand messaging for increased conversions in all layers of the funnel. Testing is also useful when optimizing your landing pages for user activations and revenue conversions. In the following sections, I introduce the testing strategies that are most commonly deployed in growth and discuss how you can use those strategies to optimize your efforts. I also provide you with a few tips on what applications are available to make testing easier and more fun.

Checking out common types of testing in growth

When you use data insights to increase growth for e-commerce businesses, you're likely to run into the three following testing tactics: A/B split testing, multivariate testing, and mouse-click heat map analytics.

An *A/B split test* is an optimization tactic you can use to split variations of your website or brand messaging between sets of live audiences in order to gauge responses and decide which of the two variations performs best. A/B split testing is the simplest testing method you can use for website or messaging optimization.

Multivariate testing is, in many ways, similar to the multivariate regression analysis that I discuss in Chapter 5. Like multivariate regression analysis, multivariate testing allows you to uncover relationships, correlations, and causations between variables and outcomes. In the case of multivariate testing, you're testing several conversion factors simultaneously over an extended period in order to uncover which factors are responsible for increased conversions. Multivariate testing is more complicated than A/B split testing, but it usually provides quicker and more powerful results.

Lastly, you can use *mouse-click heat map analytics* to see how visitors are responding to your design and messaging choices. In this type of testing, you use the mouse-click heat map to help you make optimal website design and messaging choices to ensure that you're doing everything you can to keep your visitors focused and converting.

REMEMBER

Landing pages are meant to offer visitors little to no options, except to convert or to exit the page. Because a visitor has so few options on what he can do on a landing page, you don't really need to use multivariate testing or website mouse-click heat maps. Simple A/B split tests suffice.

Data scientists working in growth hacking should be familiar with (and know how to derive insight from) the following testing applications:

>> **Webtrends** (http://webtrends.com): Offers a conversion-optimization feature that includes functionality for A/B split testing and multivariate testing.

>> **Optimizely** (www.optimizely.com): A popular product among the growth-hacking community. You can use Optimizely for multipage funnel testing, A/B split testing, and multivariate testing, among other things.

>> **Visual Website Optimizer** (https://vwo.com): An excellent tool for A/B split testing and multivariate testing.

Testing for acquisitions

Acquisitions testing provides feedback on how well your content performs with prospective users in your assorted channels. You can use acquisitions testing to help compare your message's performance in each channel, helping you optimize your messaging on a per-channel basis. If you want to optimize the performance of your brand's published images, you can use acquisition testing to compare image performance across your channels as well. Lastly, if you want to increase your acquisitions through increases in user referrals, use testing to help optimize your referrals messaging for the referrals channels. Acquisition testing can help you begin to understand the specific preferences of prospective users on a channel-by-channel basis. You can use A/B split testing to improve your acquisitions in the following ways:

>> **Social messaging optimization:** After you use social analytics to deduce the general interests and preferences of users in each of your social channels, you can then further optimize your brand messaging along those channels by using A/B split testing to compare your headlines and social media messaging within each channel.

>> **Brand image and messaging optimization:** Compare and optimize the respective performances of images along each of your social channels.

>> **Optimized referral messaging:** Test the effectiveness of your email messaging at converting new user referrals.

Testing for activations

Activation testing provides feedback on how well your website and its content perform in converting acquired users to active users. The results of activation testing can help you optimize your website and landing pages for maximum sign-ups and subscriptions. Here's how you'd use testing methods to optimize user activation growth:

>> **Website conversion optimization:** Make sure your website is optimized for user activation conversions. You can use A/B split testing, multivariate testing, or a mouse-click heat map data visualization to help you optimize your website design.

>> **Landing pages:** If your landing page has a simple call to action that prompts guests to subscribe to your email list, you can use A/B split testing for simple design optimization of this page and the call-to-action messaging.

Testing for retentions

Retentions testing provides feedback on how well your blog post and email headlines are performing among your base of activated users. If you want to optimize your headlines so that active users want to continue active engagements with your brand, test the performance of your user-retention tactics. Here's how you can use testing methods to optimize user retention growth:

>> **Headline optimization:** Use A/B split testing to optimize the headlines of your blog posts and email marketing messages. Test different headline varieties within your different channels, and then use the varieties that perform the best. Email open rates and RSS view rates are ideal metrics to track the performance of each headline variation.

>> **Conversion rate optimization:** Use A/B split testing on the messaging within your emails to decide which messaging variety more effectively gets your activated users to engage with your brand. The more effective your email messaging is at getting activated users to take a desired action, the greater your user retention rates.

Testing for revenue growth

Revenue testing gauges the performance of revenue-generating landing pages, e-commerce pages, and brand messaging. Revenue testing methods can help you optimize your landing and e-commerce pages for sales conversions. Here's how you can use testing methods to optimize revenue growth:

>> **Website conversion optimization:** You can use A/B split testing, multivariate testing, or a mouse-click heat map data visualization to help optimize your sales page and shopping cart design for revenue-generating conversions.

>> **Landing page optimization:** If you have a landing page with a simple call to action that prompts guests to make a purchase, you can use A/B split testing for design optimization.

Segmenting and targeting for success

The purpose of segmenting your channels and audiences is so that you can exact-target your messaging and offerings for optimal conversions, according to the specific interests and preferences of each user segment. If your goal is to optimize your marketing return on investment by exact-targeting customized messages to entire swathes of your audience at one time, you can use segmentation analysis to group together audience members by shared attributes and then customize your messaging to those target audiences on a group-by-group basis. In the following sections, I tell you what applications can help you make user segmentation easier and how you can use segmentation and targeting tactics to grow the layers of your sales funnel.

Segmenting for faster and easier e-commerce growth

Data scientists working in growth hacking should be familiar with, and know how to derive insight from, the following user segmentation and targeting applications:

>> **Google Analytics Segment Builder:** Google Analytics (www.google.com/analytics) contains a Segment Builder feature that makes it easier for you to set up filters when you configure your segments within the application. You can use the tool to segment users by demographic data, such as age, gender, referral source, and nationality. (For more on the Segment Builder, check out the Google Analytics Help page at https://support.google.com/analytics/answer/3124493.)

>> **Adobe Analytics (**www.adobe.com/solutions/digital-analytics/marketing-reports-analytics.html**):** You can use Adobe Analytics for advanced user segmentation and customer churn analysis — or analysis to identify reasons for and preempt customer loss.

REMEMBER

Customer churn describes the loss, or churn, of existing customers. *Customer churn analysis* is a set of analytical techniques that are designed to identify, monitor, and issue alerts on indicators that signify when customers are likely to churn. With the information that's generated in customer churn analysis, businesses can take preemptive measures to retain at-risk customers.

>> **Webtrends (**http://webtrends.com**):** Webtrends' Visitor Segmentation and Scoring offers real-time customer segmentation features that help you isolate, target, and engage your highest-value visitors. The Conversion Optimization solution also offers advanced segmenting and targeting functionality that you can use to optimize your website, landing pages, and overall customer experience.

>> **Optimizely (**www.optimizely.com**):** In addition to its testing functionality, you can use Optimizely for visitor segmentation, targeting, and geotargeting.

>> **IBM Product Recommendations (**www-01.ibm.com/software/marketing-solutions/products-recommendation-solution**):** This solution utilizes IBM Digital Analytics, customer-segmentation, and product-segmentation methods to make optimal product recommendations to visitors of e-commerce websites. IBM Product Recommendations Solutions can help you upsell or cross-sell your offerings.

Segmenting and targeting for acquisitions

You can optimize your acquisition efforts to meet the exact preferences and interests of your prospective users. If you want to maximize your user-acquisition return on investment, you can use segmenting and targeting to group your prospective users and channels by interest and style preferences, and then use those groupings to send out exact-targeted messaging to prospective users en masse. Acquisitions segmentation and targeting helps you build your channels by providing solid facts about the preferences of particular segments. After you have prospective users grouped by preference, it's just a matter of marketing to those preferences and avoiding messaging that's unfavorable within the segments.

Prospective user and channel segmentation and targeting is the low-lying fruit of acquisitions growth because after you figure out what works with each segment, it's just a matter of continuing to provide that content in order to make your user acquisition numbers grow. Here's how you can use segmentation and targeting tactics to optimize your user acquisitions (which is the same goal as the tactics discussed in the section "Accessing analytics for acquisitions," earlier in this chapter):

>> **Audience discovery:** By performing segmentation analysis on your website visitor data, you can successfully group your website visitors in certain and distinctive classes according to their shared characteristics. This approach is far more definitive than the simple inference-based method used for analytics, but the purpose is the same — to use visitor data to better understand who your audiences are, what they're interested in, and how you can best target your messaging and offerings to appeal to them.

>> **Social media channel optimization:** You can use the insights you've gleaned via segmentation analysis to better understand and cater to the distinct preferences of your social media network audiences.

Targeting for activations

You can increase your user activations by understanding and responding to the interests and preferences of your website users. If you want to optimize your website and its content for increased user activations, segmentation analysis can help you get a better understanding of your audiences' interests. Here's how you can use segmentation and targeting tactics to optimize your user activation growth:

>> **Audience discovery:** You can perform segmentation analysis of your website visitor data in order to understand and substantively group users according to their types and preferences. These groupings help you develop more strategically targeted messages to pique the interests of people in your audience segments.

>> **Strategic channel messaging:** After you have a solid understanding of your user segments and their preferences, you can use this information to help you develop strategic, highly targeted messaging that performs well within each of the separate segments. This targeted approach can lead to increased social media followings and increased website subscriptions.

Segmenting and targeting for retentions

You can increase your user retentions by understanding and responding to the interests and preferences of your website users. To help increase user retention by reducing customer churn, you can deploy user segmentation and targeting strategies. Simply segment your customer–churn data into *cohorts* — subsets that are grouped according to similarities in some shared characteristic — and then analyze those cohorts to uncover trends and deduce the factors that contribute to churn within each of the groups. After you understand why particular segments of users are churning, you can take preemptive measures to stop that churn before you lose the customers for good.

Segmenting and targeting for revenues

You can increase your brand's revenues by understanding and responding to the interests and preferences of your e-commerce customers. User segmentation and targeting strategies can help you increase revenues and sales volumes. Here's how:

>> **Landing and e-commerce page optimization:** You can use segmentation analysis on your website visitor data to better understand visitor behavior patterns per customer category, where a customer category could be defined by age, race, gender, income, referral source, or geographic region. After you distinguish clear user segments, and the preferences thereof, you can use that information to create separate, customized landing or e-commerce pages that are targeted for optimal sales conversions within the segments.

>> **Recommendation engines:** Whether you build them yourself or use a recommender application instead, recommendation systems use collaborative filtering or content-based filtering to segment customers according to shared characteristics. It's useful to segment customers in this way so that you can exact-target offers per customers' known preferences, in order to upsell and cross-sell your brand's offerings.

Chapter **21**

Using Data Science to Describe and Predict Criminal Activity

I n recent years, data science has been increasingly incorporated into criminological methodologies in a practice that's been referred to as *predictive policing.* Predictive policing offers promising results, and law enforcement decision-makers have high hopes that they can use predictive intelligence to help them formulate more effective tactical strategies. Judges hope to use predictive insights for support when deciding when to grant bail to suspects. Police agencies want to use the technology for improved offender monitoring. Consequently, there's a very high demand for crime analysts who are skilled at using data science to build descriptive and predictive information products to support the decisions of law enforcement officials.

To practice data science in criminal analysis, you need to be skilled in GIS, data visualization, coding, and basic math and statistics. If you want to go deeper into descriptive, predictive, or resource modeling, you need strong skills in spatial statistics. To practice as a data scientist in crime analysis, you also need a strong subject-matter expertise in the criminal justice field.

Criminal data science practitioners aren't replacements for crime analysts — rather, they enhance the work that crime analysts do. Crime analysts are responsible for analyzing and reporting crime data trends as they happen to keep law enforcement officials and public citizens aware so that they can take proactive measures to prevent future criminal activity. Crime analysts work with law enforcement officials to develop strategies and tactics to attack and reduce criminal activity. Data scientists in crime analysis, however, assume a more technical role in the data analysis. They use advanced math, statistics, and coding to uncover spatial and temporal trends hidden deep within crime datasets. Data scientists in crime analysis work to describe, predict, and model resources for the prevention of criminal activity.

Two distinct types of data analysis are relevant to criminology — temporal data analysis and spatial data analysis. *Temporal data analysis* involves the analysis of tabular datasets that contain temporally relevant but not geo-referenced data. *Spatial data analysis* involves analyzing geo-referenced datasets without regard to time. Spatial analysis can also involve analyzing tabular data that's included within geo-referenced spatial datasets. It may even involve analyzing temporal data that pertains to the locations in question — which is known as *spatio-temporal data analysis.*

Temporal Analysis for Crime Prevention and Monitoring

The temporal analysis of crime data produces analytics that describe patterns in criminal activity based on time. You can analyze temporal crime data to develop prescriptive analytics, either through traditional crime analysis means or through a data science approach. Knowing how to produce prescriptive analytics from temporal crime data allows you to provide decision-support to law enforcement agencies that want to optimize their tactical crime fighting.

For purposes of this discussion, consider *temporal data* to be tabular data that's earmarked with date/time entries for each record in the set. You use temporal data analysis to make inferences and draw correlations that you can use to monitor and predict what crimes are happening when and why. In crime analysis, an example of a temporal dataset would be a dataset that describes the counts of different types of crimes that have been committed, broken into count per day and recorded on a daily basis for an entire month.

To be successful at deriving simple, yet useful, insights from temporal crime data, you need only a basic skill level in data science. You should know how to draw fundamental statistical and mathematical inferences, how to spot and investigate outliers, how to analyze patterns in time series, and how to draw correlations or causations through regression techniques. When deriving insights from temporal crime data, you generally produce decision-support products in the form of tabular data reports and simple data visualizations — such as bar charts, line charts, and heat map charts.

Spatial Crime Prediction and Monitoring

Spatial data is tabular data that's earmarked with spatial coordinate information for each record in the dataset. Many times, spatial datasets also have a field that indicates a date/time attribute for each of the records in the set — making it *spatio-temporal data.* If you want to create crime maps or uncover location-based trends in crime data, use spatial data analysis. You can also use spatial analysis methods to make location-based inferences that help you monitor and predict what crimes will occur where, when, and why. In the following sections, I show how you can use GIS technologies, data modeling, and advanced spatial statistics to build information products for the prediction and monitoring of criminal activity.

Crime mapping with GIS technology

One of the most common forms of data insight that's used in law enforcement is the crime map. A *crime map* is a spatial map that visualizes where crimes have been committed during any given time interval. In olden days, you might have drawn this type of map out with pencil and paper, but nowadays you do the job using a GIS software, such as ArcGIS Desktop or QGIS.

REMEMBER

Although crime mapping has become increasingly sophisticated while advances have been made in spatial technologies, the purpose has remained the same — to provide law enforcement decision makers and personnel with location information that describes on-the-ground criminal activities so that they can use that information to optimize their efforts in protecting public safety. GIS software can help you make crime maps that can be used as a descriptive analytic or as a source for simple inference-based predictions. (For much more about mapmaking and basic spatial analysis, check out Chapter 13.)

Going one step further with location-allocation analysis

Location allocation is a form of predictive spatial analytics that you can use for location optimization from complex spatial data models. For example, in law enforcement, location optimization can predict optimal locations for police stations so that dispatched officers can travel to an emergency in any part of the city within a 5-minute response-time window. To help your agency predict the best locations to position officers so that they can arrive immediately at any emergency in any part of town, use location-allocation analysis.

You can most easily do a location-allocation analysis by using the ArcGIS for Desktop Network Analyst add-on to carry out a maximum coverage analysis. (Check out ArcGIS for Desktop at www.esri.com/software/arcgis/arcgis-for-desktop.) In this form of analysis, you input data about existing facilities, *demand points* — points that represent places in the study area that exhibit a demand for law enforcement resources — and any spatial barriers that would block or severely impede law enforcement response times. The model outputs information about the optimal locations to place officers for the fastest, most well-distributed response times. Packages such as the Network Analyst add-on are easy to use, which is one of the feature benefits that might have you choose ArcGIS over open-source QGIS. Figure 21-1 shows map results that are derived from a location-allocation analysis.

FIGURE 21-1:
A map product derived from location-allocation analysis.

Analyzing complex spatial statistics to better understand crime

You can use your skills in GIS, mathematics, data modeling, and spatial statistics in many ways to build descriptive and predictive information products that support the decision making of law enforcement officials. Proprietary spatial-analysis software applications have greatly simplified this work by providing special add-on tools specifically designed for spatial analysis of crime data. In addition, free open-source applications such as the CrimeStat III program (www.nij.gov/topics/technology/maps/pages/crimestat.aspx) are available to help you carry out more advanced forms of statistical analysis. In the following sections, I introduce how you can use your data science skills to derive descriptive and predictive spatial data insights that help law enforcement agencies optimize their tactical response planning.

Delving into descriptive methods

You can incorporate descriptive spatial statistics into crime analysis in order to produce analytics you can then use to understand and monitor the location-based attributes of ongoing criminal activities. You can use descriptive spatial statistics to provide your law enforcement agency with up-to-date information on the location, intensity, and size of criminal activity hot spots, as well as to derive important information about the characteristics of local areas that are positioned between these hot spots.

This list includes types of approaches that are helpful when using spatial statistics for descriptive methods in crime analysis:

>> **Clustering:** Use methods such as nearest neighbor algorithms (hierarchical and nonhierarchical) and the k-means algorithm to identify and analyze criminal hot spots, to describe the properties of inter-incident distances, or to describe spatial autocorrelation that exists between dense areas of criminal activity. To learn more about clustering methods, be sure to check out Chapter 6 of this book.

Spatial autocorrelation is a term that refers to the natural phenomenon that when things are closer to one another in physical location, they exhibit more average similarity than things that are far away from one another.

>> **Advanced spatial mathematics:** You can use spatial mathematical metrics, such as the Euclidian metric or the Manhattan metric (otherwise known as the taxicab metric) to describe the distances between criminal incidents or sets of incidents. The *Euclidean metric* is a measure of the distance between points plotted on a Euclidean plane. The *taxicab metric* is a measure of the distance

between points, where distance is calculated as the sum of the absolute value of the differences between two points' Cartesian coordinates.

>> **Descriptive statistics:** Use statistics to generate a description about the location distribution of criminal activities — including information on the directional mean and mean center of criminal incidents.

Building predictive spatial models for crime analysis

You can incorporate predictive statistical models into crime analysis methods to produce analytics that describe and predict where and what kinds of criminal activity are likely to occur.

Predictive spatial models can help you predict the behavior, location, or criminal activities of repeat offenders. You can also apply statistical methods to spatio-temporal data to ascertain causative or correlative variables relevant to crime and law enforcement.

The following list includes types of approaches that are helpful in spatial predictive modeling for crime analysis:

>> **Clustering:** You can use kernel density estimation methods to quantify the spatial density of criminal activities and to generate comparative measures between the densities of criminal activity relative to the base population of the affected area.

REMEMBER

Kernel density estimation (KDE) is a smoothing method that works by placing a *kernel* — or, a weighting function that is useful for quantifying density — on each data point in the dataset and then summing the kernels to generate a kernel density estimate for the overall region.

>> **Advanced spatial statistics:** One example of this is to use regression analysis to establish how one or more independent crime variables directly cause, or correlate with, a dependent crime variable. Lastly, advanced spatial statistics are used to make behavioral predictions for repeat offenders and to predict future criminal activity based on historical records on criminal behavior and information about present conditions.

Modeling travel demand in criminal activity

Modeling the travel demand of criminal activity allows you to describe and predict the travel patterns of criminals so that law enforcement can use this information in tactical response planning. If you want to predict the most likely routes that criminals will take between the locations from where they start out and the locations where they actually commit the crimes, use crime travel modeling.

Travel demand modeling is the brainchild of civil engineers and was developed to facilitate improved transportation planning. Although you can use four different approaches in travel demand modeling — trip-based, integrated trip-based, tour-based, and activity schedule-based — the trip-based approach (see Figure 21-2) is most relevant to crime analysis.

The trip-based approach is broken into the following four steps:

1. Trip generation.

   Model the *trip production* (the quantity of crime trips that originate in a *zone of origination* — a spatial region, like a neighborhood or subdivision) and the *trip attractions* (the quantity of crime trips that end in the *zone of destination* — the spatial region where the criminal act is executed).

2. Trip distribution.

   Incorporate a *trip matrix* — a matrix of rows and columns that covers a study area and depicts the patterns of trips across it— and a *gravity model* — a model that describes and predicts the locational flow of objects across space — to quantify the count of crime trips that occur between each zone of origination and each zone of destination.

3. Modal split.

   A *modal split* is the portion of travelers that uses particular trip paths across a study area. For travel demand modeling, you'd generate a count of the number of trips for each zone-of-origination/zone-of-destination pair that occurs via each available route. The choice between routes can be modeled statistical or mathematical.

4. Network assignment.

   Assign probability and predict the most likely routes that a criminal would take when traveling from a particular zone of origination to a particular zone of destination across the network of potential travel paths.

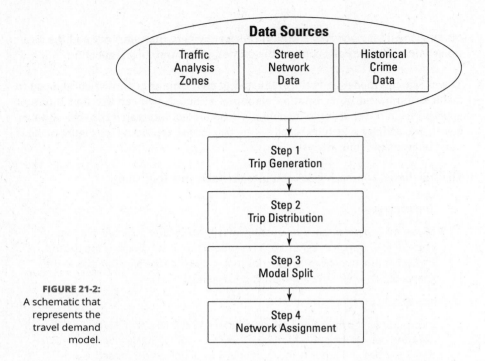

FIGURE 21-2:
A schematic that represents the travel demand model.

Probing the Problems with Data Science for Crime Analysis

Although data science for crime analysis has a promising future, it's not without its limitations. The field is still young, and it has a long way to go before the bugs are worked out. Currently, the approach is subject to significant criticism for both legal and technical reasons.

Caving in on civil rights

The legal systems of western nations such as the United States are fundamentally structured around the basic notion that people have the right to life, liberty, and the pursuit of property. More specifically, the U.S. Constitution's Fourth Amendment explicitly declares that people have a right "to be secure . . . against unreasonable searches and seizures, shall not be violated . . . but upon probable cause." Because predictive policing methods have become more popular, a consternation has arisen among informed U.S. citizens. People are concerned that predictive policing represents an encroachment on their Fourth Amendment rights.

To see how this rights violation could occur, imagine that you've developed a predictive model that estimates a car theft will occur on the afternoon of January 15 at the corner of Apple Street and Winslow Boulevard. Because your predictions have proven accurate in the past, the agency dispatches Officer Bob to police the area at said time and day. While out policing the area, Officer Bob sees and recognizes Citizen Daniel. Officer Bob had arrested Citizen Daniel five years earlier for burglary charges. Officer Bob testified against Citizen Daniel and knows that he was subsequently convicted. Citizen Daniel is also a racial minority, and Officer Bob finds himself being suspicious on that basis alone (known as *racial profiling*, this is illegal, but it happens all the time).

Officer Bob, on said street corner, has a predictive report that says a theft crime is about to occur, and he's in the presence of a man of a racial minority whom he knows has a history of committing theft crimes. Officer Bob decides that the predictive report, combined with what he knows about Citizen Daniel, is enough to justify probable cause, so he performs search-and-seizure on Daniel's person.

The conundrum arises when one considers whether a predictive report combined with knowledge of past criminal activity is sufficient to support probable cause. Even if the predictive report were guaranteed to be accurate — which it's not — couldn't this decision to search Citizen Daniel just be mostly racial profiling on the part of Officer Bob? What if Officer Bob is just using the predictive report as a justification so that he can harass and degrade Citizen Daniel because Daniel is a minority and Officer Bob hates minorities? In that case, Officer Bob would certainly be violating Daniel's Fourth Amendment rights. But because Officer Bob has the predictive policing report, who's to say why Officer Bob acts in the way that he does? Maybe he acts in good faith — but maybe not.

Predictive policing practices open a gray area in which officers can abuse power and violate civil rights without being held liable. A significant portion of the U.S. population is against the use of predictive policing measures for this reason, but the approach has technical problems as well.

Taking on technical limitations

Data science for crime analysis is a special breed, and as such, it's subject to certain problems that may not generally be an issue in other domains of application. In law enforcement, criminal perpetrators are acting according to their own intellects and free will. A brief analogy is the best way to describe the problem.

Imagine that you build a crime travel demand model. Based on the zone of origination, this model predicts that Criminal Carl will almost certainly travel on Ventura Avenue or Central Road when he goes to pick up his next shipment of drugs.

In fact, the model predicts these same two routes for all drug criminals who depart from the same zone of origination as Criminal Carl.

Based on this prediction, the agency sets up two units, one on Ventura Avenue and one on Central Road, in the hope of catching Criminal Carl after the buy. Criminal Carl, of course, doesn't know about all these plans. He and his buddy Steve travel Ventura Avenue, purchase their drugs, and then return back along the same route. It's nighttime, so Steve isn't so worried about wearing his seatbelt since he figures no one could see that anyway. As Criminal Carl and Steve make their way back, Officer Irene begins to tail them and look for a reason to pull them over; Steve's seatbelt infraction is just cause. When Officer Irene talks to the men, she can tell they're high, so she has probable cause to search the vehicle. Criminal Carl and Steve go to jail on drug charges, and when they're released, they tell their criminal friends all the details about what happened.

The agency uses this model to catch six more drug offenders in rapid time, on either Ventura Avenue or Central Road. Each time they make an arrest, the offenders go out and tell their criminal associates the details of how they got caught. After six busts on these two roads within a relatively short period, local drug criminals begin to catch on to the fact that these roads are being watched. After word is out about this fact, no criminal will take these streets any more. The criminals change their patterns in random ways to avert police, thus making your predictive model obsolete.

This kind of common pattern makes it ineffective to use predictive models to reduce crime rates. After criminals deduce the factors that put them at risk, they avoid those factors and randomly assume a different approach so that they can perpetrate their crimes without being caught. Most of the time, agencies continually have to change their analysis strategies to try to keep up with the criminals, but the criminals are almost always one step ahead.

This is a more severe version of an issue that arises in many applications, whenever the underlying process is subject to change without notice. Models must always be kept up to date.

6

The Part of Tens

Chapter **22**

Ten Phenomenal Resources for Open Data

O pen data is part of a larger trend toward a less restrictive, more open understanding of the idea of intellectual property, a trend that's been gaining tremendous popularity over the past decade. *Open data* is data that has been made publicly available and is permitted to be used, reused, built on, and shared with others. Open data is part of the open movement. Beyond open data, this aptly named *open movement* also includes open-source software, open hardware, open-content creative work, open access to scientific journals, and open science — all committed to the notion that content (including raw data from experiments) should be shared freely.

The distinguishing feature of open licenses is that they have copyleft instead of copyright. With *copyleft,* the only restriction is that the source of the work must be identified, sometimes with the caveat that derivative works can't be copyrighted with a more restrictive license than the original. If the second condition is in force, successfully commercializing the work itself becomes difficult, although people often find plenty of other indirect, creative avenues of commercialization.

WARNING

Be aware that sometimes work that's labeled as open may not fit the accepted definition. You're responsible to check the licensing rights and restrictions of the open data you use.

People often confuse *open* licenses with Creative Commons licenses. *Creative Commons* is a not-for-profit organization that's dedicated to encouraging and spreading creative works by offering a legal framework through which usage permissions can be granted and obtained, so that sharing parties are safe from legal risks when building on and using work and knowledge that's been openly shared. Some Creative Commons licenses are open, and some explicitly forbid derivative works and/or commercialization.

As part of more recent open government initiatives, governments around the world began releasing open government data. Governments generally provide this data so that it can be used by volunteer analysts and *civic hackers* — programmers who work collaboratively to build open-source solutions that use open data to solve social problems — in an effort to benefit society at large. In 2013, the G8 nations (France, the United States, the United Kingdom, Russia, Germany, Japan, Italy, and Canada) signed a charter committing themselves to open data, prioritizing the areas of national statistics, election results, government budgets, and national maps.

The open government movement promotes government transparency and accountability, nurtures a well-informed electorate, and encourages public engagement. To put it in computing terms, open government facilitates a read/write relationship between a government and its citizenry.

Digging through data.gov

The Data.gov program (at www.data.gov) was started by the Obama administration to provide open access to nonclassified U.S. government data. Data.gov data is being produced by all departments in the executive branch — the White House and all Cabinet-level departments — as well as datasets from other levels of government. By mid-2014, you could search for over 100,000 datasets by using the Data.gov search. The website is an unparalleled resource if you're looking for U.S. government-derived data on the following indicators:

>> **Economic:** Find data on finance, education, jobs and skills, agriculture, manufacturing, and business.

>> **Environmental:** Looking for data on energy, climate, geospatial, oceans, and global development? Look no further.

>> **STEM industry:** Your go-to place for anything science-, technology-, engineering-, and mathematics-related — data on energy science and research, for example.

>> **Quality of life:** Here you can find data on weather patterns, health, and public safety.

>> **Legal:** If your interests go in a more legalistic direction, Data.gov can help you track down data on law and ethics.

TIP

Data.gov's data policy makes federal data derived from this source extremely safe to use. The policy says, "U.S. Federal data available through Data.gov is offered free and without restriction. Data and content created by government employees within the scope of their employment are not subject to domestic copyright protection." And because it comes in countless formats — including XLS, CSV, HTML, JSON, XML, and geospatial — you can almost certainly find something that you can use.

Datasets aren't the only things that are open on Data.gov. You can also find over 60 open-source application programming interfaces (APIs) available on the platform. You can use these APIs to create tools and apps that pull data from government departments listed in the Data.gov data catalog. The catalog itself uses the popular open-source CKAN API. (CKAN here is short for Comprehensive Knowledge Archive Network.) Even the code used to generate the Data.gov website is open source and is published on GitHub (at `http://github.com`), in case you're interested in digging into that.

TIP

Data.gov allocates hundreds of thousands of dollars in prizes per year for app development competitions. If you're an app developer and you're looking for a fun side project that has the potential to provide you with financial rewards, while also offering you an opportunity to make a positive impact on society, check out the Data.gov competitions. Popular apps developed in these competitions include an interactive global hunger map and an app that calculates and tracks bus fares, routes, and connections in Albuquerque, New Mexico, in real-time.

Checking Out Canada Open Data

For many decades, Canada has been a world leader for its data collection and publication practices. Both *The Economist* and the Public Policy Forum have repeatedly named Statistics Canada — Canada's federal department for statistics — as the best statistical organization in the world.

If you take a look at the Canada Open Data website (`http://open.canada.ca`), the nation's strong commitment to data is overwhelmingly evident. At the Canada Open Data website, you can find over 200,000 datasets. Among the 25 most popular offerings on the Canada Open Data site are datasets that cover the following indicators:

>> **Environmental:** Such as natural disasters and fuel consumption ratings

>> **Citizenship:** Permanent resident applications, permanent resident counts, foreign student entry counts, and so on

>> **Quality of life:** For example, cost-of-living trends, automobile collisions, and disease surveillance

WARNING

Canada Open Data issues its open data under an *open government license* — a usage license that's issued by a government organization in order to specify the requirements that must be met in order to lawfully use or reuse the open data that the organization has released. Canada Open Data releases data under the Open Government License – Canada — you're required to acknowledge the source every time you use the data, as well as provide backlinks to the Open Government License – Canada page at http://open.canada.ca/open-government-licence-canada.

Diving into data.gov.uk

The United Kingdom got off to a late start in the open government movement. Data.gov.uk (http://data.gov.uk) was started in 2010, and by mid-2014, only about 20,000 datasets were yet available. Like Data.gov (discussed in the section "Digging through Data.gov," earlier in this chapter), data.gov.uk is also powered by the CKAN data catalog.

Although data.gov.uk is still playing catch-up, it has an impressive collection of Ordnance Survey maps old enough — 50 years or more — to be out of copyright. If you're looking for world-renowned, free-to-use survey maps, data.gov.uk is an incredible place for you to explore. Beyond its stellar survey maps, data.gov.uk is a useful source for data on the following indicators:

>> **Environmental** (data.gov.uk's most prolific theme)

>> **Government spending**

>> **Societal**

>> **Health**

>> **Education**

>> **Business and economic**

Interestingly, the dataset most frequently downloaded from data.gov.uk is a dataset that covers the Bona Vacantia division — the government division charged with tracking the complicated processes involved in determining the proper inheritance of British estates.

WARNING

Like the Canada Open Data website (see the preceding section), data.gov.uk uses an Open Government License, which means you're required to acknowledge the data source every time you use it, as well as provide backlinks to the data.gov.uk Open Government License page at www.nationalarchives.gov.uk/doc/open-government-licence.

TIP

Although data.gov.uk is still young, it's growing quickly, so check back often. If you can't find what you're looking for, the data.gov.uk website offers functionality through which you can specifically request the datasets you want to see.

Checking Out U.S. Census Bureau Data

The U.S. Census is held every ten years, and since 2010, the data has been made freely available at www.census.gov. Statistics are available down to the level of the census block — which aggregates by 30-person counts, on average. The demographics data provided by the U.S. Census Bureau can be extremely helpful if you're doing marketing or advertising research and need to target your audience according to the following classifications:

>> Age

>> Average annual income

>> Household size

>> Gender or race

>> Level of education

In addition to its census counts on people in the United States, the U.S. Census Bureau conducts a census of businesses. You can use this business census data as a source for practical industry research to tell you information such as the number of businesses, the number of employees, and the size of payroll per industry per state or metropolitan area.

Lastly, the U.S. Census Bureau carries out an annual American Community Survey to track demographics with a statistically representative sample of the population during noncensus years. You can check this data if you need specific data about what has happened during a particular year or set of years.

WARNING

Some census blocks have a population density that's far greater than average. When you use data from these blocks, remember that the block data has been aggregated over a person count that's greater than the average 30-person count of census blocks.

With respect to features and functionality, the U.S. Census Bureau has a lot to offer. You can use QuickFacts (`http://quickfacts.census.gov/qfd`) to quickly source and pull government data from the U.S. federal, state, county, or municipal level. Also, the U.S. Census offers Census Explorer (`www.census.gov/censusexplorer`), a useful feature that you can use to create and display web-based interactive charts or maps of census data. Although you can find all this data by reviewing the Data.gov website (which you can read about in the section "Digging through Data.gov," earlier in this chapter), these extra features and functions make Census.gov worth a visit.

Knowing NASA Data

Since its inception in 1958, NASA has made public all its nonclassified project data. It has been in the open-data game so long that NASA has tons of data! NASA datasets have been growing even faster with recent improvements in satellite and communication technology. In fact, NASA now generates 4 terabytes of new earth-science data per day — that's equivalent to over a million MP3 files. Many of NASA's projects have accumulated data into the petabyte range.

NASA's open data portal is called data. NASA (`http://data.nasa.gov`). This portal is a source of all kinds of wonderful data, including data about

>> Astronomy and space (of course!)

>> Climate

>> Life sciences

>> Geology

>> Engineering

Some examples from its hundreds of datasets include detailed data on the color of Earth's oceans, a database of every lunar sample and where it's stored, and the Great Images in NASA (GRIN) collection of historically significant photographs.

Wrangling World Bank Data

The World Bank is an international financial institution run by the United Nations. It provides loans to developing countries to pay for capital investment that will lead (one hopes) to poverty reduction and some surplus so that the recipient nations can repay the loan amounts over time. Because World Bank officers need to make well-informed decisions about which countries would be more likely to repay their loans, they've gathered an enormous amount of data on member nations. They've made this data available to the public at the World Bank Open Data page (http://data.worldbank.org).

If you're looking for data to buttress your argument in a truly interesting data-journalism piece that's supported by global statistics, the World Bank should be your go-to source. No matter the scope of your project, if you need data about what's happening in developing nations, the World Bank is the place to go. You can use the website to download entire datasets or simply view the data visualizations online. You can also use the World Bank's Open Data API to access what you need.

World Bank Open Data supplies data on the following indicators (and many, many more):

>> **Agriculture and rural development:** Here you'll find data on major contract awards, contributions to financial intermediary funds, forest area, and rural population size data.

>> **Economy and growth:** For the Big Picture — data on gross domestic product (GDP), gross capital formation, and agricultural value-added data, for example — no source is more exhaustive than World Bank Open Data.

>> **Environment:** Data here can tell you all about methane emissions, nitrous oxide emissions, and water pollution.

>> **Science and technology:** It's great for tracking patent applications and trademark applications data.

>> **Financial sector:** Research the health (or lack thereof) of a national economy by looking at a nation's bank capital-to-assets ratio, foreign direct investment, market capitalization, and new or supplemental project data.

>> **Poverty income:** For a clearer sense of how a country's poorer population is faring, analyze the data associated with gross national income (GNI) per capita, income shares, and the poverty gap.

World Bank Data also includes *microdata* — sample surveys of households and businesses in developing countries. You can use microdata to explore variations in your datasets.

Getting to Know Knoema Data

Knoema (pronounced "no-mah") purports to be the largest repository of public data on the web. The Knoema platform houses a staggering 500+ databases, in addition to its 150 million *time series* — 150 million collections of data on attribute values over time, in other words. Knoema includes, but isn't limited to, all these data sources:

>> **Government data from industrial nations:** Data from Data.gov, Canada Open Data, data.gov.uk, and Eurostat.

>> **National public data from developing nations:** Data from countries such as India and Kenya.

>> **United Nations data:** Includes data from the Food and Agriculture Organization, the World Health Organization, and many other UN organizations.

>> **International organization data:** There's more to the international scene than the United Nations, so if you're looking for data from organizations such as the International Monetary Fund and the Organization for Economic Co-operation and Development, Knoema is where you want to be.

>> **Corporate data from global corporations:** Knoema offers data made public by private corporations such as British Petroleum and BASF.

Knoema is an outstanding resource if you're looking for international data on agriculture, crime statistics, demographics, economy, education, energy, environment, food security, foreign trade, health, land use, national defense, poverty, research and development, telecommunications, tourism, transportation, or water.

In addition to being an incredible data source, Knoema is a multifaceted tasking platform. You can use the Knoema platform to make dashboards that automatically track all your favorite datasets. You can use the platform's data visualization tools to quickly and easily see your data in a tabular or map format. You can use the Knoema Data Atlas (http://knoema.com/atlas) to drill down among categories and/or geographic regions and quickly access the specific datasets you need. As an individual, you can upload your own data and use Knoema as a free hosting service. Above and beyond all of this, Knoema even offers the Knoema Market — a place where you can go to get paid just for being part of data-driven projects. Check it out at http://knoema.com/market.

TIP

Although a lot of Knoema's data is pretty general, you can still find some surprisingly specific data as well. If you're having a hard time locating data on a specific topic, you might have luck finding it on the Knoema platform. Figure 22-1 illustrates just how specific Knoema data can be.

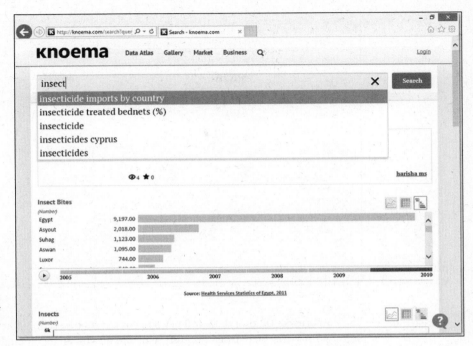

FIGURE 22-1:
The index of insect records in Knoema's search.

Queuing Up with Quandl Data

Quandl (www.quandl.com) is a Toronto-based website that aims to be a search engine for numeric data. Unlike most search engines, however, its database isn't automatically generated by spiders that crawl the web. Rather, it focuses on linked data that's updated via *crowdsourcing* — updated manually via human curators, in other words.

Because most financial data is in numeric format, Quandl is an excellent tool for staying up-to-date on the latest business informatics. As you can see in Figure 22-2, a search for *Apple* returns over 4,700 datasets from 11 different sources with time series at the daily, weekly, monthly, quarterly, or annual level. Many of these results are related to the United Nations' agricultural data. If you're looking for data on Apple Computers, you can narrow the scope of your search by replacing the *Apple* search term with the company's stock abbreviation, *AAPL*.

The Quandl database includes links to over 10 million datasets (although it uses a generous metric in declaring what distinguishes one dataset from another). Quandl links to 2.1 million UN datasets and many other sources, including datasets in the Open Financial Data Project, the central banks, real estate organizations, and well-known think tanks.

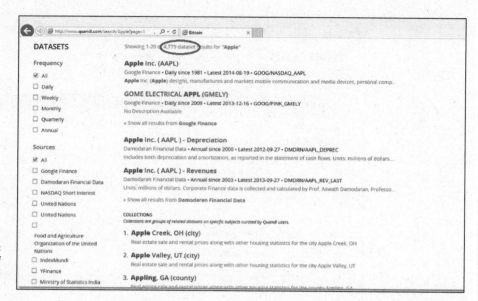

You can browse Quandl data and get instant charts based on what you find. If you sign up for a free registered account, you can download as much data as you want or use the Quandl application programming interface (API). The Quandl API includes wrappers to accommodate platforms such as Java, Python, Julia, R, MAT-LAB, Excel, and Stata, among others.

Exploring Exversion Data

Modeled after GitHub — the cloud-hosted platform across which programmers can collaboratively share and review code — Exversion aims to provide the same collaborative functionality around data that GitHub provides around code. The Exversion platform offers version control functionality and hosting services to which you can upload and share your data. To illustrate how Exversion works, imagine a platform that would allow you to first *fork* (or copy) a dataset and then make the changes you want. Exversion would be there to keep track of what has changed from the original set and every change that you make to it. Exversion also allows users to rate, review, and comment on datasets.

Datasets hosted on the Exversion platform are either provided by a user or created by a spider that crawls and indexes open data to make it searchable from a single application programming interface (API). Like GitHub, with a free user account, all the data you upload to Exversion is public. If you're willing to pay for an account, you can create your own, private data repositories. Also, with the paid account, you get the option to share your data with selected users for collaborative projects.

TIP

When you work on collaborative projects, version control becomes vitally important. Rather than learn this lesson the hard way, just start your project on a version-enabled application or platform — this approach will save you from a lot of problems in the future.

Exversion is extremely useful in the data-cleanup stage. Most developers are familiar with data-cleanup hassles. Imagine you want to use a particular dataset, but in order to do so, you must put tabs in all the right places to make the columns line up correctly. Meanwhile, the other 100 developers out there working with that dataset are doing exactly the same thing. In contrast, if you download, clean, and then upload the data to Exversion, other developers can use it and don't have to spend their time doing the same work later. In this way, everyone can benefit from each other's work, and each individual person can spend more time analyzing data and less time cleaning it.

Mapping OpenStreetMap Spatial Data

OpenStreetMap (OSM) is an open, crowd-sourced alternative to commercial mapping products such as Google Maps and ESRI ArcGIS Online. In OSM, users create, upload, or digitize geographic data into the central repository.

REMEMBER

The OSM platform is quite robust. Governments and private companies have started contributing to, and pulling from, the shared datasets. Even corporations as big as Apple are relying on OSM data. OSM now has over 1 million registered users. To illustrate how a person can create data in OSM, imagine that someone links the GPS systems on her mobile phone to the OSM application. Because of this authorization, OSM can automatically trace the routes of roads while the person travels. Later, this person (or another OSM user) can go into the OSM online platform to verify and label the routes.

The data in OSM isn't stored as maps, but as geometric and text representations — points, lines, polygons, and map annotation — so all of OSM's data can be quickly downloaded from the website and easily assembled into a cartographic representation via a desktop application. (For more on mapmaking and GIS, see Chapter 13.)

» Using open-source tools for scraping, collecting, and handling data

» Analyzing your data with free open-source tools

» Having fun with visualizations in advanced open-source applications

Chapter **23**

Ten Free Data Science Tools and Applications

Because visualizations are a vitally important part of the data scientist's toolkit, it should come as no surprise that you can use quite a few free web-based tools to make visualizations in data science. (Check out Chapter 11 for links to a few.) With such tools, you can leverage the brain's capacity to quickly absorb visual information. Because data visualizations are an effective means of communicating data insights, many tool and application developers work hard to ensure that the platforms they design are simple enough for even beginners to use. These simple applications can sometimes be useful to more advanced data scientists, but at other times, data science experts simply need more technical tools to help them delve deeper into datasets.

In this chapter, I present ten free web-based applications that you can use to complete data science tasks that are more advanced than the ones described in Chapter 11. You can download and install many of these applications on your personal computer, and most of the downloadable applications are available for multiple operating systems.

WARNING

Always read and understand the licensing requirements of any app you use. Protect yourself by determining how you're allowed to use the products you create with that app.

Making Custom Web-Based Data Visualizations with Free R Packages

I discuss some easy-to-use web apps for data visualization in Chapter 11, so you may be wondering why I'm presenting yet another set of the packages and tools that are useful for creating cool data visualizations. Here's the simple answer: The tools I present in this section require you to code using the R statistical programming language — a programming language I present in Chapter 15. Although you may not have much fun coding things up yourself, with these packages and tools, you can create results that are more customized for your needs. In the following sections, I discuss using Shiny, rCharts, and rMaps to create neat-looking web-based data visualizations.

Getting Shiny by RStudio

Not long ago, you needed to know how to use a statistics-capable programming language like R if you wanted to do any kind of serious data analysis. And if you needed to make interactive web visualizations, you'd have to know how to code in languages like JavaScript or PHP. Of course, if you wanted to do both simultaneously, you'd have to know how to code in an additional two or three more programming languages. In other words, web-based data visualization based on statistical analyses was a cumbersome task.

The good news is that things have changed. Due to the work of a few dedicated developers, the walls between analysis and presentation have crumbled. After the 2012 launch of RStudio's Shiny package (http://shiny.rstudio.com), both statistical analysis and web-based data visualization can be carried out in the same framework.

RStudio — already, by far, the most popular integrated development environment (IDE) for R — developed the Shiny package to allow R users to create web apps. Web apps made in Shiny run on a web server and are *interactive* — with them, you can interact with the data visualization to move sliders, select check boxes, or click the data itself. Because these apps run on a server, they're considered *live* — when you make changes to the underlying data, those changes are automatically reflected in the appearance of the data visualization. Web apps created in Shiny are also *reactive* — in other words, their output updates instantly in response to a user interaction, without the user having to click a Submit button.

If you want to quickly use a few lines of code to instantly generate a web-based data visualization application, use R's Shiny package. What's more, if you want to customize your web-based data visualization app to be more aesthetically appealing, you can do that by simply editing the HTML, CSS, and JavaScript that underlies the Shiny application.

WARNING

Because Shiny produces server-side web apps, you need a server host and the know-how to host your web app on a server before you can make useful web apps by using the package.

TIP

Shiny runs the public web server ShinyApps.io (`www.shinyapps.io`). You can use that server to host an app for free, or you can pay to host there if your requirements are more resource-intensive. The most basic level of service costs $39 per month and promises you 250 hours of application runtime per month.

Charting with rCharts

Although R has always been famous for its beautiful static visualizations, only just recently has it been possible to use R to produce web-based interactive data visualizations.

Things changed dramatically with the advent of rCharts (`http://ramnathv.github.io/rCharts`). The rCharts open-source package for R takes your data and parameters as input and then quickly converts them to a JavaScript code block output. Code block outputs from rCharts can use one of many popular JavaScript data visualization libraries, including NVD3, Highcharts, Rickshaw, xCharts, Polychart, and Morris. To see some examples of data visualizations created by using rCharts, check out the data visualizations located on its GitHub page.

Mapping with rMaps

rMaps (`http://rmaps.github.io`) is the brother of rCharts. Both of these open-source R packages were crafted by Ramnath Vaidyanathan. Using rMaps, you can create animated or interactive choropleths, heat maps, or even maps that contain annotated location droplets (such as those found in the JavaScript mapping libraries Leaflet, CrossLet, and Data Maps).

rMaps allows you to create a spatial data visualization containing interactive sliders that users can move to select the data range they want to see.

TECHNICAL STUFF

If you're an R user and you're accustomed to using the simple R Markdown syntax to create web pages, you'll be happy to know that you can easily embed both rCharts and rMaps in R Markdown.

REMEMBER

If you prefer Python to R, Python users aren't being left out on this trend of creating interactive web-based visualizations within one platform. Python users can use server-side web app tools such as Flask — a less–user-friendly but more powerful tool than Shiny — and the Bokeh and Mpld3 modules to create client-side JavaScript versions of Python visualizations. The Plotly tool has a Python application programming interface (API) — as well as ones for R, MATLAB, and Julia — that you can use to create web-based interactive visualizations directly from your Python IDE or command line. (Check out Flask at `http://flask.pocoo.org`, Bokeh at `http://bokeh.pydata.org`, Mpld3 at `http://mpld3.github.io`, and Plotly at `https://plot.ly`.)

Examining Scraping, Collecting, and Handling Tools

Whether you need data to support a business analysis or an upcoming journalism piece, web-scraping can help you track down interesting and unique data sources. In *web-scraping,* you set up automated programs and then let them scour the web for the data you need. I mention the general ideas behind web-scraping in Chapter 18, but in the following sections, I elaborate a bit more on the free tools you can use to scrape data or images, including import.io, ImageQuilts, and DataWrangler.

Scraping data with import.io

Have you ever tried to copy and paste a table from the web into a Microsoft Office document and then not been able to get the columns to line up correctly? Frustrating, right? This is exactly the pain point that import.io was designed to address.

import.io — pronounced "import-eye-oh" — is a free desktop application that you can use to painlessly copy, paste, clean, and format any part of a web page with only a few clicks of the mouse. You can even use import.io to automatically crawl and extract data from multipage lists. (Check out import.io at `https://import.io`.)

TIP

Using import.io, you can scrape data from a simple or complicated series of web pages:

>> **Simple:** Access the web pages through simple hyperlinks that appear on Page 1, Page 2, Page 3.

>> **Complicated:** Fill in a form or choose from a drop-down list, and then submit your scraping request to the tool.

import.io's most impressive feature is its capability to observe your mouse clicks to learn what you want, and then offer you ways that it can automatically complete your tasks for you. Although import.io learns and suggests tasks, it doesn't take action on those tasks until after you've marked the suggestion as correct. Consequently, these human-augmented interactions lower the risk that the machine will draw an incorrect conclusion due to overguessing.

Collecting images with ImageQuilts

ImageQuilts (http://imagequilts.com) is a Chrome extension developed in part by the legendary Edward Tufte, one of the first great pioneers in data visualization — he popularized the use of the data-to-ink ratio to judge the effectiveness of charts.

The task that ImageQuilts performs is deceptively simple to describe but quite complex to implement. ImageQuilts makes collages of tens of images and pieces them all together into one "quilt" that's composed of multiple rows of equal height. This task can be complex because the source images are almost never the same height. ImageQuilts scrapes and resizes the images before stitching them together into one output image. The image quilt shown in Figure 23-1 was derived from a "Labeled for Reuse" search at Google Images for the term *data science*.

ImageQuilts even allows you to choose the order of images or to randomize them. You can use the tool to drag and drop any image to any place, remove an image, zoom all images at the same time, or zoom each image individually. You can even use the tool to covert between image colors — from color to grayscale or inverted color (which is handy for making contact sheets of negatives, if you're one of those rare people who still processes analog photography).

Wrangling data with DataWrangler

DataWrangler (http://vis.stanford.edu/wrangler) is an online tool that's supported by the University of Washington Interactive Data Lab. (At the time DataWrangler was developed, this group was called the Stanford Visualization Group.) This same group developed Lyra, an interactive data visualization environment that you can use to create complex visualizations without programming experience.

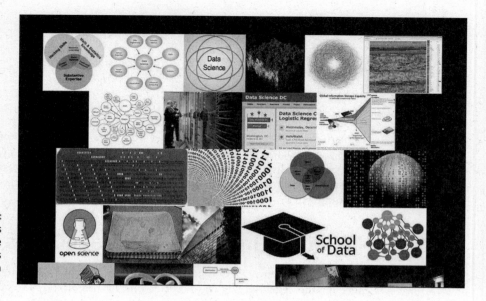

FIGURE 23-1:
An ImageQuilts output from the Google Images search term *data science.*

If your goal is to *sculpt* your dataset — or clean things up by moving things around like a sculptor would (split this part in two, slice off that bit and move it over there, push this down so that everything below it gets shifted to the right, and so on) — DataWrangler is the tool for you.

You can do manipulations with DataWrangler similar to what you can do in Excel using Visual Basic. For example, you can use DataWrangler or Excel with Visual Basic to copy, paste, and format information from lists on the Internet.

DataWrangler even suggests actions based on your dataset and can repeat complex actions across entire datasets — actions such as eliminating skipped rows, splitting data from one column into two, and turning a header into column data. DataWrangler can also show you where your dataset is missing data.

Missing data can indicate a formatting error that needs to be cleaned up.

TIP

Looking into Data Exploration Tools

Throughout this book, I talk a lot about free tools that you can use to visualize your data. And although visualization can help clarify and communicate your data's meaning, you need to make sure that the data insights you're communicating are correct — that requires great care and attention in the data analysis phase. In the following sections, I introduce you to a few free tools that you can use for some advanced data analysis tasks.

Getting up to speed in Gephi

Remember back in school when you were taught how to use graph paper to do math and then draw *graphs* of the results? Well, apparently that nomenclature is incorrect. Those things with an *x*-axis and *y*-axis are called *charts*. Graphs are actually *network topologies* — the same type of network topologies I talk about in Chapter 9.

If this book is your first introduction to network topologies, welcome to this weird and wonderful world. You're in for a voyage of discovery. Gephi (http://gephi. github.io) is an open-source software package you can use to create graph layouts and then manipulate them to get the clearest and most effective results. The kinds of connection-based visualizations you can create in Gephi are useful in all types of network analyses — from social media data analysis to an analysis of protein interactions or horizontal gene transfers between bacteria.

To illustrate a network analysis, imagine that you want to analyze the interconnectedness of people in your social networks. You can use Gephi to quickly and easily present the different aspects of interconnectedness between your Facebook friends. So, imagine that you're friends with Alice. You and Alice share 10 of the same friends on Facebook, but Alice also has an additional 200 friends with whom you're not connected. One of the friends that you and Alice share is named Bob. You and Bob share 20 of the same friends on Facebook also, but Bob has only 5 friends in common with Alice. On the basis of shared friends, you can easily surmise that you and Bob are the most similar, but you can use Gephi to visually graph the friend links between you, Alice, and Bob.

To take another example, imagine you have a graph that shows which characters appear in the same chapter as which other characters in Victor Hugo's immense novel *Les Misérables*. (Actually, you don't have to imagine it; Figure 23-2 shows just such a graph, created in the Gephi application.) The larger bubbles indicate that these characters appear most often, and the more lines attached to a bubble, the more he or she co-occurs with others — the big bubble in the center-left is, of course, Jean Valjean.

When you use Gephi, the application automatically colors your data into different clusters. Looking to the upper-left of Figure 23-2, the cluster of characters in blue (the somewhat-darker color in this black-and-white image) are characters who mostly appear only with each other. (They're the friends of Fantine, such as Félix Tholomyès — if you've only seen the musical, they don't appear in that production.) These characters are connected to the rest of the book's characters through only one character, Fantine. If a group of characters appear only together and never with any other characters, they'd be in a separate cluster of their own and not attached to the rest of the graph in any way.

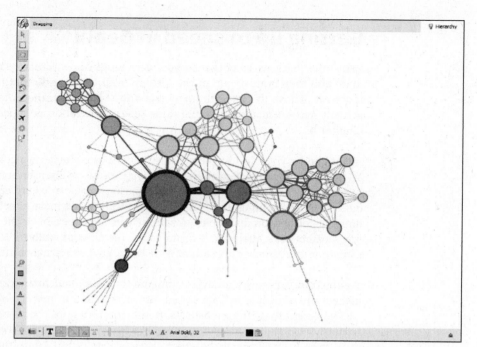

FIGURE 23-2:
A moderate-size graph on characters in the book *Les Misérables.*

To take one final example, check out Figure 23-3, which shows a graph of the U.S. power grid and the degrees of interconnectedness between thousands of power-generation and power-distribution facilities. This type of graph is commonly referred to as a *hairball* graph, for obvious reasons. You can make it less dense and more visually clear, but making those kinds of adjustments is as much of an art as it is a science. The best way to learn is through practice, trial, and error.

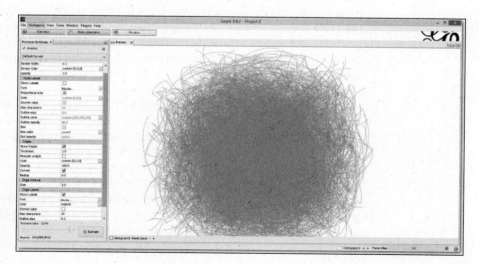

FIGURE 23-3:
A Gephi hairball graph of the U.S. power grid.

Machine learning with the WEKA suite

Machine learning is the class of artificial intelligence that's dedicated to developing and applying algorithms to data, so that the algorithms can automatically learn and detect patterns in large datasets. Waikato Environment for Knowledge Analysis (WEKA; www.cs.waikato.ac.nz/ml/weka) is a popular suite of tools that is useful for machine learning tools. It was written in Java and developed at the University of Waikato, New Zealand.

WEKA is a stand-alone application that you can use to analyze patterns in your datasets and then visualize those patterns in all sorts of interesting ways. For advanced users, WEKA's true value is derived from its suite of machine-learning algorithms that you can use to cluster or categorize your data. WEKA even allows you to run different machine-learning algorithms in parallel to see which ones perform most efficiently. WEKA can be run through a graphical user interface (GUI) or by command line. Thanks to the well-written Weka Wiki documentation, the learning curve for WEKA isn't as steep as you might expect for a piece of software this powerful.

Evaluating Web-Based Visualization Tools

As I mention earlier in this chapter, Chapter 11 highlights a lot of free web apps you can use to easily generate unique and interesting data visualizations. As neat as those tools are, two more are worth your time. These tools are a little more sophisticated than many of the ones I cover in Chapter 11, but with that sophistication comes more customizable and adaptable outputs.

Getting a little Weave up your sleeve

Web-Based Analysis and Visualization Environment, or *Weave,* is the brainchild of Dr. Georges Grinstein at the University of Massachusetts Lowell. Weave is an open-source, collaborative tool that uses Adobe Flash to display data visualizations. (Check it out at www.oicweave.org.)

WARNING

Because Weave relies on Adobe Flash, you can't access it with all browsers, particularly those on Apple mobile devices — iPad, iPhone, and so on.

The Weave package is Java software designed to be run on a server with a database engine like MySQL or Oracle, although it can be run on a desktop computer as long as a local host server (such as Apache Tomcat) and database software are both installed. Weave offers an excellent Wiki (http://info.iweave.com/projects/weave/wiki) that explains all aspects of the program, including installation on Mac, Linux, or Windows systems.

TIP

You can most easily install Weave on the Windows OS because of Weave's single installer, which installs the desktop middleware, as well as the server and database dependencies. For the installer to be able to install all of this, though, you need to first install the free Adobe Air runtime environment on your machine.

You can use Weave to automatically access countless open datasets or simply upload your own, as well as generate multiple interactive visualizations (such as charts and maps) that allow your users to efficiently explore even the most complex datasets.

Weave is the perfect tool to create visualizations that allow your audience to see and explore the interrelatedness between subsets of your data. Also, if you update your underlying data source, your Weave data visualizations update in real-time as well.

Figure 23-4 shows a demo visualization on Weave's own server. It depicts every county in the United States, with many columns of data from which to choose. In this example, the map shows county-level obesity data on employed women who are 16 years of age and older. The chart at the bottom-left shows a correlation between obesity and unemployment in this group.

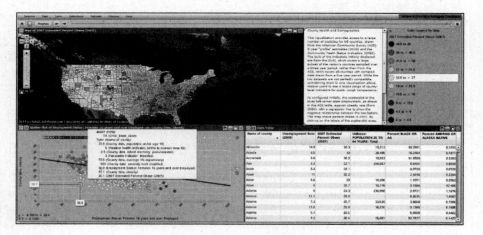

FIGURE 23-4:
A figure showing a chart, map, and data table in Weave.

Checking out Knoema's data visualization offerings

Knoema (http://knoema.com) is an excellent open data source, as I spell out in Chapter 22, but I would be telling only half the story if I didn't also mention Knoema's open-source data visualization tools. With these tools, you can create visualizations that enable your audience to easily explore data, drill down on geographic areas or on different indicators, and automatically produce data-driven timelines. Using Knoema, you can quickly export all results into Power-Point files (.ppt), Excel files (.xls), PDF files (.pdf), JPEG images (.jpg), or PNG images (.png), or even embed them on your website.

REMEMBER

If you embed the data visualizations in a web page of your website, those visualizations automatically update if you make changes to the underlying dataset.

Figure 23-5 shows a chart and a table that were quickly, easily, and automatically generated with just two mouse clicks in Knoema. After creating charts and tables in Knoema, you can export the data, further explore it, save it, or embed it in an external website.

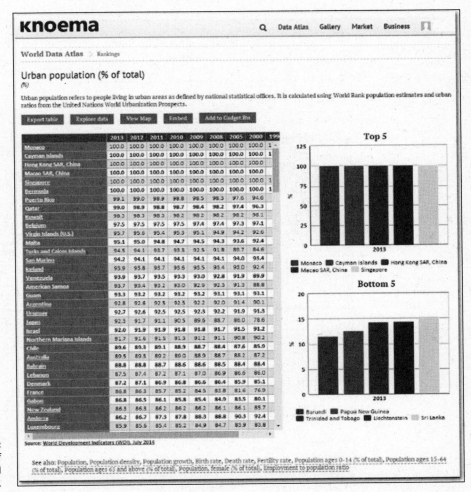

FIGURE 23-5:
An example of data tables and charts in Knoema.

You can use Knoema to make your own dashboards as well, either from your own data or from open data in Knoema's repository. Figures 23-6 and 23-7 show two dashboards that I quickly created using Knoema's Eurostat data on capital and financial accounts.

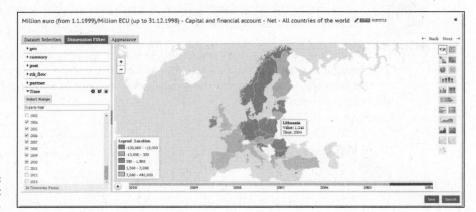

FIGURE 23-6:
A map of Eurostat data in Knoema.

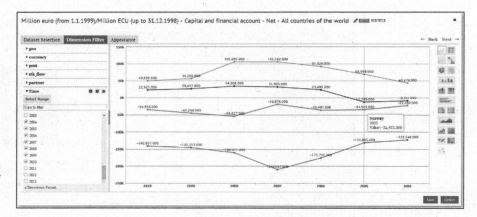

FIGURE 23-7:
A line chart of Eurostat data in Knoema.

Index

image file data, 42

ImageQuilts, 343

import statement, 210

import.io, 342–343

in-batch, 24

index, 242

individual strategy, 15

inferential statistics, 62–65

Infogr.am, 170–171

infographics, 170–172

in-house teams, assembling, 14–15

__init__ function, 210

inner join, 250, 251

insight-to-action arc, 38

instance, in machine learning, 53

instance-based algorithm, 56

instance-based learning classifiers

  about, 93–94

  average nearest neighbor algorithms, 98–101

  clustering compared with classification, 94–97

  k-nearest neighbor algorithms, 44, 101–104

  nearest neighbor analysis, 97–98, 104–105

instances, modeling with, 93–105

integers, 204

interactions, 153–155

interactive mode, 226

interface, QGIS, 191–192

internal datasets, 41

Internet of Things (IoT)

  about, 20, 107–108

  artificial intelligence (AI), 113–114

  contextual-awareness, 111

  deep learning, 113

  geospatial analysis, 112

  hardware platforms, 110

  Spark streaming, 110–111

  terms for, 108–110

  time series, 112

interpreter, 250

inter-quartile range (IQR), 76

intersection operations, 189

IoT. *see* Internet of Things (IoT)

IoT cloud, 108

IoT cloud application developers, 109

IoT hardware platforms, 110

IoT software platforms, 110

IQR (inter-quartile range), 76

iterating, in R, 232–234

iterative, 38

J

Jaccard distance metric, 85

Java, 28

JavaScript, 145

JobTracker, 28

JpGraph PHP library (website), 141

jQuery Javascript library (website), 141

K

KDE (kernel density estimation), 87–88, 320

kernel, 87

kernel density estimation (KDE), 87–88, 320

key-value format, 25

key-values, 30

k-means algorithm, 86–87, 319

k-means clustering, 44

k-Nearest Neighbor algorithms, 44, 101–104

KNIME, using for advanced data analytics, 264–266

Knoema, 334–335, 348–350

Kriege, 296

Kriging methods, 296

L

Lall, Upmanu (director), 294–295

landing page optimization, 311, 314

landing pages, 309, 310

latent variables, 69

layer overlay analysis, 189–190

lazy learners, 93

learns form, 103

left join, 251

letter_grade function, 220–221

N

Naïve Bayes, 44, 56, 65–66
narratives, creating, 285
NASA data, 332
Natural Language Toolkit (website), 253
natural resources, modeling, 293–295
n-dimensional plot, 85, 211
nearest neighbor analysis, 97–98, 104–105, 319
neighborhood clustering, 90–91
network analysis, 265
network topologies, 345
networks, analyzing with `statnet` and `igraph`, 239–240
neural network, 56–57
nodes, 27
non-core samples, 90
nonglobular clustering, 90
non-interactive mode, 226
non-intersection operations, 189
non-numeric, 65
nonstationary processes, 78
normal distributions, 64
normalization, of databases, 247–248
NoSQL databases, 29–30
NULL values, 248
number of centroids present, 86
numbers, in Python, 203, 204
numeric continuous, 64
numeric dataset, 85
numeric discrete, 64
numerical data type, 246
NumPy library, 211–212

O

objects, 202, 234–236
OLAP (Online Analytical Processing), 40
OLS (ordinary least squares), 74–75
Online Analytical Processing (OLAP), 40
online geographic tools, visualizing spatial data with, 162–166
open data, 292, 327–337
open government license, 329, 331

open movement, 327
open source web-based applications, for data visualization, 166–169
OpenHeatMap, 163–164
open-source QGIS, 191–197
OpenStreetMap (OSM), 337
operators (R), 229–232
optimized referral messaging, 310
Optimizely, 309, 312
ordinal variables, 65
ordinary least squares (OLS), 74–75
OSM (OpenStreetMap), 337
outer join, 250
outliers, 70, 75–78, 281–282
outputs, of business-centric data science and business intelligence, 45
outsourcing, 15
overfitting, 95–97
overgeneralization, 96–97

P

packed circle diagrams, 130, 132
Pandas library, 213–214
parallel distributed processing, 25
partitional algorithms, 82–84
PCA. *see* principal component analysis (PCA)
PDF file data, 42
Pearson coefficient, 66, 282
persuasive design, 127
PHP, 146–147
pie charts, 128, 129
Piktochart, 172
Pinterest Analytics, 305
pivot charts, 262
pivot tables, reformatting and summarizing with, 261–262
Plotly, 159–160, 342
point map, 138–139, 163
point outliers, 75
polygons, 183
PostgreSQL, 243
predictant, 73
predictive analytics, 35

Y

Z

About the Author

Lillian Pierson, P.E., is a leading expert in the field of big data and data science. She equips working professionals and students with the data skills they need to stay competitive in today's data-driven economy. In addition to this book, she is the author of two highly referenced technical books by Wiley: *Big Data / Hadoop For Dummies* (Dell Special Edition) and *Managing Big Data Workflows For Dummies* (BMC Special Edition).

Lillian has spent the past decade training and consulting for large technical organizations in the private sector, such as IBM, BMC, Dell, and Intel, as well as government organizations, from the local government level all the way to the U.S. Navy. As the founder of Data-Mania LLC, Lillian offers online and face-to-face training courses as well as workshops and other educational materials in the area of big data, data science, and data analytics.

Dedication

I dedicate this book to my family — Vitaly and Ariana Ivanov. Without your love and companionship, life wouldn't be even half as good.

Author's Acknowledgments

I extend a huge thanks to all the people who've helped me produce this book. Thanks so much to Russ Mullen, for your technical edits. Also, I extend a huge thanks to Katie Mohr, Paul Levesque, Becky Whitney, and the rest of the editorial and production staff at Wiley.

Publisher's Acknowledgments

Acquisitions Editor: Katie Mohr
Project Manager: Paul Levesque
Project Editor: Becky Whitney
Copy Editor: Becky Whitney
Technical Editor: Russ Mullen
Editorial Assistant: Serena Novosel
Sr. Editorial Assistant: Cherie Case

Production Editor: Magesh Elangovan
Cover Image: iStock.com